EDUCATION AND MANPOWER

NATIONAL MANPOWER COUNCIL

Education
and Manpower

EDITED BY HENRY DAVID

New York 1960

COLUMBIA UNIVERSITY PRESS

COPYRIGHT © 1960 COLUMBIA UNIVERSITY PRESS, NEW YORK

PUBLISHED IN GREAT BRITAIN, INDIA, AND PAKISTAN
BY THE OXFORD UNIVERSITY PRESS
LONDON, BOMBAY, AND KARACHI

LIBRARY OF CONGRESS CATALOG CARD NUMBER: 60-14796

MANUFACTURED IN THE UNITED STATES OF AMERICA

THE NATIONAL MANPOWER COUNCIL

ACKNOWLEDGMENTS

The National Manpower Council is grateful for the permission granted by Harper & Brothers to reprint "Manpower Problems and Education" by Henry David from *Public Education in America;* by the World Book Company, which holds the copyright, to reprint "Education and National Efficiency: The United States" by Eli Ginzberg from the *International Yearbook of Education, 1956;* and by the Association for Higher Education to reprint "Higher Education and the American Economy" by Henry David from *Current Issues in Higher Education, 1955.*

CONTENTS

TABLES

FIGURES

FOREWORD

"EVERYONE KNOWS," John W. Gardner has remarked, "that education is a primary means of achieving the aims which the American people have set themselves." It is, in his words, "the servant of all our purposes," as well as an aspiration and a value. But Mr. Gardner also observes, as have many others, that "Most Americans honor education; few understand its larger purposes." Hopefully, the present debate over the state of American education will not only help establish its instrumental importance—that is, its importance as "the servant of all our purposes"—but also its central position in American life as a value and an aspiration.

Much can be and has been accomplished to remedy educational deficiencies and to provide a wider range of richer educational opportunities in order to serve national security objectives, rather than the aim of education itself. The point has been made, for example, that the National Defense Education Act of 1958 probably would not have become law had the word "Defense" been lacking in the title. Similarly, significant steps have been suggested and taken to improve and strengthen the nation's vast educational enterprise on the ground that they are dictated by manpower objectives. The National Manpower Council itself has, of course, pressed for educational improvements on this very score. Consequently, its work has no doubt reenforced the tendency to view education primarily as a means for achieving immediate, practical purposes, rather than as an aim in itself. However, because the Council also has recognized the shortcomings embedded in every single and restricted view of education, I venture the hope that the present debate over its state will help establish its larger significance for the individual and the society. Whatever other ends it serves, it is a way "not only to satisfy the curiosity and perfect the spirits of individual men, but also to advance civilization."

Some of the participants in the debate on American education are so passionately committed to their particular diagnoses of its ills and to the cures they propose that I am prompted to express one further hope. And that is, that no one engaged in it will emerge from it with the conviction that he has found definitive and final solutions for any of the problems which have finally won public attention. For such a conviction would misconceive both the nature and functions of education and the requirements of a dynamic society. The nation's educational enterprise should be the subject of permanent discussion and debate, and should receive at least as much continuing concern and scrutiny as the public and public officials have given to the state of the economy.

The concern of the National Manpower Council, since its founding in 1951, with education both as means and aim, as well as the emphasis it has placed upon educational issues and problems in each of its studies, do not require elaborate explanation. Whether in the guise of formal schooling or informal learning, the nation's educational enterprise constitutes the foundation for the development of its manpower resources. The knowledge, skills, competence, and creativity of the American people are in large part products of the society's educational institutions. Their scale, diversity, and quality—and, equally important, the opportunities for access to them—are of key importance in determining the extent to which labor force skills and capacities are developed and subsequently utilized.

The schools, colleges, and universities, however, constitute only part of the nation's resources available for education and manpower development. For a number of years, now, the armed services have also functioned as a major educational enterprise, and private industry has been increasing its investment in education and training. In the sector of public employment, too, there has been an expansion of educational opportunities and in-service training programs. Work itself, of course, must be viewed as a critical learning experience, contributing enormously to the acquisition of occupational knowledge, skill, and competence.

Educational institutions play a major, if not frequently a decisive role in the complex process of occupational choice. The vocational guidance and counseling responsibilities with which they are charged—or which they inevitably assume—have, consequently, also been part of the National Manpower Council's concern with education. It is a commonplace that enormous gains could be effected in reducing the present waste of manpower and in raising the skill level of the population as a whole through improved educational and vocational guidance and counseling at the secondary level.

The intimate relationship between education, broadly conceived, and manpower development and utilization is reflected in the fact that almost half of the recommendations made by the Council with an eye to enhancing the quality of the nation's manpower resources deal in one fashion or another with issues of education, training, and guidance. The connection between the two is also reflected in the substantial number of staff chapters in the Council's studies devoted to educational themes, and in the consideration given to them in the national conferences held by the Council at Arden House, the Harriman Campus of Columbia University.

The contents of *Education and Manpower* represent a selection of educational materials from four of the seven volumes published by the Council to date and from the many papers published by members of its staff in connection with the Council's work. The decision to make these materials available in a single volume was prompted by two considerations: they are the products of a common approach—namely, a manpower approach—to education, and they are still relevant to the continuing discussion of basic educational problems. Where needed, more recent information has been provided in the extensive Notes.

The Executive Director of the Council, Dr. Henry David, was responsible for selecting the contents of *Education and Manpower* and editing the volume. Dale L. Hiestand and Albert R. Vogeler, members of the National Manpower Council staff, assisted in the editing.

ERWIN D. CANHAM
Chairman
National Manpower Council

Boston
May, 1960

Part One

INTRODUCTION

I. MANPOWER PROBLEMS AND EDUCATION

Henry David

IT IS A COMMONPLACE that formal education is the foundation upon which the development of the nation's manpower resources is built. This commonplace, however, bears constant reiteration.

"Manpower Problems and Education" indicates the sources of contemporary concern with manpower development and utilization, and sets forth the key reference points for the making of sound manpower policies. It was originally written for an Italian audience as one of a series of articles contributed by Americans to a special issue of *Problemi della Pedagogia* (July–October, 1957). This issue was designed by its editor, Luigi Volpicelli of the Istituto della Pedagogia, the University of Rome, to illuminate some of the distinctive features of the American educational enterprise.

"Manpower Problems and Education" is reprinted from George Z. F. Bereday and Luigi Volpicelli, Public Education in America: A New Interpretation of Purpose and Practice (New York: Harper & Brothers, 1958), pp. 144–53, in which it first appeared in this form.

MANPOWER is the nation's most precious and critical resource. Such an assertion represents a relatively new understanding of the extent to which our national well-being is a function of the quantitative and qualitative characteristics of our human resources and, consequently, of the significance of soundly conceived, long-range policies which aim at the maximum development of our manpower and of its more effective utilization.

The United States, like other democratic societies, has historically been more or less indifferent to the idea of human resource development, although we affirm that a belief in the importance, the dignity, and the sanctity of the individual human being is the cornerstone of a democratic value system. We have been less concerned with "the investment in human beings" than with problems of capital investment. It was not until the close of the nineteenth century that we became self-conscious about the state and utilization of our physical resources, and it is only in recent years that we have developed anything like a comparable concern with our manpower resources.

For most of its history the United States has pursued only two national policies which may be strictly described as manpower policies. One is immigration, and the other is publicly supported education. Following the growth of the movement for the conservation of physical resources, a movement got under way during the first decade of the present century for the conservation of human resources. Its primary aim, however, was the reduction of the death rate through improved hygiene, preventive medicine, and industrial and other safety measures. It was preoccupied with the wastage of human life in physical terms, so to speak, rather than with the wastage of human ability or with the development of skills and capacities.

The present concern with the manpower resources of the nation dates essentially from World War II. It has been shaped very largely by a realization of the costly consequences produced by severe shortages under conditions of full mobilization and of the manpower difficulties experienced during the partial mobilization necessitated by the fighting in Korea and by the cold war. We have been living for some years with shortages of engineers, physicists, chemists, and other physical scientists. For many years we have been aware that we require more doctors and other types of medical personnel, particularly nurses, than have been available to provide the standard of health services that we desire. Shortages of qualified school teachers have constituted a problem since World War II—in the first instance, of elementary school teachers and now of high school teachers, particularly of competent teachers of science and mathematics. The expansion of the college student population, certain to come in the next few years, has already produced warnings that there will be severe shortages of competent college and university teachers.

We have also been pressed periodically during the last fifteen years to secure adequate numbers of skilled workers of various kinds, such as tool and die makers, all-around machinists, and electronic and paramedical technicians. For some time now the armed services have failed to secure all of the trained workers they require. Recent estimates claim that the armed forces are short as much as 30 percent of the skilled personnel needed for critical military jobs. Newspaper advertisements continue to hammer home the fact that, in the new fields of nuclear energy and electronics, as well as in aircraft and chemicals, highly trained manpower is still at a premium. In the field of automation research and development, there are complaints about shortages of scientists, engineers, and technicians.

The important point to be noted in connection with the various trained groups of workers to which attention has been and is currently directed—whether they are teachers, nurses, solid state physicists, or electronic technicians—is not the precise numbers lacking. For we know from experience that estimates of shortages are susceptible to error and that they can be quite drastically reduced by changes in utilization practices. Thus, if draftsmen and engineering aides are used for certain functions in the place of professionally trained engineers, the intensity of demand for the latter may be altered.

We also know that arithmetical expressions of what is lacking in the way of trained personnel may obscure rather than reveal critical qualitative shortages. This problem of qualitative shortages may be illuminated by two instances. It does not follow that a significant increase in the supply of internists or surgeons will result in relieving a shortage of psychiatrically trained doctors. On the other hand, take the current stress upon finding an adequate number of qualified teachers to man the growing number of classrooms required by the increasing size of the school population. Even if this effort were to meet with success, there would be little ground for assuming that the shortage of first-rate teachers would be alleviated. And a shortage of first-rate teachers is one from which we have always suffered, even during the depressed 1930's, when the supply of applicants for the teaching profession was relatively large.

What is important about the shortage situations which have won attention is the explicit story they tell of a continuing high level of demand for highly trained manpower—a level of demand that almost appears to be a built-in factor of American life in recent years. If the question is asked whether this high level of demand promises to continue in the foreseeable future, the answer must be given that it does, even if such considerations as the continuing threat of Soviet power and the possibility of a full-scale mobilization are ignored. The reasons for being concerned with inadequacies in our highly trained manpower resources would be compelling, even if there were no Communist threat to the free world.

It is significant that, since the opening of the present century, the number of men and women engaged in the sciences and the professions has grown about twice as rapidly as the total population. Skilled workers now make up a larger proportion of the United States labor force than they did fifty or sixty years ago. There has, in short, been a growing demand for highly trained manpower as a result of advances in science, technology, and an expanding national income. This development is, interestingly enough, reflected in striking changes in educational patterns. In 1890, out of every 100 young people, only 3 or 4 graduated from high school, and only 1 from college. Today, 6 out of every 10 are high school graduates, and 1 in 8 is a college graduate.[1]

If one looks ahead and tries to calculate the nation's future requirements for highly trained manpower, every important basis for judgment points to higher, rather than lower, levels of demand. For example, if it is assumed that a rising national income will be accompanied by a substantially higher demand for health services, then it follows that more doctors, dentists, nurses, and semi-professionally trained workers and technicians in the health field will be needed. Or, let us assume, as there is good reason, that private and governmental expenditures for research and development, which have undergone an explosive growth in recent decades, will remain fairly high in the future. Experience indicates that the availability of personnel has been a far more important limiting factor on the expansion of such expenditures than the availability of dollars. Research and development efforts, of course, not only accelerate the advances made in science and technology, but they also create heavy demands for highly trained manpower.

An expansion in the school plant which will involve every level of education must be taken for granted, and this, too, will mean an increased demand for professionally trained personnel. The long-run results of increasingly automatic systems which utilize the idea of a continuous process or flow in production— generally spoken of as automation—also promise to raise the demand for various kinds of highly trained manpower to work with and control the new self-directing and self-tending machines, as well as to make, install, maintain, and repair them. Another determinant of high future demand is embedded in the growing appreciation of the extent to which highly trained manpower is itself a major factor in continued technological and economic development. We are now much more sharply aware than ever that the availability of such manpower is capable of hastening economic growth, just as its absence can act as a brake on economic advance.

Recent estimates by the United States Department of Labor of labor force growth for the period 1955–1965 show an expected increase of 10 million workers. This is reasonable if it is assumed that there will be no major depression on the scale of the 1930's and no large-scale war attended by catastrophic destruction of human life; that past rates of growth in the economy and in scientific and technological knowledge will be maintained; and that no sudden transformations in social values and attitudes which decisively influence the behavior of individuals with respect to education and training, work, leisure, and consumption will occur. More important than the anticipated expansion of the labor force to over 79 million by 1965 are the qualitative changes expected. It is estimated that the professional and technical groups in the labor force—most of whose members are prepared for work through college or graduate school education—will be one-third larger than in 1955. The estimated increase over that year in the skilled worker segment of the labor force is put at about 25 percent. The expected growth in clerical and sales workers is roughly of the same dimension. The semi-skilled group is expected to grow a little more than one-fifth, but it is estimated that the unskilled segment of the labor force will decline, perhaps by as much as 3 or 4 percent.[2]

The shortage situations which have developed since 1940 have, without question, been costly to the nation. However, they have also had the virtue of helping to shape a basically new posture toward the country's resources of highly trained manpower. It is not an accident that a new field of manpower study has grown up almost overnight. In the past Americans acted for the most part as if the numbers and kinds of highly trained people needed would always be available without it being necessary to undertake any extraordinary measures to insure their presence. True, we did, from time to time, take special steps of a limited character to expand the supply of certain kinds of highly trained personnel. For the most part, however, we were content to believe that free immigration, a publicly supported compulsory school system and, compared with other nations, a large college and university enrollment would take care of our manpower needs.

We are now sensitive to the strategically important roles played by a relatively small proportion of the working population in the production and distribution of goods and in the provision of critical services. The highly trained manpower resources of the nation account for about 15 of the 68 million persons in the civilian labor force—approximately 22 out of every 100 workers.[3] These consist of over 5 million scientific and professional workers and about 9 million skilled workers. There are in addition about half a million skilled workers who are described as technicians or technical workers.

An examination of the occupational groups comprised within these grosser categories indicates that they vary enormously in size. Thus, of the teachers in the nation, those employed in the elementary and secondary schools alone now number about one and one-third million.[4] There are some 600,000 engineers; over 200,000 doctors; and approximately 700,000 dentists, nurses, and other health workers. On the other hand, there are only about 160,000 physical and natural scientists in the labor force. Of more than 20,000 physicists, only about a fourth have Ph.D. degrees. This range in size is reproduced among the groups of skilled workers and technicians, many of which are smaller than the larger professional occupational groupings. Thus, the school teachers outnumber the carpenters, while the physical and natural scientists combined outnumber the draftsmen, the surveyors, the skilled metal workers, and others.

In the striking growth in scientific and professional manpower from a total of just over 1,200,000 in 1900 to approximately 5,000,000 in 1950, not all the groups underwent similar experiences. The sharpest increase occurred in the technological and scientific fields, whereas the proportions represented by each of the traditional professional fields of law, health, religion, and social welfare have been declining. The teaching profession, which just about maintained its relative importance in size among professional and scientific occupations up to 1940, has since been declining, even though the total number of teachers increased almost threefold from 1900 to 1950.

Broadly speaking, for that whole cut of the labor force which may be described as highly trained, there can be no ready substitution or replacement for the distinctive abilities and the competences which set it apart from other segments of the working population. These abilities and competences have been acquired by dint of some special effort, continued over fairly long periods of time, requiring an investment in education and training not only on the part of the individuals involved, but also by the society. This gives the factor of time special significance and immediately suggests the complex of institutions and forces related to the development of highly trained manpower.

The importance of this second point is indicated by the implications of the change in the way in which individuals are prepared for skilled work. At one time professional skills were largely acquired through a form of apprenticeship, but today professional workers are, with few exceptions, trained for their occupations through college and university education. Consequently, the scale and availability of educational and training facilities, the size and the quality of the population prepared for and actually continuing with a college education, and the incentives and disincentives attracting individuals to and repelling them from specific occupations are key determinants of our resources of professional and scientific manpower.

Obviously, a number of other factors are important in determining the size of the supply initially entering upon the course of education and training required for a given profession. It must also be borne in mind that different things happen to different professions with respect to the proportions of those who remain in a profession for which they have been trained. While relatively few graduates of medical schools subsequently fail to make professional use of their training, the same assertion cannot be made about such fields as engineering, nursing, and teaching. It has been reported that in New York State, for example, between 85 and 90 percent of those who prepare for teaching in the four institutions which comprise the College of the City of New York actually do enter the teaching profession.[5] However, a far smaller proportion of the graduates of the state teacher colleges become teachers, largely because these institutions are used by many young people to secure a college degree, which they otherwise would not be able to attain for financial or other reasons.

It is necessary to note, without arguing the point, that the size of the supply trained for certain professional fields, notably nursing and teaching, can be subsequently decimated because of relatively poor working conditions and pay, low prestige, and other factors. In these two professions, as well as others, the retention of individuals already trained is as significant a problem as the attraction of new entrants into the occupations.

The point has been made that shortage situations have compelled Americans to rethink a whole range of issues bearing on the development of our human resource potential and the more effective utilization of our highly trained manpower. Shortages have, in fact, offered us an opportunity to be creative in making qualitative gains with respect to our manpower. We should, in consequence, now be prepared to recognize the fundamental weakness in approaching our manpower resources and their use in a fragmented fashion, as if each manpower problem existed in isolation from the others. That we should have followed this latter course in the past is understandable. Voluntary organizations, whether they are professional societies, employer associations, or unions, are the reflection of particular interests, and tend to deal with manpower questions from the point of view of special, and frequently very narrow, concerns.

The development of our human resource potential, however, not only implies but requires an over-all national approach and an understanding that what is done with one part of the supply capable of a high degree of education and training will affect other parts of the supply. There is a kind of competition among manpower resources in short supply which is self-defeating. Suppose we steal from the potential supply of young women who might become teachers a significant number who become nurses; or deflect young men and women who might become doctors into the physical sciences and engineering; or discourage young men of ability from teaching science and mathematics in high school and make them available for employment in private industry, where they are also needed. If this is done—and to some degree that is what we have been doing—we may be compounding our manpower problems under the impression that we are solving them.

In a dynamic and free society, imbalances in manpower demand and supply relationships are to be expected. The problem is to minimize the costs they exact and the difficulties they create by establishing those conditions which will reduce the likelihood of severe and enduring imbalances. These considerations have certain clear-out implications for policy thinking. The first is that any naive belief that there are simple solutions for extremely complex human problems can only create additional difficulties. Next is the recognition that the basic directions of manpower policy can be achieved only by action on many fronts. This observation needs no argument once these directions are specified. They are: (1) the search for ways to reduce the wastage of able people in our society; (2) strengthening and improving the institutions through which people are educated and trained; (3) expanding the supply of young people who are educated and trained for professional and scientific work; (4) securing better utilization of our highly trained manpower resources; and (5) an indispensable instrument for achieving these directions—the search for improved knowledge in the human resources field.

The investment which is made in education lies at the heart of intelligent action on the manpower front. Aside from health, the field of education constitutes the society's major investment in people. The industrial capital of the United States—that is, the buildings, equipment, working capital and public capital, housing excluded—can now be replaced by the equivalent of one and a quarter years of the gross national product. We seem to have reached the point where education has to be recognized as a field for investment in quite new and different terms. It is the nation's largest social enterprise. There is now a school population of youngsters and adults of some 41 million.[6] By 1965, that school population is likely to reach between 54 and 55 million. We can expect to have about 36 million youngsters enrolled in elementary schools; about 12 million will be attending high schools; about 5 million are likely to be enrolled in colleges and universities; and perhaps another 1.5 million will be attending special trades and business schools.

Many Americans are disappointed with, if not angry about, the state of the schools and the education they provide. This is a healthy development. The schools, colleges, and universities of the nation are indispensable tools in any effort to raise the quality of its manpower resources. Complacency about the country's manpower resources, the National Manpower Council has asserted, is both "short-sighted and dangerous." This is another way of saying that complacency about the nation's educational resources is short-sighted and dangerous.

One special aspect of the educational problem we face has to do not only with the shortage of teachers, but also with the more effective utilization of those now employed in the schools. It has already been suggested that the supply of teachers cannot be viewed independently of the total supply of professionally trained personnel, and that the demand for teachers partly depends upon the way in which available resources of teaching personnel are utilized. The time is long overdue for recognizing that teachers are probably the most poorly utilized of all groups of professionally trained manpower. It is about the only profession in which the poorest and the best people are likely to be utilized in precisely the same fashion. Certainly the complex question of the productivity of the teaching profession has never been seriously investigated, and it is quite clear that under current utilization practices the unique qualities and abilities of first-rate teachers are to a large extent being wasted.

Perhaps nothing is more revealing of the key part which education plays in manpower development than the extent to which our human resource potential is being wasted. There is in the nation a substantial reserve, relatively speaking, of young men and women whose first-rate abilities will not be developed largely because they will be traveling only a short distance in terms of formal schooling. If we take the youth of the country with an I.Q. of 110 and over, it appears that about 46 percent complete high school, but do not go on to college; another 11 percent enter college, but do not complete a four year program; about a third graduate from college; and 10 percent do not even finish high school.[7] Less than half of the youth of the country capable of acquiring a college degree do not enter college, and two-fifths of those who do enter college do not graduate. Almost one-fifth of the top 10 percent of the young people in the country, measured in terms of I.Q., are not now graduating from college. For every youngster who graduates from high school with the ability to earn a Ph.D. degree, there are another 25 who do not. Only 1 out of every 300 women with the intellectual ability to earn a doctoral degree actually does so. These figures testify to a loss of "brainpower" which the nation can ill afford.

It may be comforting to believe that there are several simple devices—which only need be invented—that would assure the country of adequate resources of highly trained manpower. But this is simply not so. Yet there is reason for optimism because Americans are coming to understand the challenge and the promise of a new and imaginative development and use of human resources. They have, consequently, been searching for a fuller grasp of the complex interplay among forces, institutions, attitudes, and public and private actions which determine the quality of the nation's manpower resources expressed in the skills, capacities, competence, and creativity of its people.

II. EDUCATION AND NATIONAL EFFICIENCY

Eli Ginzberg

WRITTEN FOR *The International Yearbook of Education*, this article sought to portray for a non-American audience the extent to which the strength of the United States and its material well-being are related to its educational institutions, and the degree to which the latter are shaped by the dominant values of the society. It also points to shortcomings in American education—the world's most ambitious effort in mass education—which may be viewed as significant sources of loss from the viewpoint of national efficiency.

> *"Education and National Efficiency" is reprinted with some editorial changes from* The International Yearbook of Education, 1956 *(New York and London, 1956), pp. 507–18, in which it first appeared.*

ABOUT two years ago,[1] when the National Manpower Council was engaged in its study of skilled manpower, its staff called a conference of leading American educators to explore the interrelations between secondary education and the way in which young people prepare for work and life. The staff hoped to learn from the educators what, in their opinion, had been the contribution of the schools to the economic progress of the country and how this contribution could be enhanced.

The educators were not inclined to move from broad claims to detailed proofs of the ways in which an expanding educational system had contributed to the economy and welfare of society. One participant argued that the subject did not warrant exploration since it was self-evident that the prosperity of the nation was directly dependent upon the American educational system. In support, he pointed out that the expansion of the economy had coincided with the expansion of education.

The purpose of this paper is to probe more deeply into the connections, past and present, between America's high level of economic productivity and her great and highly diversified educational system. The scale of this system is suggested by the fact that the teaching personnel in elementary and secondary schools numbers over one and a quarter million, and that there are more than 1,800 institutions of higher learning in the country, with a total faculty of approximately a quarter of a million. Two additional facts may help to reinforce this picture. In the fall of 1950 there were five and a half million pupils between the ages of 16 and 22 enrolled in all schools, representing 37 percent of the total population in this age-group. In terms of expenditure, the educational effort of the country amounts to over 11 billion dollars.[2]

It would be difficult to gainsay the conclusions dictated by these data—that Americans are currently investing very substantial resources in the maintenance and operation of a far-reaching educational system. However, impressive though these figures may be, alone they do not make very clear the particular contributions that education has been making to national efficiency. To explore the extent and limits of these contributions, it is necessary, first, to identify some of the outstanding characteristics of the American economy; next, to make explicit the salient features of the American educational effort; and then to study the relationship between the two. Since both the American economy and the American educational system are constantly in a state of flux, it will also be helpful to point to the major directions of likely change. And, finally, it would be well to sort out that part of the American experience which is unique and those lessons which may be transferable—in whole or in part—to other countries, whether industrial or non-industrial, that are struggling to raise the productivity of their economies.

The economist faces a difficult task when he seeks to select for special emphasis a few of the welter of factors responsible for the shape and functioning of the American economy. There is the danger—in fact, the certainty—that by restricting himself to a limited number of factors he will fail to provide himself with an adequate base for interpreting accurately such a highly specialized and productive economy. However, such a selective procedure is permissible when the reader is forewarned that the facets selected represent characteristic and essential elements, and that the author does not pretend to take in all that are of strategic importance. With this warning, three important aspects of the American economy may be briefly considered: the extent to which that economy is driven by the money-making propensities of large numbers of the society; secondly, the extent to which almost the entire society is willing to accept and adjust to change; and, finally, the strong motive power exercised by the prevailing belief in equality—that is, that men should be judged by what they do, not by who their parents were.

THE MONEY-MAKING PROPENSITY

Without seeking to explain why so many Americans are deeply concerned with the making of money and more money (the simplest explanation might be that the American scene has been unique in terms of the opportunities it has offered people to make money), it would be difficult to deny the potency of this drive and the contribution that it makes to keeping the American economy highly dynamic. Of course, as the distinguished American economist, Frank H. Knight, pointed out many years ago, making money is not only work geared to improving the consumption levels of the individual and his family, but has become in the United States a sort of game that pre-empts a man's leisure time as well as his working hours. It is not accidental that much American business is transacted around the luncheon table, at cocktail bars, and on the golf links.

There is probably no other country in the world where the sons of middle-class and even wealthy parents are so encouraged early in childhood to engage in activities the end of which is the making of money. Here is seen the early and heavy indoctrination with respect to money-making activities. At the same time the extent to which these activities are turned into a game should be noticed. Every society must make a selection among the values it stresses. No society can be equally distinguished in all respects. Economic expansion and the increase of personal and national wealth are unquestionably at the forefront of American life, and have been from the earliest days of colonial settlement. There may come a point in American development when significant re-adjustments will take place, but as yet there is no evidence of this. Men give up the highest positions in government to enter or return to money-making activities. Talented young people turn their backs on academic careers in order to carve out successful niches for themselves in the world of business and so on.

THE VALUE PLACED ON CHANGE

The progress of a modern economy depends in very large measure on the rate at which improvements in technology take place and, equally important, on the speed with which these improvements are assimilated. An outstanding characteristic of American life is the high value placed upon change, in contrast to the value that other societies place upon custom and tradition. In the major industries of the country, labor has long been willing to accept technological changes, subject only to getting its share of the increases in profit due to increases in productivity. The American consumer is constantly on the look-out for new and improved products and places great faith in even the most modest changes in style or performance. To Americans, last year's car is an old car; a house constructed five years ago is an old house.

Another aspect of the American attitude toward change is reflected in the mobility of the population. Millions of people are constantly on the move. Year after year the South sees much of its surplus rural population leave for the major manufacturing cities of the North and, more recently, for the expanding Far West. There have also been sizable movements, although somewhat less spectacular, in the other regions of the country, from rural to urban communities and from one urban community to the next. A new plant located in one of the Southeastern states will find, on the day that it begins hiring, applicants who have come from a distance of a thousand miles. In short, we can see, then, that the employer with a new and improved process need not fear that his labor will refuse to accept it. The manufacturer with a new product need not fear that the public will turn it down simply because it is new; its very newness will give him an edge over competitors. It would be hard to exaggerate the contribution that this cultural desire for the new, this pervasive social acceptance of change, makes to the vitality of the economy.

THE CONCEPT OF EQUALITY

A third characteristic of the American economy that has contributed greatly to its continuing vitality is summarized by the concept of equality. Americans proceed on the assumption that what some men have done others can do; that success is the result of a combination of brains, initiative, hard work, and luck; and that there is no need to respect a man only because of the accomplishments of his father or his grandfather. The doctrine that a man can be whatever he wants to be if he is willing to strive has gone far to unleash the potential that is locked up in many men born into modest circumstances. The ideal of the self-made man, the son of immigrant parents who moves to the top, has substantial validity in a country where literally thousands and tens of thousands of children born into modest, or even poverty-stricken, homes have made their way up the ladder.

Quite another aspect of this doctrine that any man can be as good as any other is reflected in the consumption patterns of the population. With the exception of a few luxuries, there are no items purchased only by a particular class. America is the land of the mass market. The aspiration of the American working man is to provide for his family as many of the good things of life as his employer is able to provide for his family. Automobiles, radios, television sets, college education—all of these and other good things are good not only for the minority, but for all. Much of American prosperity in recent years is the result of the constant growth in demand by the population as a whole for all kinds of consumer goods, consumer durables, and, not least important, for private housing.

There is a further aspect of this equalitarian doctrine which warrants consideration. The family corporation has been replaced in the United States by the public corporation to the extent that nearly every large enterprise in the country is managed by individuals who do not own it. Management is becoming increasingly professionalized, and the decisions of management more and more rationalized. Consequently, no decisions play a larger part in the efficiency of American business than the selection and development of key personnel. Although it would be foolish to argue that all nepotism has been eliminated, or that favoritism and personal factors play no role, it can be said that the personnel practices of large corporations are becoming increasingly objective.

EDUCATIONAL OPPORTUNITY AND VOCATIONALISM

The first, and undoubtedly the most outstanding, characteristic of the American educational system is the extent to which public funds have been used to support increasingly extended educational preparation for all young people. Within the last two decades there has been a gain of not less than three years in the amount of formal schooling that the average young person receives prior to entering work. At the present time this schooling averages slightly more than twelve years.[3] The important points to note in this connection are, first, that the support for this schooling comes from public funds and represents no untoward burden upon the poor, other than the very small contribution which they make through taxes, and, secondly, that the educational process has now been extended to provide on the average for more than the completion of high school. Still another point worth mentioning is the extent to which there has been no sex discrimination in the development of American education. Ever since 1870 the number of girls graduating from high school has been greater than the number of boys.[4] At the collegiate and postgraduate level it is true that boys have consistently outnumbered girls, but the gap between the two has been substantially narrowed within recent decades.

The American educationl structure has been characterized by a pronounced utilitarianism, in which the responsibility of the schools for preparing individuals for work and life was narrowly and specifically, rather than broadly, defined. The large-scale contributions of the Federal government in making grants of land available to the states in the 1860's to facilitate the establishment and expansion of state universities was motivated by the understanding that the embryonic industrial economy of the United States would soon need more engineers and technicians. The importance of vocational education at the high school level was greatly stimulated by shortages of skilled manpower during World War I. Additional evidence of this vocational trend can be found in the great increases in enrollment at the collegiate level in recent decades in such "practical" fields as engineering and business administration. The elaboration of professional schools at university centers is further testimony of the same trend. Today the larger universities boast schools of journalism, business administration, hospital administration, social work, pharmacy, optometry, and dentistry, as well as the classical triad of law, medicine, and theology.

It is unlikely that up to 25 percent of the appropriate age-group—in some states it is now as high as 50 percent—would have entered advanced courses at collegiate or university levels unless such courses had been rather closely geared to preparation for work. There is undoubtedly a close relationship between the vocational orientation of American education and the continued expansion in enrollment.

One of the most striking and perhaps unique features of the American educational system at every level, surely from the secondary level on, has been the difference in quality between institutions and even between departments within the same institution. This reflects the fact that the United States, although a single nation, spans an entire continent, and further reflects that financial support for public education has been exclusively local and by the states. The large variations in wealth and taxing power have been reflected inevitably in the educational systems of the several states and localities. At the collegiate and university level there have been at least three major types of institution: the famous, heavily endowed institutions, few in number but very important in terms of educational leadership; the many state-supported institutions, ranging from outstanding universities to poorly staffed teachers colleges in states that have been hard-pressed to maintain their position in the expanding economy; and the ubiquitous private smaller colleges, many of which originally were denominational institutions, some well supported and well led, others poorly supported and with little intellectual leadership.

ACADEMIC STANDARDS

In the face of the trend to draw ever larger numbers of the population into secondary schools, so that at the present time more than 55 percent graduate from high school and 25 percent of the males attend college,[5] it has been next to impossible to maintain rigid standards. Many graduates of the poorer, smaller colleges would have been unable to gain admission to a good college. In turn, many high school graduates from weaker school systems would be unable to match first-year students at strong high schools. The same differences prevail at the upper end of the scale. A Ph.D. degree from one of the weaker universities simply does not represent the same achievements as a Ph.D. degree from a major institution.

Although there are obvious and deep-seated weaknesses in an educational system with this range in standards, there are also some important strengths in the very diversity of the system. Many students who would be unable to gain entrance to a good college are afforded, under this flexible structure, an opportunity not only to enter but to do well at a weaker institution. Many positions in society, even in a society that places as limited a value on status and tradition as does the United States, become open to individuals because they have some kind of college degree. Except in the sciences, an individual seeking work is seldom asked what he knows. Emphasis is placed merely upon his satisfactory completion of a required level of education, which often means that he has acquired a bachelor's degree. Moreover, individuals who have been handicapped by inadequate schooling are often able to compensate by an opportunity to continue their education. Although it is not easy even for a well-endowed student to develop his capacities in the absence of stimulating teachers and a strong curriculum, the fact remains that many are able to do so. Included among the most distinguished American scientists and scholars are a considerable number of men who are graduates of these weaker institutions.

EDUCATION AND THE ECONOMY

We have now considered some major characteristics of the economy and of the American educational system; what connection and interrelations can be found between the two? More particularly, what can be said about the contribution of the American educational system to the vitality of the American economy?

The drive for economic aggrandizement which is found among large numbers of the population is of strategic importance for the American economy; the equalitarian bias of the American educational system strongly supports and encourages this underlying goal. Every youngster who comes to school is told not by a single teacher, but by many, that his future will be what he determines to make it. He learns about presidents who came from humble beginnings. The American school must be given major credit for inspiring the youth of each generation with the model of the self-made man. What this means is well illustrated by a table presented by Dael Wolfle in *America's Resources of Specialized Talent*, in which he estimates the distribution of college graduates according to the occupation of their fathers. Of 100 graduates, only about 40 come from the professional, semi-professional, and managerial classes, while the fathers of the remaining 60 are lower in the socio-economic scale: half are skilled, unskilled, or factory workers; the other half, farmers and clerical and related workers.

It is not necessary to believe that the constant prolongation of education is pure gain, in order to recognize that there are many advantages in a situation where young people are permitted to find themselves late in their adolescence rather than in a situation of having their life determined for them by their educational accomplishments when they are 10 or 11. My associates and I have shown in our study of occupational choice (*Occupational Choice, An Approach to a General Theory*) [6] the serious handicaps under which the children of the poor grow up because they leave school before they have reached the emotional and intellectual maturity that enables them to choose their occupations wisely and to prepare themselves in accordance with their choices. At present, young people in certain states can secure their working papers at the age of 14, although 15 or 16 is typical.[7] But it is important to note that the concept of public education is being stretched in the richest states, such as California and

New York, to include fourteen years of free education for all. This means that a young person need not make any serious decisions about an occupation until he is 18. In California there is strong pressure to remove all vocational education from the high schools and relocate it in the junior colleges. This would mean that a young person would not commit himself until his nineteenth year.

The most obvious and direct connection between the sizable and constantly expanding American investment in education and the economy is reflected in the levels of education and training that young people have completed at the time when they first look for work. In passing, note must be taken of the fact that this training process has been extended further in recent years by the introduction of compulsory military service, which means that young men serve between two and four years, and much of this time is devoted to acquiring some sort of specialized skill. One of the most interesting findings of the National Manpower Council's study, *A Policy for Skilled Manpower,* was the extent to which large American corporations have shifted their interest over the last generation or two from young people who have completed a vocational course in high school to young people with substantial control over the fundamentals of mathematics, communication, and basic science. This attitude of employers has a simple explanation. They are interested in young people who have acquired a sound foundation; they are willing to undertake the specific skill instruction. It is possible to discount to a considerable extent the official statements of American industry about its serious predicament resulting from the fact that too few young men are graduating in engineering and in the sciences. Yet, there is no denying that American industry around the turn of the century employed 1 engineer for every 255 workers in manufacturing, mining, construction, transportation, and public utilities; twenty years later the ratio was much higher: it was 1 for every 78 workers; the data for 1950 show that industry employs 1 engineer for every 62 workers.[8] The absorption by American industry of these large numbers of engineers is only one outstanding illustration of the general trend to constantly enlarge the number of staff personnel.

DEFICIENCIES

Significant as the contributions of American education to the expansion of the American economy have been, it would be a serious misreading of the facts to omit to say that this contribution has fallen seriously short in several respects. One of the most striking shortcomings is the extent to which individuals with good intellectual potential are not educated and trained, despite the great public and private investment in education. In the most able sector of the population, not more than one out of every two young persons completes college. Although every young man or woman with the intellectual potential need not necessarily go to college to ensure his own personal development or his place in the economy and the society, the fact that so large a percentage fails to receive advanced training is of major concern to an increasingly large number of Americans. This concern is the deeper because, on the one hand, people have come to recognize the extent to which the progress of the economy and the security of the nation depend upon the development of its brainpower and, on the other, because it runs counter to American principles to admit that in many cases the barrier which prevents young people from going on with their education is financial. Because of the deep belief in the right of every individual to develop his potentialities to the full, the fact that so many are unable to do so because of straitened economic circumstances of their parents is a challenge that will not long remain unanswered.

Other weaknesses that cannot easily be rectified have developed in the secondary school system. Having turned the high school into a common school, the educators have had to develop all types of curricula in order to meet the varying intellectual, emotional, and vocational needs of the vastly expanded student body. In responding to these democratic pressures, many compromises and adjustments have been made which have not necessarily resulted in a sound educational foundation. It is not easy to generalize about any facet of American education because of its great variability. However, many well-informed observers have reached the conclusion that secondary schools need strengthening, and by this they usually mean two things: first, that more stress should be placed upon instruction in mathematics, language, and science; and secondly, that to ensure that students profit from such instruction it is definitely necessary to strengthen the teaching staffs. This, they believe, can be accomplished only if the salaries of teachers and the conditions under which they work are vastly improved. Because of the striking increases in enrollments that loom on the horizon as a result of the much increased birth rate of the 1940's, this challenge is even more formidable.

World War II revealed one of the more serious consequences of primary and secondary education being originally the responsibility of localities, and, now, to a great extent, the states. The well-to-do and highly industrialized regions of the nation suddenly realized that conditions in backward economic areas, such as the Southeast and the Southwest, had produced substantial numbers of young adults who were either totally illiterate or so poorly educated that the military forces, even during a major emergency, did not accept them for service. There is a close relationship between *per capita* income, expenditures for education, and illiteracy rates.[9] Although the over-all problem is complicated in the Southeast by the heavy concentration of Negroes, whose schooling has long lagged behind that of the white population, the roots of the problem go deeper. The population of the Southeastern states is prolific—the rural South has by far the highest birth rates in the country; it has lagged far behind most other regions in industrialization; and it has far smaller revenues available for education.

One of the major issues facing the country that is certain to agitate the public and that may well lead to legislative action relates to the advantages of Federal aid to education, the level of such aid, and the conditions under which it should be proffered. Were it not for two extraneous issues—whether Federal funds should be available to parochial schools, and, secondly, whether the granting of Federal funds should be made contingent on the introduction of non-segregated practices in the South—there can be little question that substantial Federal aid would have been forthcoming long before now. This much is certain: if the legislators can get around these two issues, Federal aid of one sort or another will definitely be forthcoming to the states so that they can better cope with the marked rise in enrollments which coincides with a public awareness that education has been less well-nourished than it should have been during the past fifteen years of prosperity.

Within a few years the substantially increased enrollments will press against the facilities available for higher education. A public policy already exists regarding the expansion of state-supported colleges. Recognizing that the major costs of a college education are represented not by tuition but by the cost of living away from home, some of the wealthier and more farsighted states have moved toward the establishment of junior colleges in communities large enough to provide a student body of reasonable size. At present the junior college can have three distinct objectives. It can represent two years of terminal education beyond high school in liberal arts studies; this type of institution provides half of the usual college course. In other instances it serves as a feeder to the larger colleges and universities in the state, thus reducing the living costs of some young people in acquiring baccalaureates. Thirdly, it is geared to providing a large number of vocationally oriented courses to prepare people more specifically to enter an occupation. Another objective which is likely to develop is that of providing refresher training and education for older women who will be entering or re-entering the labor market at the age of 35 to 40 after their children are no longer a major demand on their time. During the past few years this particular group of married women has represented one of the most important additions to the labor force, and there is every indication that more and more of them will seek employment in the future. It is no easy matter for a junior college to achieve all these objectives simultaneously; yet concentrating on one or two leaves other community needs unprovided for.

The great strength of American education has been its expansion so that more and more citizens have acquired the appurtenances of learning. Although the United States has been able to develop at every level a small number of outstanding institutions and a considerable number of strong institutions, the system has also encouraged the survival of a very large number of weak institutions. One consequence of the increasing preoccupation of various leadership groups with education has been to create an increasing awareness that quantity and quality are antithetical concepts. Several of the nation's leading colleges have already announced their intention not to expand their facilities and their staffs to any substantial extent to meet the oncoming rush of students. They plan to maintain standards and do the best job they possibly can with a selected number of students. Another facet of this same awareness is the trend among the best engineering colleges to add a fifth year to the curriculum for the purpose of providing the student body with a broader education in the liberal arts and more fundamental grounding in advanced mathematics and physics. Still another piece of evidence is the repeated warnings of leading scientists that the present research and development program is out of balance because it neglects basic research in favor of applied work.

Clearly, most Americans do not exactly understand how an improved educational system can contribute to economic welfare and national security. Nevertheless, there is enough understanding of these interrelations to have built up substantial pressure for constructive action to ensure that a larger number of intellectually able people in the community have an opportunity to go on to college and graduate school; to strengthen the teaching staffs and improve the curriculum of secondary education; to provide financial assistance from the Federal government to the poorer states so that they can more readily discharge their obligation to provide a reasonable level of public education for all of their citizens; to expand further the educational plant through the establishment of a larger number of junior or community colleges with the objective of providing more and more citizens with fourteen years of basic education; and, finally, to place more stress than heretofore on raising the quality of American education.

In seeking to understand the reasons that lie behind the phenomenal productivity of the American economy, it would be an error to neglect the unique factors in the American scene, factors that derive from the history of the country. The wealth of natural resources available cannot be over-emphasized. Freedom from rigid class structures and traditions, though on occasion a serious disability, has proved a great boon as far as the American economy is concerned, because of the encouragement thus given to individuals to develop their full potential.

The educational system must be given substantial credit for the ways in which it has contributed to the reality of the opportunity story. American schools have encouraged the individual to take his future in his own hands and set high aspirations for himself. Furthermore, the ever greater extension of the educational system has increasingly avoided the wastage which takes place when young people must make occupational decisions at too early an age. Young Americans have had the opportunity to mature emotionally and intellectually before they have had to commit themselves. Finally, the ability of large numbers of individuals to receive specialized training within the educational system at no cost at all, or at a very minimal cost, has prepared them to enter many preferred occupations. In short, the school system itself has been a major source of occupational mobility.

The ability of other countries to profit from the American lesson will depend upon the structure of their society, their economic well-being, and the extent to which their present educational system is developed. But every country in the world can profit by establishing the following as criteria for its educational system: that it should contribute as much as possible to the enlargement of personal opportunities, that it should avoid the necessity for premature commitments, and that it should provide specialized training at the lowest possible cost for all who are capable of profiting from it and who desire it.

Part Two

SECONDARY EDUCATION

III. OUR SECONDARY SCHOOLS AND NATIONAL MANPOWER NEEDS

Clarence Faust

TO HELP FOCUS attention upon the need to improve the work skills of the nation, the National Manpower Council held a conference at the close of April, 1955, at Arden House, the Harriman Campus of Columbia University. This conference was an outgrowth of the Council's study, *A Policy for Skilled Manpower*, published the preceding year.

"Our Secondary Schools and National Manpower Needs," an address by Dr. Clarence Faust, President of the Fund for the Advancement of Education, served as a point of departure for discussions of one of the major themes of the conference—the relationship of secondary education to the development of skill. The roles of private industry and of the community in the complex process of skill development were the other themes considered.

Dr. Faust's plea for "a fundamental rethinking of our educational system, especially of our secondary school program," is no less valid today than when he first made it in 1955. The continuing debate over the purposes, structure, and quality of secondary education in the United States testifies to this. That debate also provides overwhelming evidence of the compelling need which exists for American secondary education to find an effective means of escaping from the restraints imposed, according to Dr. Faust's diagnosis, by "success," rigid institutionalization, and historical accident.

"Our Secondary Schools and National Manpower Needs" is reprinted without change from the National Manpower Council's Improving the Work Skills of the Nation: Proceedings of a Conference on Skilled Manpower *(New York: Columbia University Press, 1955), pp. 21–35.*

IT IS a truism that our present strength as a people and our future security depend, not so much upon our numbers, as upon our technical development, our "know-how." Certainly our tremendous progress as a nation, from thirteen colonies huddled on the eastern seaboard to our present territorial size and our international position, is in no small part due to our technological knowledge and skill.

Know-how is not passed on from father to son. Knowledge and the skill to apply it are acquired rather than inherited characteristics. A study of our future manpower must, therefore, necessarily involve an analysis of the possibilities of education. And in this context education must be taken to include, not merely the work of schools and colleges or the efforts of those who make teaching a career, but all of those processes by which the young pick up the ideas and modes of activity of their elders.

Here, however, my concern is with the role of one of the formal educational institutions of our society in meeting one of our important needs—the role of the secondary school in the development of American manpower.

I should like to begin with a point less frequently stressed than I think it should be—namely, the greatness of our existing educational resources. During the past few generations, the American high school has developed until it serves a very large proportion of American youth. Because the needs of the American educational system are so constantly brought to our attention, and justifiably so, we are likely to forget how fully it has already been developed. Hearing of the enormous need for more classrooms and more teachers, we tend to forget the already magnificent scope of our educational system. We possess the educational machinery in this country to give practically every American youth twelve years of schooling and to give a large number considerably more. Twelve years is a long time in the life of the individual, and the period when the school has its opportunity with youngsters is a critical, formative one. What society in history has developed an educational system, established educational institutions, enlisted and trained a sufficient number of professional teachers, and released young people from other obligations so as to provide twelve years of formal education for all of its youth? Americans take the principle of universal education and its extensive application in this country so much for granted that it requires an effort to appreciate the extent and power of our educational resources.

To appreciate our great advantage, consider what it would mean to any of the countries we describe as underdeveloped—for example, India, Pakistan, or Burma—to possess the educational resources enjoyed in this country. Yet, having said this, I am immediately obliged to add that we are far from making the best use of the instruments we have developed. The feeling that we are not doing the best we can with the educational means available grows in part out of the high ideals and large expectations we hold with respect to education, and in part from our sense of the tremendous needs the schools must meet.

These needs may be generally described as of three kinds. One of these, with which the National Manpower Council is especially concerned, is the need to maintain and develop our specialized and technological skills. Ours is a highly specialized society, and one of the functions of education is to help prepare young people for the special roles they must take in such a society.

Ours is also a democratic society. We depend upon the judgment of all in determining our internal affairs and our external relations. We can survive only if we have sufficient wisdom to exercise good judgment with respect to at least the major issues that confront us.

It is therefore not enough that our educational system prepare people for the specialized tasks required in our specialized society. It must, in addition, prepare them for their responsibilities as citizens. For, in our society, thinking about important questions is everybody's business. If government itself becomes a specialty, if our people, content to be effective specialists in their own labors, turn over the major decisions respecting the nation's internal affairs and foreign relations to specialists in these matters, the people will have abdicated and we shall have government by aristocracy or dictatorship.

It may be important to make a distinction here between major matters of policy and the day-by-day operations of government, but even when responsibility for the latter is placed more fully, as perhaps it should be, upon those who have been chosen for government posts, the responsibility of all our people to deal wisely with major issues still remains. And so long as this responsibility remains, it is essential that our educational system prepare people to exercise their powers as citizens wisely. As Jefferson put it, "Our liberties can be safe only in the hands of the people, and that of a people with a measure of education."

A third function of our educational system which, like training for specialized activity and education for citizenship, lies heavily upon the secondary schools, is providing the kind of education that will enable each individual in our society to realize his capacities for development as a human being to the fullest possible extent. Men do not live to carry on an occupation. We develop occupational and professional skills in order to live. We desire a strong society not as an end in itself, but to provide the conditions under which the capacities of individuals may flower fully. In a democratic society, man does not live for the state any more than he lives for the profession or occupation. The state exists for the individual. The full force of this point is expressed by the obvious fact that in exercising their rights and responsibilities as citizens, individuals may remake the nation or state.

It is true that a man's occupation, his exercise of his rights as a citizen, and his personal development as a human being are interrelated. These are not compartments of his life nor are they the products of three separate sets of human faculties. Nevertheless, the fullest development of one does not necessarily guarantee an adequate development of the others.

These three needs of the young members of a democratic society make education in such a society much more complex and much more difficult than in the totalitarian state. The totalitarian state may be concerned with the development of specialized skills, but it can handle the matter of preparation for citizenship by simple processes of indoctrination and it can simplify education for personal development by assuming the subordination of the individual to the state and by limiting individual development to minor and unimportant areas.

The problems of education for all youth in a democratic and specialized society devoted to the fullest possible development of each individual member are difficult enough. The difficulties are critically increased in a society devoted not to the status quo, but to progress in a world changing as rapidly as ours. We expect the next generation of doctors to do far more than the present one. We expect inoculation for polio to be followed by discoveries for the cure of cancer. At a lower level, we expect the invention of the railroad and the airplane to be followed by even more rapid modes of transportation. We expect the telegraph and the telephone and radio and television to be followed by even more effective modes of communication. Most of us hope for social progress. We expect the abolition of slavery and, now, desegregation in education to be followed by further steps in the elimination of racial prejudice. We hope that better opportunities will be provided for the development of individual human capacities. We hope that the removal of illiteracy will be followed by widespread creative activities in the arts and a more general appreciation of them.

This means that our educational system must not only make sure that the knowledge, the insights, and the skills developed by preceding generations are transmitted to oncoming ones, but that the next generation be prepared to make advances in technology, in social justice, and in the realization of the full range of individual capacities. In short, the educational system of a democratic society committed to the idea of progress must prepare the next generation to be better than ourselves—more skillful and more wise.

Viewed in this light, the task of the American educational system is tremendous in scope and difficulty. But even in this view of the needs to be met, its resources are tremendous. It is equipped with buildings and teachers for almost all American youth. It has twelve years of the life of almost every young American during which no other serious social demand is placed upon him.

The system is not failing, but I believe every thoughtful educator will admit it is not making the most of its opportunities and resources. Our school system does need more buildings, more money for operating expenses and teachers' salaries, and more and better prepared teachers, but it needs even more to find ways of making better and more effective use of its resources for the major purposes of education.

The many devoted people who man our schools face several difficult obstacles. One of these is, in a sense, a price of success. The rapidity with which our educational system has been built has resulted in a good deal of jerry-building. Ideal use of twelve years of education would make these years a sequential, cumulative, comprehensive educational experience. But as the system has been put together, this ideal is difficult to achieve.

We began in America with an ungraded public school in which each student was carried as far as his interests and capacities and the competence of the teacher permitted. As larger numbers were accommodated, we borrowed from the Prussian educational system the idea of an eight-year terminal school. Thus our present elementary school came into being. As larger numbers of young people and their parents demanded further education, we developed a high school on the model of earlier Latin schools and academies. This four-year unit we perched uneasily on the elementary school. In New England we had developed four-year colleges modeled largely on those of old England. As a larger proportion of our youths sought education beyond the high school level, the four-year college was perched on the high school. When in the middle of the nineteenth century we became enamored of German scholarship, we began to develop graduate schools and these were perched on the college. It is small wonder that the parts of this system are poorly articulated and that in consequence the educational experience of the student passing through this series of institutions is neither properly sequential nor cumulative.

The lack of articulation between parts of the system has been accentuated by the differences in the modes of preparation of our teachers at various levels. The educational philosophy of the elementary school differs markedly from that of the liberal arts college. Teachers for the former are trained in schools or departments of education. College teachers are trained in graduate schools. All too frequently schools of education and graduate schools exist in separate educational worlds. Even when they sit side by side on the same campus, communication between them is slight, generally inadequate, and not infrequently painful.

The greatest sufferer in this system, if it can be called a system, is the secondary school. It is uncertainly and uneasily connected with the college on one side and with elementary school on the other. Its curriculum may bear the mark of the college and it may think of itself as preparatory to college, but its students come to it from elementary school, which differs from the college not merely in being elementary but in commitment to a different educational philosophy. Its students may have no intention of going to college. Or the curriculum may be constructed to meet the needs of students for vocational training and fail to satisfy the requirements for college preparation. The problem of the purposes of secondary school is exhibited in the development of such ideas as are expressed in the common phrase "the dual-purpose high school." What is reflected in this title is the problem of the several purposes of the secondary school. And with respect to this, there is to say the least, a great deal of uncertainty and confusion.

If the high school devotes itself to preparing students for college, it will be objected that only about one third of its graduates go on to higher education. If, in an effort to be realistic, it devotes itself to vocational training, it will be objected that as citizens and human beings its students need more than vocational know-how. If, furthermore, it attaches itself closely to the community it serves and prepares its students for the vocations practiced in the community, it will be objected that, although this sounds practical, it is unrealistic. In our fluid society, young people frequently do not spend their lives in the community of their birth and education. Even if they do, communities change rapidly. Occupations practiced in a community today may not be the ones that will be practiced there in ten years. Even if they were, the sweep of technological progress is likely to change them so radically that new and different skills will be required for them. Consider the high school that offers courses in automobile mechanics. How can it keep up in equipment and methods with the rapid developments of the automobile industry? At graduation the student is likely to find the machinery and practices of the trade for which he has prepared radically different from those of the high school shop in which he was trained.

If, to meet these difficulties, the high school tries to be all things to all students, both its academic and its so-called vocational training are likely to suffer. The list of things the high school is pressed to undertake is appalling. Among the objectives stated for it are the development of the student's skill as a worker; instruction with regard to health; education in the rights and duties of citizenship; education in the significance of the family; training in how to purchase and use goods; a grasp of the methods of science; an appreciation of music, literature, and art; preparation for the use of leisure; development of respect for others and insight into ethical and social principles; a capacity to think rationally; and a command of the powers of expression. I have not invented this list. It is a list of recognized "objectives" of the secondary school. The high school may be expected to give courses in family living, personal relations, consumer education, safe driving, sewing, dancing, cooking, hobbies, music and art, and international relations.

The task of the high school is so difficult because, instead of beginning with a set of limited and clear purposes and devising an institution to carry them out, we have inherited an institution and have constantly added to its list of obligations. And the obligations successively thrust upon it too frequently confuse, or frustrate, or erode its basic purposes.

The difficulties of an institution having this origin and loaded with so many and such confusing tasks are increased further by the diverse and conflicting theories and practices with respect to the learning process. Even if the high school were made responsible for an easily manageable set of educational achievements, it would suffer from the conflicts between differing concepts of how learning takes place. There is, for example, the conflict between the proponents of learning by doing and those who believe that learning is primarily a disciplining of the mind to understand and apply general principles. The first group insists that youngsters must be educated by having them engage in specific activities for the specific tasks they must undertake as adults. They regard attempts at education through other than such specific activities as academic, verbal, and futile. The second group insists that education worthy of the name must involve a clear understanding of principles and that an examination of general principles is the essence of the educational process and that attempts to avoid the verbal level of education are unrealistic in preparing people for life in human society. These two views underlie sharply opposed practices at the secondary school level.

It would seem fair to say that our high schools suffer, on the one hand, from being too rigidly institutionalized along lines explainable only as historical accidents, and on the other hand, from having to undertake too large and too diverse a collection of objectives by conflicting methods supported by opposing schools of educational theory.

But I come back to my opening statement. Despite these difficulties, our resources are great. High schools suffer, as do all institutionalized endeavors, from the twin dangers of institutionalization: (1) As means of education are institutionally established they come to be mistaken for ends; and (2) after a time institutionalized procedures that are merely devices for achieving the institution's purpose come to be regarded not as contrivances to serve specific purposes but as the "natural" ways of proceeding.

Courses, programs, degrees come to be regarded as ends in themselves, rather than as more or less useful ways of achieving important purposes. Particular procedures, because they are long established, come to be viewed as the "natural" way of doing things and therefore inevitable. If, in this situation, purposes become multitudinous and confused and if underlying theory becomes diverse and conflicting, resolute rethinking is essential. Such rethinking, it seems to me, is demanded with respect to secondary education.

I am disheartened—though not in despair—about the prospects of secondary education. As a people, we are progressive and ingenious. If under the urgent necessity we could think out the principles and develop the appropriate techniques to produce an atomic bomb, we can certainly think our way to the basic principles and develop the appropriate institutional organization to provide the kind of secondary school education the country needs.

There are several lines, it seems to me, along which we need to proceed in our rethinking of the problem. For one thing, we need to re-examine the concept of "terminal" education. One of the consequences of institutionalizing education is that we think of formal beginnings and conclusions. We think of a child's first day at school as the initiation of his education, forgetting that during the first five years of his life he has probably learned more than he will ever learn in the same number of years any time later. We think of graduation from eighth grade, or high school, or college as somehow terminating his education, forgetting that an alert mind grows in knowledge and wisdom to the end of life and that even a sluggish mind cannot avoid making some additions to its store of information and insight.

Several controversies about secondary school education involve such artificial conceptions. The high school, it is said, must provide terminal education for the majority of its students, that is, for all but the thirty-five percent who go on to college. It is sometimes urged that the first two years of high school be regarded as terminal with respect to general education and the last two years be devoted to vocational training, as though knowledge required for good citizenship and a good life could be so completely packaged that at the end of the second year of high school, or at the end of four years of high school, or at the end of the second year of college general education was complete, had been terminated, and could be forgotten. We seem to assume that at some point the student has completed his preparation for life and then begins to live.

I suggest that it may be useful to reconsider these views, to ask whether we should not regard both formal and informal education as going on concurrently, though perhaps in different proportions, throughout life. Suppose, to put the matter specifically, instead of assuming a point at which formal education ends and the informal educational processes of life begin, we planned an educational system in which some formal education continued through life and in which responsible participation in the world's work began as early as the youngster was ready for it. I have in mind more than merely the addition of night school classes for adults. Suppose that at some appropriate point, say age fourteen or fifteen, students began to work part time at apprenticeships in various trades, occupations, and professions. Suppose that the so-called leaving of school were a gradual process and even the young person who eventually entered college began at the secondary school level to give some part of his time to an occupation, or the youngster who entered a trade did so in graduated steps and continued through life some formal education.

One consequence of such rearrangement might be that the increasing leisure our technological developments are bound to make possible might then be put to better use than it is likely to be when based on the assumption that education is terminated at age fifteen or seventeen or nineteen or twenty-one. For the secondary school, a second consequence of such an arrangement would be to relieve it of its present difficult problem of determining how to complete education for different individuals at the various arbitrary points set by our relatively rigid educational system.

Such reconsideration of the question of terminal education would require rethinking the nature and purpose of education. If secondary schools are currently obliged to do too many different things for too many different people (different in interests, needs, and capacities) in too arbitrarily fixed a time, it is necessary to establish priorities. For this purpose, it is necessary to try to determine the essence of education.

On this point, I would like to suggest that the essence of education of all kinds at all levels is the fullest possible development of man's capacity for taking thought about himself, about his world, about what he is doing, about future possibilities, and about his choice of alternatives with respect to them. For want of a better word, let me call this peculiar and powerful capacity of man his capacity for reflection. The development and utilization of this capacity—this mysterious and amazingly reproductive ability of human beings to be aware of the world, of their fellow men, of themselves and to recall and compare impressions, to weigh them, to make judgments, to construct systems of ideas, and to hold in imagination that which only the future can bring to objective reality—this is the basis for human achievement and progress.

Animals attain in their own way results that are astonishing. The hive constructed by the bee is an amazing thing. But it is not the result of awareness, thought, imagination, planning. It is the consequence of animal instinct. It is not the product of reflection, deliberation, and choice. Thought, imagination, and deliberate planning are subject to error in ways that instinct is not. But they open doors closed to instinct. They enable man to meet new situations, to improve his lot, to enjoy the satisfactions of achieving consciously formulated objectives.

It is the cluster of capacities I have designated by the word reflection that makes education necessary and that gives to education its tremendous potentialities. If the activities of human beings were directed purely by instinct, human beings could profit from training, but could not be educated. In his *Education and Democracy* John Dewey made an important distinction, worth frequent attention, between education and training. Animals are trained rather than educated, since the actions they are taught to perform are carried on without a view of the ends to be achieved and without choice of possible means of procedure. The horse and the dog may be trained to carry out the purposes of a master, but not educated to reflect upon their experience or see and choose among possible consequences, and then fulfill their aspirations. Human beings may also be trained, that is, taught to perform tasks without full awareness of what they are doing and why. But human beings should not be trained, they should be educated.

Without attempting a precise analysis of reflection, let me summarize what I have in mind. Reflection enables us to profit from sense experience. The shimmering and buzzing world about us brings to our senses hundreds of reports of itself. By a power so mysterious that it would be incredible if we did not experience it every day, we are capable of becoming aware of these reports, of arranging and classifying them, of establishing cause and effect connections between them, of generalizing about them. Between the first primitive judgments of the baby reporting that this is "hot" and this is "cold" and the sweeping formulae of an Einstein explaining the universe, there is only a matter of degree in the development of a capacity for reflecting on the data of sensation.

Our capacity for reflection enables us not only to become aware of the world about us but to bend our minds upon our own feelings—to be aware that we love and hate, to judge the appropriateness of these feelings, and to understand something of the operations of our own minds. Between the first dim awareness of a child that it is at a particular moment happy or unhappy, content or discontented, and the development of such psychological insights as a William James or a Sigmund Freud provides, there is only a matter of degree in the development of our capacity to reflect on our own states of mind.

Again, we have a capacity not only to entertain ideas but to bend our thoughts back upon our notions. We can review, arrange, discover consistencies and inconsistencies among them, develop systems of thought as a consequence of our capacity to be aware of our own emotions and reflect upon them. The capacity to see the connection of ideas, to be aware of inconsistencies among them is one of the most important of human resources. It is the basis of much of the progress mankind has managed to make in understanding ourselves and the world about us and in improving our behavior and our social institutions.

It is the fundamental purpose of education to develop as fully as possible the range of this mysterious and amazing human capacity for reflecting upon sense experience, our own states of mind, our beliefs and ideals. Deprive a man or a society of these capacities and education becomes meaningless—indeed, impossible. At best, it becomes mere training—an unthinking channeling of instincts in obedience to some superior will. If the development of the human capacity for reflection is the essence of education and consequently the essential task of educational institutions, the mere accumulation of information is not education. Indoctrination in even the noblest ideas and ideals is not education. Nor is the mastering of vocational skill true education if all that it involves is the training of hands to perform a task efficiently.

Education is sometimes conceived of as tripartite: the education of the hand; the education of the mind; and the education of the heart, or character. But the critical question in each case is whether what is taking place is education or training—whether or not the hand is merely being trained to unthinking efficiency, the mind merely being stored with information or indoctrinated in ideas without becoming independently thoughtful, the character simply being fixed to guarantee the habitual performance of right actions or to develop an understanding of right principles of action. To stress the importance of reflection is not to deny the importance of action. It is to deny the value of action not based upon reflection. To make the development of the capacity for reflection the essence of education is not to dismiss the power of emotion and other nonrational forces in human affairs. It is to insist that it is the application of man's reflective powers, however their scope may be narrowed by nonrational pressures, that has lifted mankind from barbarism to civilization and is essential to prevent a relapse.

To regard the development of the capacity for reflection as the purpose of education is not to reject the idea of the education of the whole child or man. It is to view the child as a whole, generally capable of being in a critical degree governed by its most important human power—the power of thought. Current theories of education of the whole child tend, it seems to me, to view the whole as merely a conglomeration of parts—the physical part, the social part, the mental part, the vocational part, the citizen part, and so on. The whole is educated when each part has received some attention. I suggest that the child be regarded as truly a whole, as a human whole in which the coordinating element, the element which binds all other powers together as parts of a whole, is the source of man's distinction and the hope of his survival and progress—the capacity to imagine, weigh, and judge, to develop civilization and technology—the capacity, in short, to reflect.

I believe that if we fastened our attention on what is essential in education we might make progress in resolving the current difficult conflicts between academic and vocational education, conflicts that are especially troublesome at the secondary school level. We should perhaps become equally impatient with merely vocational training and with merely academic training. Induction into vocations might on the more mechanical side be handled through apprenticeship carried on while the school gave itself to the development of basic knowledge and the understanding of basic principles in the light of which vocational activities could be carried on with an understanding of the reason for particular operations, in short, in a truly reflective manner. So-called academic subjects would be taught not with a view to transmitting information concerning the present state of an academic discipline (the latest views of the historian, the political scientist, the specialist in languages and literature, the geologist, and so forth) but with an eye to stimulating thoughtful attention to the persistent problems of human beings on this planet and to the current questions that trouble mankind. The curriculum of the secondary school would not be dominated either by the current practices of vocations and professions or by the current state of information in the academic disciplines. It would be controlled by the need for educating people to think profitably about the most important human problems. Such education would be given the highest priority in the educational program. It might be expected to produce specialists who knew the why as well as the how of what they were doing, independently thoughtful citizens, and men able to develop the range of their human capacities fully. If subsidiary tasks had to be performed in the secondary school, they would be carried on in the recognition that they were subsidiary.

We would have twelve long and critical years on the elementary and secondary school levels for this task. The attainments of individuals would vary with their natural capacity, but surely in this period of years it should be possible to develop a sequential and cumulative educational experience that would develop a significant measure of the reflective power essential to dynamic vocations, wise citizenship, and the good life in all but those young people who by birth are deprived of normal human capacities. We should, furthermore, not suppose that the possibilities of education terminate abruptly at some point where the student leaves school to enter the world.

I do not believe that I am engaged here in a counsel of perfection. If a democratic society with a rapidly progressing technology is to survive, then education of the kind I have described is not a luxury that a people of great natural resources and highly developed productive capacities can choose to enjoy, but a necessity. Our tradition is not to be hampered by tradition, not to be overwhelmed by the institutionalized processes of our own social interests, but to take long steps toward the ideal even when it seems almost impossible of attainment.

Our principal danger is that we shall be content to tinker with our educational system, or, under a multitude of pressures, to yield to the temptation simply to add one function after another to the tasks of the schools without proper attention to the essence of the task and to the priorities it establishes. Or we may make the mistake of depending upon remedial measures to take care of the inadequacies of an educational program. This is the temptation that leads us into the supposition, for example, that if we add to our secondary school system a fully developed program of student guidance we could in each individual case take care of the problems the system had not adequately handled. There are signs that the growing profession of guidance is being loaded with precisely this responsibility. It is alarming to observe how frequently when the deficiencies of high school or college curricula are discussed the problem comes to be dismissed with the observation that a good system of guidance would take care of them. But guidance might easily move into an unfortunate kind of human engineering in which individuals are tested to discover the role they should play in society and are then trained to fill it.

What I am pleading for is a fundamental rethinking of our educational system, especially of our secondary school program. I am confident we are capable of taking the necessary thought and developing the needed reforms. We are confronted here with a kind of challenge Toynbee makes much of in his study of the careers of human civilizations. The promise of the future depends upon the imagination and wisdom with which we tackle the challenge that confronts us.

IV. SECONDARY EDUCATION AND PREPARATION FOR WORK

The Council Staff

THE FORMAL EDUCATION of the overwhelming majority of skilled workers and technicians stops with high school and junior college. Consequently, the National Manpower Council's *A Policy for Skilled Manpower* dealt intensively with various aspects and problems of secondary education from the viewpoint of their bearing upon the development of adequate supplies of skilled workers and technicians in the future.

In this study, the Council, noting that "the measure of skilled work is relative and changing," differentiated the skilled worker segment of the labor force on the basis of three criteria—distinctive abilities, work competence, and special training. When *A Policy for Skilled Manpower* was published, there were 8 to 9 million skilled workers and about half a million technicians. Together, they accounted at that time for about 14 percent of a total civilian working population of 64 million.

The Council estimated that "three out of every five skilled workers and technicians acquire their abilities and competence through informal training," and, therefore, emphasized the extent to which the secondary school experience, regardless of its specific vocational content, represents broad preparation for work for the youth of the nation.

"Secondary Education and Preparation for Work" is reprinted with some editorial changes from the National Manpower Council's *A Policy for Skilled Manpower* (*New York: Columbia University Press, 1954*), in which it first appeared as Chapter 5, pp. 136–58.

WHAT IS the purpose of secondary education? An attempt to answer this question is implicit in every current dispute over the public educational system. This is true whether the speaker bewails the alleged inability of contemporary students to write,

read, or mind their manners; whether he insists that more education for all is the surest way to cure the world's ills; whether he
protests that too many people are getting too much education; or
whether he calls for larger appropriations for school buildings and
teachers' salaries. No matter what his point of view, he bases his
arguments and his judgments on his concept—frequently un-
stated and unexamined—of what the educational system should
accomplish.

Lack of agreement on what should be the purpose of education is not a new phenomenon. Aristotle wrote:

All people do not agree in those things they would have a child
taught, both with respect to improvement in virtue and a happy life;
nor is it clear whether the object of it should be to improve the reason
or rectify the morals.

Just as education's purposes have been disputed, dire fore-
bodings have similarly been voiced regarding the educational
achievements of the young. Some of those who critically compare
the present with the good old days, when solid learning was sup-
posedly pounded into their own heads, would be taken aback by
a New York *Sun* editorial of 1902:

When we were mere boys, boys had to do a little work in schools.
They were not coaxed; they were hammered. Spelling, writing, and
arithmetic were not electives; and you had to learn. In these more
fortunate times, elementary education has become in many places a
sort of vaudeville show. The child must be kept amused and learns
what he pleases.

Complaints about the effectiveness of the schools were chronic
at the opening of the century—a period now often cited as a
standard for comparison—and even much earlier. Such criticism,
however, has been valuable. It is doubtful whether many of the
significant accomplishments of American public education would
have been possible if critics of the schools had not stimulated self-
examination and change. It is important, therefore, to remember
that education has been recurrently subjected to critical inspection and that the current educational controversies have long his-

tories. Today, however, they take place within a new setting distinguished by the tremendous expansion in secondary education which has taken place during the past half-century.

HOW THE SCHOOLS PREPARE FOR WORK

Before a decision can be made as to who should be educated and how, it must be decided why students should be educated—that is, the purpose or purposes of education. A review of the educational literature or an examination of any school system's curriculum reveals at once that education has a variety of purposes. Nevertheless, whatever else they do, the secondary schools are a major institution for preparing the youth of the nation, in different ways and with varying degrees of success, for work.

Training in the professions—medicine and law, for example—could once be acquired informally through a form of apprenticeship. Now, for scientists and professional personnel, high school graduation is the prerequisite for an extended period of education and training in institutions of higher education.

Skilled and technical work is evolving comparable though lesser requirements. Many technicians are trained in technical institutes and junior colleges, which usually require high school graduation for admission. Most apprenticeship programs require high school graduation of young applicants. Many employers will not hire young workers who have not graduated from high school.

Preparation for work is a need common to all students. Certain knowledge, skills, and attitudes must be acquired both by those who go on to the most advanced university education and those who will have no additional formal training after graduation from high school. Consequently, the type of high school preparation required by different students cannot be determined solely by differentiating between those for whom high school is or is not considered "terminal."

Secondary education is not really terminal for many students. Even those who do not go on to junior colleges or to regular four-year colleges may attend technical institutes or adult education classes, enter apprenticeship, take on-the-job training, or study through correspondence courses. For all who will seek some form of advanced education or training, the necessity for learning does not end with the high school diploma. They all need, to a greater or lesser extent, a common foundation in high school.

A consideration of secondary education as preparation for work is dictated by any concern for the adequacy and the quality of the nation's resources of skilled workers and technicians. Preparation for work, moreover, is one function of the schools on which all agree. It thus offers a valuable vantage point from which to analyze current educational issues and to develop criteria for assessing educational curricula and methods.

Preparation for work is not conceived of here as specific vocational training; it may be achieved through a wide variety of different subjects and by different methods. Preparation for work is not the sole purpose of education and there is no necessary conflict between it and other essential purposes. In addition, it is an intrinsic part of other goals, such as the inculcation of good citizenship.

The basic set of common skills is the ability to read with comprehension, to communicate understandably—both orally and in writing—and to use arithmetical processes accurately. The foundation for these basic skills is supposed to be laid in the elementary school, but for some students, the high school may find it necessary to use remedial techniques to bring them up to a minimum standard. For the others, the high school seeks to augment these skills. Since a high school education establishes the basis of eligibility for and adaptability to subsequent education and training, and is increasingly required for desirable employment, the high schools would do their students a disservice if they failed to provide as much academic training in these skills as students could absorb.

Another set of skills required by all students lies in the area of work habits. These, too, are provided both deliberately and indirectly by the schools. The school environment exposes youngsters to conditions and experiences comparable, in a number of important ways, to those which they will encounter when they go to work. The school enforces a regular schedule by setting hours of arrival and attendance; assigns tasks that must be completed; rewards diligence, responsibility, and ability; corrects carelessness and ineptness; encourages ambition. Of all the cultural institutions a youngster encounters—his family, the church, his peer group—the school makes demands which come closest to those made by an employer. Because the school's manner of operation resembles the employment situation, it can be viewed as a training and preliminary testing ground in the work habits and methods, motivations, and attitudes that will be considered desirable when the student seeks employment.

Completion of high school as a prerequisite for even noncollegiate training is an increasingly common requirement for two broad reasons. First, the applicant who has completed the high school program with satisfactory grades is considered to have acquired the basic skills and knowledge most employers consider desirable in young workers who are potential trainees. The second reason is that high school graduation is considered an indication of a youngster's commitment to his own development and, therefore, of his willingness to undertake further training. Large firms, especially, place particularly heavy emphasis on the young worker's attitudes toward work even more than on his specific aptitudes and his high school courses.

The young man or woman with a satisfactory school record is felt to have shown at least fundamental ability to complete a task and accept work discipline. With the enormous expansion in high school enrollment, most employers look dubiously at the young job applicant who had not availed himself of this opportunity for education. He is usually considered inadequately prepared for work, both academically and psychologically—and more particularly, for the training through which he can become a skilled worker.

It is one thing to point out that there are certain needs common to all students to which the high school must respond in order to fulfill its responsibilities. It is another to determine how this obligation can be met most effectively with today's large and diverse high school population. What methods and curricula are to be employed? At what point should the schools begin differentiating their offerings in order to meet the particular needs of different segments of the student population?

THE GROWTH OF SECONDARY EDUCATION

The United States is the only country where high school education has been made freely available to those not seeking college preparation. School-leaving age laws have, in fact, made at least some high school education virtually compulsory for most youngsters. In Western Europe general education for those who will become workers—skilled or not—usually stops at fourteen or fifteen. The same holds true in Australia and the situation is similar in New Zealand. Only in this country has it been considered desirable to extend secondary education to everyone who wants it—and frequently to many who do not.

Equal educational opportunity is part of the nation's social philosophy. The United States has a tradition of faith in the beneficent value of expanding popular education. Working class parents have viewed education as the means by which their children could achieve social and economic advancement.

In addition, economic factors have influenced the expansion of secondary education. A crucial factor is that only this country could afford it. Because of the extensive use of machinery and the increase in worker productivity, the economy could afford to let part of the labor supply remain unused. The spread of urbanization and industrialization; the development of mechanized farming; the decline in the agricultural population and the reduced demand for unskilled farm labor—all these changes made it possible for boys and girls to spend what used to be working years in school.

When the major depression of the early 1930's struck, economic pressures to prolong schooling became more immediate. With millions of unemployed, youngsters seeking work would only add to the surplus labor supply. The unions wanted to keep them out of the labor market. One way of doing this was by raising the school-leaving age and providing additional school facilities.

The pressures exerted in response to the unemployment problem probably were more effectual than school-leaving age laws in lengthening the period of secondary education for many students. Today,[1] school-leaving age laws are still flexible enough in most states to allow students under 16 to leave school in case of family need, if they are employed, and if they have completed the eighth grade. Twenty-two states allow children to leave school at 14 and have no general restrictions on child labor above this age. The laxity of these laws was demonstrated during World War II, when many students left high school to take jobs.

Secondary education is now generally considered to begin with the seventh grade, the beginning of junior high school, and continues through the twelfth grade. In some communities, secondary education is often considered to last through the fourteenth grade, the end of junior college.

The traditional division of public schooling in this country has been eight years of elementary school and four years of high school. In recent years the trend in secondary education has been away from the four-year high school toward a system that includes some form of junior high school. The biggest growth has been among junior-senior high schools, which span a five- or six-year period. The next largest growth has been among the separately organized junior high schools. The three-year senior high schools, as distinct from "regular" four-year high schools, constitute the smallest group of secondary schools. But in recent years the number of senior high schools and their enrollment has been growing rapidly. Currently,[2] the annual cost of running the public high schools is probably more than $1.75 billion.

In 1952, with a total of 7,688,919 daytime students enrolled in 23,746 public secondary schools, the enrollment in the different types of schools was as follows:

1,526,998 students were in the 3,227 junior high schools.

1,528,006 students were in the 1,760 senior high schools.

1,937,210 students were in the 10,168 regular high schools.

2,696,707 students were in the 8,591 junior-senior high schools.

The following figures prepared by the Office of Education illustrate how secondary education has expanded in this country:

The number of students enrolled in the last four years of the public high schools rose from 202,963 in 1890 to 5,695,514 in 1952.

In 1890, 3.8 percent of the fourteen-seventeen year olds were enrolled in the ninth through twelfth grades. In 1952, the figure was 65.3 percent.

In 1890, 3.5 percent of the seventeen-year-olds graduated from high school. In 1949–50, 59 percent graduated.

With the nation committed to making at least some secondary education available to practically the entire teen-age population, and with a national birth rate that in recent years has remained at record highs, the secondary school population will continue to expand enormously. High school enrollment in 1960, it has been predicted, will be more than 9 million; by 1965, it is expected to reach 12 million.[3] For some regions of the country—the South particularly—the cost of expanding secondary education will be disproportionately high. The South is faced with a particularly acute expansion problem because its present level of secondary education is far below the national average. Two other difficulties that add to the problem are the high rural birth rate and the realization of desegregation.

About 80 percent of the country's fourteen-seventeen year olds acquire some secondary school education.[4] Not counting the South, the percentage would be even higher. In the South, only 65 percent of the white, and 45 percent of the Negro youngsters are attending high school. The Southern Regional Education Board estimates that by 1967–68, 71 percent of the whites and 64 percent of the Negroes will attend high school.

The effort required to provide the present percentage of the expanding high school age group with schools—and, in the case of the South, to catch up with the rest of the country's current standards—cannot be minimized. The schools are not only trying to accommodate an increasing school population, but they are also trying constantly to bring an increased percentage of the total age group into the schools and to hold them in school longer.

The high school now must cope with many students who have not been motivated to learn—or lack the ability for further education—and do not wish to remain in high school. Compulsory education laws or inability to find employment because of their age force most of them to attend school until they are at least 16. The number of such low-ability or inadequately motivated students varies in different communities. In New York City, for example, it has been estimated that such students constitute 20 percent of those in the early years of high school.

Several decades ago, youngsters such as these would rarely have been admitted to high school. They may lack the fundamental ability in the Three R's that entitles them to graduate from elementary school. But the general introduction of a continuous promotion policy, which keeps students moving along with their own age group at a lower level of scholastic achievement, pushed them into high school. Now that the high schools have been forced to retain a substantial number of students who are recalcitrant or inept, or both, they must devote a great deal of attention to disciplinary problems.

In theory, continuous promotion is supposed to apply only so long as a student's achievements measure up to his abilities. In practice, continuous promotion too often produces cases like one reported in Washington, D. C. There, a fourteen-year-old juvenile delinquent, who had led a gang that terrorized his junior high school, had been promoted through elementary school although he was barely able to read. Not until he reached junior high school, did he get the lessons in remedial reading that, it was believed, might have helped alleviate his behavior problems.

If the school is to perform effectively its function of preparation for work, the introduction of an ever-increasing percentage of the young population into high school will require more than enlarged school facilities. If educators are seeking the beneficial psychological effects continuous promotion is supposed to confer, remedial efforts will be needed for students retained in school and pushed too rapidly for their ability. Otherwise, as one observer pointed out, continuous promotion often creates frustrated, resentful academic failures. To educate them effectively, and not detrimentally affect the education of other students, requires special provisions.

Such students usually need courses tailored to meet their needs and teachers specially trained to handle them. They probably need a school-work program and special vocational opportunities and guidance. Exactly how much education, and what kind of education, would be most worthwhile for such youngsters is a problem both educators and the community will need to consider in terms of these students themselves and of the total resources of education available in the community.

The expansion of secondary education has created a wide diversity in the functions demanded of the high school. About fifty years ago, 75 percent of those who graduated from high school went to college. Compared to today's student body, the students of that time were comparatively homogeneous in social background, intellectual ability, and scholastic purpose. The high school's purpose was college preparation; it attempted to discipline its students' minds through training in literature, languages, and mathematics.

Although the actual number of college entrants is close to record levels, only about 40 percent of high school graduates go on to college. Contemporary high school students are vastly diversified in social background, in intellectual ability, in their level of previous scholastic achievement, in their life goals, and, consequently, in their reasons for attending high school.

Another obstacle that makes it difficult to formulate common goals generally applicable to the high schools is the wide diversity in the standards and facilities of schools throughout the country. Some high schools have 5,000 students, others have 50; some send almost all their students on to college, others send almost none. Such differences in size and occupational goal also influence the variety of courses offered and the level of achievement demanded.

The continuing expansion of the secondary schools may obscure the need to define their purpose. By itself expansion will not solve the most fundamental problems of the secondary schools. The process of alleviating shortages of facilities may, however, postpone their consideration. The difficulties created by an expanding school system that does not clearly define its major purposes is illustrated by the problems secondary education faces today after half a century of extraordinary growth.

THE INFLUENCE OF VOCATIONAL EDUCATION

The rapid growth of the high school population during the past half-century compelled the high school to acquire other purposes than college preparation. But, at the same time, the introduction of vocational courses into secondary education in turn helped spur the remarkable expansion of the high schools. It seems safe to say that, to a large extent, the high school population and high school offerings expanded together, with each helping to spur the growth of the other.

In his study of *American Apprenticeship and Industrial Education*, published in 1921, Paul H. Douglas remarked that, "Perhaps the most important educational movement of the past decade has been that of industrial education." Beginning in the 1880's, there was a growing preoccupation in educational circles with the vocational or industrial content of the public school curriculum. This was reflected first in the introduction of manual training courses and schools and, later, in the appearance of specialized trade and industrial schools. Next it was manifested in the growth of vocational schools and in the expansion of vocational courses in the general high schools.

These innovations in the kinds of secondary schools and in the curricula offered indicate that, early in the century, a special effort was already being made to serve the vocational needs of high school students who did not plan to enter college. In addition, cooperative courses, consisting of alternate work and study periods, and continuation schooling for those who left school early, also were established in the public school system.

The widespread diffusion of vocationally directed courses and facilities throughout the general high schools is indicated by the fact that Federally reimbursed trade and industry vocational courses are today [5] given in 2,000 high schools. Only 400 of these are vocational schools. The rest are general high schools. About 10,000 high schools have agricultural vocational courses. Over 85 percent of the public secondary schools have shop facilities.

Exact figures on the number of general high school students taking vocational courses of one kind or another are not available. Probably more than one million students in the general high schools take Federally supported courses in trade and industry, home economics, and vocational agriculture.[6] At least as many study industrial courses outside of the Federal-state vocational program. More than 50 percent of the students in the general high schools are enrolled in at least one commercial course.

The available data thus indicate that the general high schools have assumed certain responsibilities in the area of vocational preparation. In fact, the larger part of all the vocational education offered by the secondary schools is provided by the general high schools.

The growth of the vocational high school has been limited for a number of reasons. The general high school has thus acquired the task of educating a large body of students who will seek immediate employment or specific skill-training after they graduate. At the same time it retains its old function of preparing students for college entrance.

THE GOALS OF SECONDARY EDUCATION

At the same time that the high schools face the task of educating an enormously enlarged and highly variegated student body, they are supposed to assume the educative functions formerly performed by various other institutions. Thus the high school is often expected to train the student in personal relations and family living. It may try to teach the student how to swim, dance, drive, cook; it may try to make him into a hobbyist, a knowing consumer, an athlete. Not many schools aim at all these targets, but to offer instruction along these lines is frequently declared to be the duty and function of the high school. In any case, it is clear that in addition to its earlier preoccupation with formal learning, the school now frequently assumes many of the duties of the church, the family, and voluntary groups.

The public's differing, and often contradictory, views of what the school's functions should be are illustrated by a study conducted under the auspices of Harvard's Graduate School of Education. Interviews with 105 Massachusetts school superintendents during 1952–53 showed that they were subjected to the following contradictory demands:

50 percent were pressured to put more emphasis on the Three R's; 64 percent received demands that more courses and subjects be taught.

39 percent received protests against the introduction of new school services, such as guidance and health programs; 63 percent were urged to have the schools introduce such services.

40 percent faced demands from the community for less emphasis on athletics; 58 percent were under pressure to put more emphasis on athletics.

Many vocational or avocational courses—such as driver-training—have been added to the curriculum as the result of local demands. Often they have had no clear relationship to an all-embracing concept of the function of education. They have simply been instituted in response to what was considered a local need—which may sometimes be a sufficient reason.

A good part of curricular expansion, however, has grown out of a conscious attempt to broaden the scope of secondary education. This broadening has gone far beyond the introduction of traditional vocational courses. Many educators have maintained that the student body's many needs were not met solely by adding vocational courses to the older classical curriculum. They have also emphasized that the high school cannot be satisfied only to train students to enter college when most students do not plan to go to college. These educators have insisted that the school must expand its offerings to meet the highly varied needs of youth and to stimulate and explore their interests. They have advocated that the high school seek to give the student what has been described as "preparation for life."

Consequently, there have been introduced into the curriculum courses in personal relations, family living, consumer education. Preparation for life attempts to arouse the student's interest in learning by presenting school activities related to his outside interests and activities. It is concerned with the student's psychological adjustment and his ability to get along with others. It places as much importance on achieving personal adjustment as on amassing knowledge of subject matter. It stresses the need to diversify the curriculum in order to fill the needs, stimulate the interests, and discover the abilities of the diversified student body.

CRITICISMS OF SECONDARY EDUCATION

The critics of the contemporary educational trends inspired by these expanded concepts of the school's function claim that secondary education has virtually abandoned intellectual training. These critics, however, differ widely in the substance of their criticism.

One group, typically businessmen, maintains that high school graduates are applying for jobs without having mastered the fundamentals of spelling, penmanship, and arithmetic. They claim that many young men seeking admission to skill-training programs have not mastered basic mathematics sufficiently well to make them eligible without extensive prior training. These critics call on the schools to place greater emphasis on the fundamentals of computation and communication.

The other principal group of critics, for which the spokesmen are mainly faculty members of liberal arts colleges, makes a more sweeping attack on contemporary educational trends. They claim that the new curriculum based on preparation for life is stunting the mental growth of capable students. By neglecting to provide intensive intellectual training, many schools are said to be undermining such students' capacity to acquire advanced education.

Many of the critics of secondary education cite the allegedly superior achievements of high school graduates a half-century or more ago. It would seem, therefore, that one way to judge the school's effectiveness in preparation for work would be a comparison of the accomplishments of present-day students with those of the past.

Several difficulties block this effort. There are little comparative objective data. Most criticisms are based on limited personal experience or the culling of a few horrendous examples. Frequently, subject matter has changed, preventing a direct comparison. For example, cube root is no longer taught in arithmetic; the content of spelling lists has changed.

Even where there are comparative data, how is it to be evaluated? Can the small percentage of the seventeen-year-old population which graduated from high school in 1890, most of whom prepared for college, be directly compared to the large proportion graduating today—most of whom go directly into employment? The effort to arrive at comparisons illustrates the need to determine what secondary education is expected to accomplish today and for whom. Still, whatever comparisons can be made will illustrate the problems that must be solved.

The following is noted in a spelling text: "For years, teachers, principals, superintendents, and school boards everywhere have been wearied by the cry of businessmen: 'The boys you send us can't spell.' " This book was published in 1909. The Chicago Board of Education observed: "It is a common complaint among businessmen that the young people seeking employment are not well grounded in the fundamentals." This comment was made 45 years ago. These remarks offer no positive comparison with the achievements of contemporary students, but it puts the matter into perspective to realize that complaints were chronic in "the good old days."

The meager evidence that is available allows the following conclusions: The best of the high school graduates are certainly as good—and probably better—than those of the past. Comparison of the test scores of average high school students with scores made on the same tests by students of 30 to 100 years ago indicates comparatively equal achievement.

The National Education Association's Research Division sought data on comparative tests in city schools during the past 30 years. Few school systems could produce objective evidence showing whether the teaching of fundamentals was more effective now or in the past. In 1950, the NEA released a report entitled *The Three R's Hold Their Own at the Midcentury*. It concluded that there was "partial evidence . . . that in general present-day pupils are holding their own in achievement in the basic skills." It found reason to believe that "present-day pupils for the most part equal, and often excel, the achievements of pupils in similar grades in the past."

However, supporting the claim that at least certain standards have changed is the fact that fewer high school students now receive intensive training in science and mathematics. The importance of such training has been stressed by Dr. James Bryant Conant, former president of Harvard, in his *Education in a Divided World:*

Mathematics, of course, is of the first importance, and probably more talent is lost to the sciences pure and applied (including medicine) by the inadequacies of our schools in this field than in any other. . . . As both a former professor of chemistry and one who has heard evidence from colleagues in the other sciences concerned with freshmen from all over the United States, I venture to be dogmatic on [this] point. . . .

Many high school students cannot study mathematics beyond the freshman year because no advanced courses are offered. This is often due to a lack of properly prepared teachers. This situation exists, for example, in more than one fourth of all the high schools in Arkansas, and it is also found in many high schools in other states.

Exact figures are hard to secure, but informed estimates are that not only a smaller percentage, but actually a smaller total number, of students are now taking fairly demanding courses in physics and chemistry. Studies made in 1952 by the Office of Education found a decline in the number of students taking chemistry and physics as compared to 1947.

These figures bear upon the problem of preparation for work in several ways. Lacking the opportunity to take mathematics and science courses, many youngsters lose the chance to acquire and develop scientific and technical interests. Many who possess such interests lose the training opportunities that would make them eligible for collegiate training in science or advanced technical training in technical institutes. The inability to develop scientific interests and skills may either deflect them from going into skilled fields or hamper them if they should desire skill-training.

Many courses in science and mathematics have been dropped from school programs because it was claimed they were beyond the capacity of most students, or that most students were not interested in taking the courses, or that equivalent educational values could be derived from other courses or forms of training. The Harvard Committee, in its report on *General Education in a Free Society*, estimates that "probably little more than half the pupils enrolled in the ninth grade can derive genuine profit from substantial instruction in algebra or can be expected to master demonstrative geometry." It is, however, impossible to say what proportion of the present student body could successfully pursue more rigorous courses if there were changes in the quality of instruction and in student motivation.

Thus far, the problem has been attacked not simply by changing teaching methods to make subject matter more interesting, but by altering, and sometimes eliminating, subject matter. Instead of algebra and chemistry, for example, courses have been offered in "general mathematics," actually arithmetic, and "general science," in which students are taught about science rather than a science itself.

As requirements have been lowered to accommodate the less able students, the usual effect has been to lower the demands made on all students. This particularly affects the most able. The result was described by one educator: "What usually happens is that the teacher assigns a task, accepts a mediocre performance from the average and superior pupils, and accepts a less than mediocre response from the less able."

Evaluating such a situation in terms of preparation for work—certainly an important part of preparation for life—would indicate that under this system students often do not learn what it means to fulfill a given task according to objective standards. They may never understand the meaning of responsibility and thoroughness in terms of an actual work assignment. Nor will they be motivated to utilize their full capacities.

Thoughtful educators have conceded that the bright students have often been the most neglected. The less able often have specially tailored programs and remedial classes; the gifted are usually expected to find their own way. Yet it is known that if bright students are allowed to coast through their earlier schooling, they may develop poor study habits, the inability to concentrate on demanding material, and an unwillingness to meet rigorous standards. These failings lead to poor preparation for work and to the waste of valuable talents.

BASIC SKILLS AND DIFFERENTIATED NEEDS

When it comes to basic skills and work habits, the needs of all students are similar. One difference is the extent to which students can develop their basic skills by taking more advanced work. Another difference is the varied types of advanced work their skills and interests lead them to study. In a sense the different yet similar needs of the most able and the least able students illuminate the major qualitative problems of secondary education and a possible solution of at least some of them.

As educators have pointed out, the secondary school is now a "common school" whose goal is to educate virtually the entire school-age population. Yet, faced with widely differentiated abilities and needs, the secondary school cannot provide equal educational opportunity by offering the same education to all. While it must have common goals for all students and, therefore, some common methods and curricula, it must also differentiate its offerings to meet the particular needs of different segments of the student population.

Since certain basic skills and knowledge, previously outlined, increase a youngster's eligibility for, and adaptability to, advanced education in school and learning on the job, one of the goals of the high school should be to provide as much education in these subjects as possible for those able to absorb it. While the high school makes education of this kind more broadly available, it must not debase the quality of the education offered to the more able students. Nor should it underestimate the average student's potential ability to absorb learning.

Regarding those who will enter employment immediately

upon graduation from high school, the testimony of businessmen and industrialists emphasizes the value of educating for versatility. Technological changes and the consequent changes in skill requirements; the nature of many production jobs, which require only a short amount of time to learn the requisite machine operations; the training facilities and opportunities available in business and industry; the high degree of job mobility in our economy—all these point to the importance, in most cases, of providing an education in the general high school that enables students to adapt to changes in industrial technology and business methods.

Since most skills are usually gained through work experience and in training programs in industry and the armed services, often the best preparation for work the student can have is to acquire the skills that will make him eligible for such training and facilitate his learning. This adaptability is best developed by acquiring competence in the basic skills and subject matter that can be used in the widest variety of occupations.

Specific training beyond the basic skills can take various forms, depending upon the student's ability and interests. For example, spelling is a basic skill for which all students have a common need. One student might advance to courses in stenography, another to courses in creative writing. Similarly, arithmetic may help lead one student to courses in bookkeeping, another to courses in mechanical drawing, a third to trigonometry.

LIFE ADJUSTMENT AND PREPARATION FOR WORK

The schools consider that one of their functions is to help students adjust to life. Although preparation for life encompasses more than preparation for work, it is clear that the area of work is one in which the schools can most feasibly contribute to life adjustment.

When they leave high school and enter either the academic world or the working world, all students will encounter a series of training situations. Satisfactory adjustment to these situations requires certain work habits, attitudes, and motivations and is necessary for the student's advancement—academically or vocationally. The training situation in school offers one of the best means of preparing for these later adjustments.

Acquisition of the work habits and methods, attitudes, and motivations already discussed as preparation for work is, of course, a necessary part of effective preparation for life. So, too, is training in analytical habits of thought. The ability to come to grips effectively and creatively with a wide range of problems can also be part of the preparation for work given by the school.

The school can inculcate in the student an acceptance of present education by demonstrating its value in terms of later vocational advancement. By informing him of the nature of the work situation, it can teach him to anticipate and willingly prepare for subsequent training. Teaching him that change distinguishes the culture in which he lives will prepare him to accept technological changes and the retraining they will make necessary.

Such training in preparation for work is one of the most important ways the school can contribute to the student's life adjustment. This training can be given through a variety of courses and can be made an integral part of varied curricula. The specific ways of achieving this objective are for educators to determine.

EDUCATIONAL PRIORITIES

Preparation for work, although an essential aim of secondary education, cannot be its only goal. An inspection of curriculum offerings underlines the fact that the schools seek to serve many purposes. The question posed at the outset of this chapter, "What is *the* purpose of secondary education?" can, therefore, be said to misstate the issue. Nevertheless, many protagonists in the current debate about secondary education continue to postulate different single goals. Even if educational philosophers could reach agreement among themselves on a unified objective, the secondary school system as it now exists is too large, too diverse, and too much under local control to be effectively directed toward a single end.

Acceptance of the position that the school must serve many purposes can, however, obscure—if not completely obliterate—the points of reference required to give direction to this country's effort to provide mass education. Almost any course in the curriculum, from courtship to automobile driving, can be justified as contributing to a socially desirable purpose. Yet, it is obviously impossible for the schools to seek to meet every student need. They should not attempt to do so. The family, the church, and community groups have important responsibilities they must continue to discharge.

Educators have always recognized that their major responsibilities were to prepare young people for work and for life. Disagreements within and outside the profession have in the final analysis centered around the alternative ways of best accomplishing these purposes. Many educational leaders are convinced that the secondary schools could not possibly provide training for the tens of thousands of specific jobs which exist in our economy. They go further and argue that even if such specific training were practical it would be a mistake for the schools to undertake it. The young person would be prepared for his first job—but not for a working career.

These educators interpose a second objection to any effort to turn the secondary school into a training institution whose major objective is to assist its graduates to gain entry into a specific sector of the job market. They argue that if too much stress is placed on specialized occupational subjects, there will be no room left in the curriculum for providing the student with an understanding of his cultural past or for preparing him to play his role properly as a citizen in the future.

If preparation for work is defined broadly rather than narrowly, there need be no conflict between this aspect of the school's objectives and the other important goals of education connected with the transmission of a cultural heritage and an inculcation of the ideals of citizenship. Preparation for work involves a mastery over the fundamentals of communication and computation by a person who has acquired good work habits and who is strongly motivated to do his best. Clearly, these attributes are compatible with the other major goals of education.

This emphasis on a broad conception of preparation for work does lead to a reaffirmation of the importance of students mastering the Three R's, but it goes far beyond. There is need for a new departure in educational practice in order to develop the elements of a curriculum that can contribute not only to student acquisition of basic skills, but also to the development of good motivations and habits of work.

This approach has additional implications for the structure of the educational system and for students' choice of courses and their timing. Accepting the premise that preparation for work requires the mastery of fundamentals rather than a large amount of specialized training re-enforces the need for a common curriculum for all students through the tenth grade. Further, there is every reason to look askance at the practice of requiring young people to make fundamental educational or occupational choices prematurely, as so many must now do at the end of the eighth grade.

At the present time, secondary education is buffeted by criticisms from within and without. It has laid itself open to these criticisms by accepting a tremendously wide range of social objectives and by splintering its curriculum in an effort to meet these objectives. There is reason to believe that by establishing "preparation for work" as a fixed point of reference, secondary education will have a useful criterion for reassessing its present position and its future prospects. In this reassessment it will want to distinguish as sharply as possible between its primary responsibilities and the host of collateral objectives it has accumulated during recent decades. In a period of serious teacher shortages and vastly expanded enrollments, secondary education must utilize its limited resources to accomplish its primary missions and must beware of dissipating its facilities on peripheral undertakings.

V. SECONDARY EDUCATION AND THE DEVELOPMENT OF SKILL

Arden House Conference Discussion

THE NATIONAL MANPOWER COUNCIL's Arden House Conference on *Improving the Work Skills of the Nation,* as has been noted, was very much concerned with the connection between secondary education, broadly conceived, and the development of skilled workers and technicians.

This report of the conference discussions shows that current criticisms of the basic shortcomings in American secondary education, however much they are inspired by the Soviet Union's successes with space satellites and missiles, turn essentially on the same basic issues as they did in pre-Sputnik days.

In retrospect, it appears that among the more important points to emerge from the conference discussions was the stress placed upon the need for secondary education to provide the foundation for subsequent self-development and adaptation, and upon its relationship to informal systems of education and training.

> *"Secondary Education and the Development of Skill" is reprinted with some editorial emendations from* Improving the Work Skills of the Nation, *in which it first appeared as Chapter 5, pp. 58–79.*

GRADUATION from high school has become in this country an almost universal prerequisite for skill-training. Hardly any training program will accept an applicant who cannot present a satisfactory high school record. Since completion of secondary school usually marks the end of formal education for the skilled worker, a consideration of how to improve the work skills of the nation begins logically with an examination of secondary education.

THE EXPANSION OF SECONDARY EDUCATION

The effectiveness of secondary education can be properly assessed, several participants maintained, only in the light of the enormous task that has been delegated to it. The high school, it was pointed out, no longer concentrates almost exclusively on preparing a small minority for college. It is now a common school for all young people. In 1890, only 43,000 students graduated from high school. But in 1930, there were 666,000 graduates; in 1940, 1,220,000; in 1960, it is estimated, there will be more than 1,700,000.[1]

A few participants questioned the wisdom of trying to give every youngster the same length of schooling. Students going on to college, it was argued, might make better use of their time if they could complete high school more quickly and enter college earlier. And students unwilling or unable to benefit from formal schooling might be better off if they could enter employment before the usual time of graduation.

The educators among the conferees maintained it would be unwise to abandon the idea of providing more secondary schooling for all. They held that the question is not whether all young people should stay in school, but what types of education should be provided for the growing numbers attending school.

THE OBJECTIVES OF SECONDARY EDUCATION

Most of the conferees did not question the value of trying to lengthen the period of secondary education for all youngsters, and turned their attention to specific educational problems such as teacher shortages, the subjects that should be emphasized in the curriculum, and the allocation of more adequate funds to meet educational needs. First, however, the conferees sought to establish a framework for the discussion of specific problems by considering the primary question: What should be the objectives of secondary education? In considering this question, the participants gave some attention to the priority that should be accorded the various objectives of secondary education in the light of their relative importance.

What the elementary schools should teach is definitely set and almost universally followed, a conferee pointed out, but the high school curriculum is not similarly agreed upon. In some cases, the high school's function is conceived to be dispensing information; in others, vocational training; some believe it should concentrate on developing the ability to think; some view it as at least partially a custodial institution, controlling youngsters until the law permits them to work.

The schools, several conferees said, are trying to do too much and, therefore, are accomplishing too little. A number of conferees maintained that the high school curriculum contains too many different courses and that extracurricular activities occupy too much of the teacher's and the student's time. One participant declared he knew of a high school with a course in baton twirling. Another was acquainted with a school that had forty-eight different extracurricular organizations. Because there is no clear concept of educational priorities, a discussant claimed, educators generally respond to the loudest pressure groups. They rely too much, another conferee declared, on the expectation that they can meet educational needs by constantly increasing the variety of courses offered. If the community faces a problem, the school's contribution is to present a course in that area. Thus there are courses in family relations, in safe driving, and many other subjects. Because the schools are constantly adding new courses and activities, he continued, too little time is devoted to genuinely important subject matter, funds are dissipated on unimportant efforts, and teachers are wasting their time and training on activities that are of little educational value.

At the same time, the schools were defended in varying degrees. Several participants insisted that a large variety of courses have a definite place in the schools. A wide variety of extracurricular activities, it was said, offers youngsters the choice of a broad range of experiences. Conducting and administering such organizations was declared to be a valuable educational experience. Another discussant acknowledged that the schools are expected to accomplish too much, but pointed out that the schools' achievement in bringing a higher level of education to more people than ever before is often ignored.

One participant declared that priorities regarding educational objectives differ in different communities. Another felt that since people move from one community to another, there should be common principles according to which all school systems would function.

A number of participants suggested particular subjects they thought should receive greater emphasis in the high school curriculum. More statistics and economics were recommended. Several thought it important for students to have a better understanding of how the economy functions. This, it was said, would help them make intelligent vocational decisions. Specific courses in economics are not necessarily required to achieve this goal, another conferee noted, since a great deal can be learned about the operation of the economy outside of school and through other courses, such as history. More instruction in mathematics, a conferee declared, would help young men to acquire more quickly the technical knowledge required by the armed forces. It would also, he said, reduce the training problem of the armed services, which must often teach draftees fundamental mathematics before they can begin to train them to use modern military equipment and techniques.

One of the participants, an educator, decried what he called the "educational fallacy"—particularly prevalent in the high schools—of packaging materials in separate courses. Then, if the courses prove inadequate, guidance is instituted as a sort of super-package on the assumption it can correct errors and weaknesses in the curriculum. If the guidance is inadequate, psychologists and psychiatrists are then brought in to correct the failings and failures of the guidance program.

This conferee declared that the school should be visualized as the focal point around which to concentrate and coordinate the educational resources of the community. Using community activities for educational purposes requires more thought and imagination, this participant said, than is now usually given to the problem. For example, just sending a class to visit a factory, a public utility, or a municipal department is rarely a worthwhile educational experience. He cited the class of students who visited the firehouse and could later recall only the big brass pole. Such an excursion, he said, does not teach a child anything about public services and the functioning of the community.

Some participants criticized the National Manpower Council's recommendation [2] that students should be permitted to specialize intensively in vocational subjects only after they have completed two years of high school on the ground that it provided tacit support for this "package" concept of education. The Council's recommendation, it was said, assumes that an academic "package" can be followed by a vocational "package."

Another participant noted that, to a large extent, the point of view just advanced suggested the scrapping of the old arguments about general education versus vocational education or life adjustment education, the value of the "core curriculum," and the other major educational disputes of the past thirty years. The essential question that had been posed, it was said, is how to produce thoughtful, adaptable, self-disciplined individuals who could intelligently pursue their self-development. With the high schools facing a period of enormous expansion, another conferee declared, it might be better to create new institutions rather than tinker with the old. This would permit a redefinition of the objectives of secondary education unhampered by the existing framework.

The school-work "cooperative" programs, in which students alternate between school and a job, were cited as one of the outstanding developments in the effort to find new means of meeting the needs of high school students. Several participants advocated the expansion of these programs. The conferees also mentioned various secondary school programs that are now functioning. One educator said the comprehensive high school is suitable for a one-high-school community. But, to provide really good education, he thought it necessary for the school to specialize either in academic or vocational education. A participant described the vocational-technical secondary school program in Connecticut. It is a three-year course beyond the ninth grade, which is an exploratory year. Shopwork takes up one half of the schooling and related and general education the other half. One week is spent in shops, the next in classrooms. Unlike vocational institutions in certain other areas, these schools restrict admission to those believed capable of genuinely benefiting from it.

In connection with the discussion of different types of secondary school education, some attention was given to the Russian and British systems. One participant noted the Massachusetts Institute of Technology studies evaluating the quality of Russian scientists and scientific training. The basic differences between the training programs go all the way back to the secondary schools. One distinctive aspect of the Russian secondary school sciences program is that the schools have standardized courses in mathematics, physics, and chemistry. Judged only in terms of the technical competence of Russian scientists, this participant said, the Russian curriculum in the sciences could be considered very good.

In Great Britain the secondary school population is divided into four groups at the age of 11, and the students then go on either to a grammar school, technical school, modern school, or special school for defectives and retarded students. The first five years of grammar school (up to 16) consist of a combined program of arts and sciences. If the student remains for the last two years, he specializes in one of the two programs. The percentage attending grammar schools in different parts of the British Isles varies widely, in some areas 60 percent, in others 15 percent. In the technical schools, the first two years are nontechnical with technical specialization coming in the last two years. At 16, most technical school students go to work. For one day and two evenings a week they continue with apprentice-related or technical courses. It is hoped that, when the money becomes available, this continuation program will be extended to all youngsters up to 18 who do not go on to college. The modern school is a comparatively recent innovation, and corresponds roughly to the comprehensive high school in this country. There has been some opposition in Britain to the examination system which determines a youngster's future opportunities for schooling when he is only 11. Traditionally, upper class children have attended the "public" (i.e., private) schools regardless of their ability. Few parallels existed, the conferees felt, between the situation in Great Britain and the problems here, where each community devises its own solutions to its educational problems.

One participant declared that, in order to increase the supply of skilled manpower, there should be an early separation of those youngsters who would eventually go into trades from those who would continue academic studies. Such early, sharp differentiation was generally rejected by the conferees. Nobody else advocated that the schools should produce specialized craftsmen.

The conferees recognized that the myriad obligations secondary education has undertaken to fulfill put it in danger of forgetting what should be its primary objectives. However, the conferees did not attempt to define specifically what these should be, nor did they seek to assign definite priorities to the varied functions that the schools have undertaken or have been assigned by the community.

From a discussion of the general goals the schools should

adopt, the conferees turned to a consideration of the type of graduate the schools should try to produce. The development of broadly educated high school graduates who command the basic disciplines of reading and computation and who are thoughtful, reflective, adaptable, well disciplined, and interested in improving their abilities was generally accepted as the fundamental purpose of secondary education. But how this is to be accomplished was a subject for argument. The discussion thereupon focused on attempts to define the type of curriculum that should be offered in order to produce as many such graduates as possible.

STUDENT MOTIVATION AND THE CURRICULUM

One of the conferees, a vocational educator, stated that students with the qualities just outlined could be developed only by having them master specific skills rather than through attempts to teach "abstractly." Students are not given sufficient opportunities to derive pleasure and experience out of making things and working in laboratories, which involve manual activities. There is too much book learning, he said, and not enough learning by doing.

Another vocational educator presented a similar point of view, but in terms of the needs of a particular type of student. The schools, he said, are obligated to retain students for whom the usual academic curriculum is unsuited and they can only be prepared for work through vocational education. Also taking issue with the National Manpower Council's recommendation regarding the point at which vocational education might be introduced, he maintained that one could not lay down a general rule. It should begin, he felt, when the student desires it.

Vocational education and general education should not be rigidly separated, another educator declared. He protested against the widespread idea that there must be two kinds of high school curriculum, one serving as preparation for further education, the other terminal and preparing the graduate to go into the working world. Preparation for further education and preparation for life are much the same, he maintained, and both can be achieved through the same curriculum.

Several conferees stressed the need for widely varied educational offerings in order to motivate students of widely differing interests and capacities to invest genuine effort in their schooling. Noting the recommendation that specialized vocational courses be postponed until a student has completed two years of high school, one participant maintained that students who most need vocational training often are no longer in school by the third year of high school.

One participant protested that it is not fair to expect the schools to solve by themselves the problem of motivating youngsters to seek education. Interest in learning begins in the home, he insisted. If not stimulated there, the schools can hardly be expected to develop it. The most the school can do about motivation, he said, is to provide good teachers. They are the best stimulant to learning. Other conferees believed that motivation can be developed by presenting materials in ways related to the students' interests. Different kinds of students, it was maintained, need different kinds of education.

How can students who want to leave school before graduating be persuaded to complete their studies, a participant asked? He wondered whether young people who drop out of high school are aware of the disadvantages they are creating for themselves and the obstacles they will encounter when they enter the armed services or look for jobs. A conferee commented that the armed services' student deferment regulations seem to have improved motivation in school. Students know they may be drafted if they do not do well. Several participants commented that returned veterans seem to have greater motivation to do well in college and technical schools than those who have not yet been in service. This was attributed in part to the fact that servicemen observe that desirable assignments usually go to those with more extensive formal education.

Although most young men now spend at least two years in the armed services, high schools and employers have by and large not made any provisions for this fact in their curricula and training programs. One educator declared that in the school systems with which he is familiar, virtually no cognizance is taken of the military training most young men will have to undertake soon after graduation. A conferee noted that more young men seem to be completing high school, but implied that they stayed in school only because they expected they would soon after be called into the service.

Is it possible, a discussant asked, to make the advantages of education apparent to more students before they begin military service? The armed forces, it was suggested, should help guidance counselors understand what the military is seeking and what will happen to young men when they enter the services. To some extent, it was said, this is being done.

GUIDANCE AND SECONDARY EDUCATION

A great deal of the effort expended on secondary education is wasted, a conferee asserted, because of the failure to provide students with adequate guidance. Those responsible for educational policy and fund allocations, however, are rarely aware of this loss. They do not accord guidance the same importance, it was said, as is given to the construction of gymnasiums and other physical facilities.

Proper guidance, it was noted, would increase youngsters' motivation to make the most of their educational opportunities. The conferees agreed that guidance could play a crucial role in secondary education and, therefore, promote the development of skills, if it performed these four functions for the high school student: (1) teach him the value of schooling so that he understands how his educational background affects his opportunities for training; (2) assist him in discovering his capabilities and then in developing them to the fullest possible extent; (3) acquaint him with the enormous number of occupations in the economy and the varied opportunities for training; (4) help him learn what occupations are best suited to his training and abilities.

Nobody questioned the important role of guidance in improving the work skills of the nation. The principal differences of opinion concerned the guidance responsibilities that should be assigned to different individuals and institutions. Several participants felt that too many parents have surrendered this function, delegating their responsibility to the school and to community organizations. The latter, it was agreed, should participate in guidance. They could perform services for which parents lacked the necessary technical knowledge. But these conferees believed that parents should play a greater role in guidance than many of them now do.

One suggestion was that the school should concentrate on vocational guidance and leave personal guidance to other agencies of the community. According to this view, the school, by trying to do both vocational and personal guidance, is doing neither well. So far as the school's role in guiding youngsters into specific vocations is concerned, another conferee stated, the school counselor should concern himself with steering a youngster away from fields for which he is obviously ill-fitted. This conferee suggested that the school provide general vocational information. Guidance into a specific vocation should be left, he said, to other agencies.

A number of participants, however, maintained that the school's role in vocational guidance could not be so narrowly delimited. One confree maintained that a guidance counselor has to know about the homes and the parents of the children he counsels, as well as about the children themselves. While the counseling movement did start as vocational counseling, a participant noted, the counselor is frequently the only person in the school with psychological training, and the teaching staff, therefore, turns to him for any assistance that it needs in that area. Even when students come to the counselor ostensibly for vocational guidance, they are often actually seeking personal counseling. A student continually meets new teachers as he advances from subject to subject and term to term. Frequently, it was said, the guidance counselor provides him with the only continuous relationship in the school.

One of the conferees cited figures from a study made in his school to support his contention that youngsters' emotional adjustment affects their educability. Of a group of 32 students with I.Q.'s over 115, five had left high school after the first term and 19 of the remaining 27 had serious emotional problems that interfered with their school adjustment. He felt that guidance counselors in the schools should pay more attention to students who drop out of school. One of the participants took issue with another's claim that bright youngsters are hardly a guidance problem, since they could do well in almost anything they might attempt. He maintained that, because they can do a number of things fairly well, it is difficult for them to decide what they really want to do.

It was pointed out that guidance in the school cannot be separated from the curriculum. An important part of the guidance specialist's job, it was said, is to show the classroom teacher how to embody elements of guidance in the course of study. How well a student does in a particular subject reveals a great deal about his interests and abilities. This does not mean he should be guided into one narrow field, but indicates a broad area in which he can be expected to do well. One conferee explained that if a student does not do well in school, not much can be learned about his abilities and there can be little effective guidance. The most important type of guidance in such cases is to seek to motivate the youngster to put more effort into his schooling.

One participant protested that the discussion of how to divide guidance responsibilities seemed to be based solely on the situation found in large cities. The vast number of small communities lack specialized personnel and the teacher must assume as much of the guidance function as possible, he declared. The problem in such a situation, he said, is to make the teacher as effective a counselor as possible.

The importance of commencing guidance early in a youngster's schooling was stressed by a number of participants. One conferee felt that youngsters could begin receiving general vocational information as early as the sixth grade. He deplored the frequent cramming of job information into a single session nearly at the end of secondary schooling, such as is often done through "career days." One example of the lack of job information, he said, is the fact that engineering students, when they are about to graduate are often still ignorant of the different fields they could enter. A participant from the field of vocational guidance pointed out that 90 percent of the high school dropouts who apply for jobs to the U. S. Employment Service do not know what they are capable of doing or what they want to do.

The inadequacy of much of the counseling available in the schools, a participant declared, is due to a variety of causes. Counselors often have so much paper work they cannot find sufficient time for the counseling that should be their main job. There are too few counselors, and their limited time must be divided among an enormous number of students. Another conferee pointed out that guidance is frequently assigned to unqualified people—teachers who have a vacant period or who can stay after school to discuss vocational problems with youngsters.

Many guidance counselors have never worked outside the schools, another participant pointed out, and are unacquainted with the requirements and opportunities of the working world. A conferee insisted that many teachers and counselors are biased against "blue-collar" work and will rarely recommend industrial skill training to capable youngsters.

Several conferees insisted that a larger proportion of youngsters can be induced to undertake skill training only if the society accords more value and dignity to the acquisition of skill than it now usually does. Too many youngsters are unwilling to devote themselves to studies, it was said, because it is often not considered a worthwhile thing to do. In addition, a participant suggested, more widespread recognition has to be given to apprentices and to apprenticeship training. He noted that guidance counselors sometimes have misconceptions about the nature of occupations which have apprentices. They frequently steer the wrong people into these fields while guiding away those who would be suitable. The consequent high attrition said to exist in many apprenticeship programs not only hurts the program itself, but raises the cost of training.

Lack of money, a conferee suggested, is preventing the schools' guidance programs from being as effective as they might be. While it was generally agreed that more funds would be helpful, one participant maintained that the schools are not using the available guidance facilities as well as they might.

SECURING MORE AND BETTER TEACHERS

To many of the conferees, the single most effective way to improve the quality of schools would be to improve the quality of teachers. A good teacher does more than teach his subject well, it was pointed out. He sets an example for his students in attitudes and behavior and, by advice or by example, often helps them make vocational decisions.

Most of the participants agreed that one of the principal ways to attract and retain more capable teachers is to offer higher salaries. In the South, a conferee noted, many of those trained at considerable local expense to be teachers go North to seek better opportunities. According to a survey that was quoted, 40 percent of the men who leave the teaching profession do so because they find their salaries inadequate. And in many communities, it was noted, women teachers are paid even less than men.

Important as income considerations are conceded to be, several participants maintained that securing a higher level of teaching requires more than raising teachers' pay. Equally important, it was said, is the need to improve teacher utilization—that is, better use must be made of the teachers who are available. Referring to Dr. Clarence Faust's emphasis upon the need to develop the capacity for reflection and analysis in students, a conferee pointed out that teachers themselves are engaged in such a merry-go-round of unceasing duties that they have little time for their own reflective thinking. Not only must teachers teach, they must supervise play, sell milk, collect funds, and perform numerous other duties unconnected with actual teaching. As much as possible, he declared, teachers should be freed from nonteaching activities.

Widespread use of closed-circuit television in classrooms was one suggested technique for making better use of the available teachers. An especially competent teacher could thus reach more students. Still, the possibilities of television should not be oversold, it was warned. By itself it is no panacea for the teacher shortage. Better utilization of teachers was said to be hampered by the fact that teaching has never gone through the professional revolution that other fields—particularly engineering—have experienced. No matter how competent and experienced a teacher is, his nonteaching duties are not reduced, he is given no assistants, his greater competence as compared to fellow teachers is not rewarded with increased responsibilities. There is no outward differentiation between the highly competent and the barely competent.

Another important way to improve the quality of teachers, a participant stated, is to improve the quality of the faculty and students in the teachers colleges. The teachers colleges were accused by one conferee of lacking an adequate philosophy of education. Poor teaching was attributed to poor administrative practices in the schools. In order to make teaching more attractive to capable young people, a conferee said, more attention must be paid to the personal needs, comforts, and desires of teachers. Management problems in industry and in the schools were said to have many parallels, and it was suggested that educational administrators might learn better school management from industry's experience and research in management methods and techniques.

One conferee maintained that the quality of the average teacher will necessarily decline because of the enormous number needed in the future. He said the schools will require an estimated 2 million new teachers by 1975.[3] Even at present, someone else noted, the rewards offered to teachers are too inadequate to compete with other fields for the brightest high school graduates. Comparatively few outstanding young people are entering teaching. One discussant noted that the number of students in teachers colleges has risen, but that the number of actual teachers will not increase for at least three years.

One suggested way to increase the number of teachers would be to bring back those who leave the field because of marriage or other reasons. It was noted that Montgomery County, Maryland, has attempted such a program. One difficulty in recruiting teachers was alleged to be the restrictions many communities still place on the personal lives of teachers. More teachers might be recruited, it was suggested, if certain formal course requirements were waived in the case of those who otherwise promised to make good teachers. Unionization, another participant declared, would improve the working conditions of teachers and thus encourage more young people to enter the profession.

THE COMMUNITY AND SECONDARY EDUCATION

During the discussions of the relationship between the school and the community, it was repeatedly pointed out that the schools alone are not entirely responsible for education. By the time a child reaches school age, he has learned a great deal—

whether what he has learned benefits him or not. The parents, the neighborhood, movies, television, the press all play an educational role. Similarly, education continues when secondary school is completed. Therefore, it was pointed out, it is necessary to recognize the community's importance in the educational process and try to have it cooperate with the schools in order to create an integrated educational effort.

As an example of how a school system consciously tries to serve the broad needs of a community, a participant cited Denver, which conducted a public opinion survey in 1950. This survey revealed there were four principal objectives the public wanted the schools to accomplish: (1) teach the fundamentals well; (2) build personality and character; (3) provide adequate guidance; (4) provide more elective courses to meet the needs of the community. The published results of the survey aroused a great deal of community interest, and the schools endeavored to keep the public informed of their efforts to meet these requirements. When the poll was repeated three years later, the public again advocated the same four objectives and the schools had risen in public favor.

One of the participants mentioned the Toronto Council as an example of educational planning by an entire community. It plans for the educational needs of the whole metropolitan Toronto area, which includes the city's suburbs. Its over-all program has permitted the development of specialized schools where needed, which would not normally be possible outside of large urban areas.

One participant was disturbed by the fact that most of the discussion seemed to be concerned with the problems of urban schools. Most schools are rather small, he pointed out. He felt that consolidation of small schools is not very widespread.

Chicago was said to be trying to decentralize its schools in order to provide more effective leadership and coordination within each area and to facilitate a readier identification by the local citizenry with their schools. At present, different types of schools are divided into administrative districts. The new plan is to divide the school system into a number of smaller school systems based on population areas of about 200,000. Another need, of course, is for more and better schools. Of the approximately 160 buildings in use in Chicago [in 1955], it was said, about 40 percent were built before 1900.

Inadequate financial support of the schools, a participant stated, is caused not so much by unwillingness to pay higher taxes as by antiquated methods of assessment and taxation. Sometimes, it was said, business seems willing to put up more money than the educators are ready to ask for. Several conferees maintained that a great display of interest in the schools by other institutions in the community would improve the schools. Industry and unions rarely appear, it was said, at local school budget hearings.

In financing the schools, one conferee stated, local tax money is the first resource that should be tapped. In the South, however, Federal aid is extremely important. He noted the funds that can be raised by local taxation are limited, not necessarily by what the community can afford to pay, but by tax rates elsewhere. The Southern county that taxes very heavily for good schools may lose its local industries. He insisted that Federal aid is essential for improving the quality of education in the South. Another participant commented that at the same time the South wants Northern money to finance its educational system, it is using tax exemption devices to attract Northern industry.

One conferee pointed out that some states lack the economic resources to finance their school adequately. For example, in Montana, 68 percent of the land is owned by the Federal government. Only a small sum is received in lieu of taxes. The necessary funds have to be raised from the remaining less than one third of the state.

Most of the comments on the current state of school-community relations were critical, but they were also sometimes contradictory. One participant felt the educators are "abdicating" their leadership and that noneducators are taking over the schools. But another thought that the public is abandoning its responsibility for determining school policies. A third claimed that the public is losing its confidence in the professional educators. A fourth maintained that the situation varied widely in different communities, but he and several others acknowledged that real estate interests often have too great a voice in educational decisions.

The public usually evaluates the school in terms of standards that are too idealistic and unrealistic, one of the conferees, an educator, declared. Everything about the schools cannot be perfect. They have a set of obligations to fulfill in providing a body of knowledge for youngsters—teaching the fundamentals, the cultural tradition, etc.—and this they accomplish. While certain aspects of the educational program often come in for criticism, he claimed that the fundamental objectives are usually successfully achieved. Several other educators among the conferees protested that the members of their profession are definitely not "abdicating" their role as educational leaders.

A number of participants pointed out that the schools are ineffective in informing the public of their problems, their objectives, and their accomplishments. Educators should interpret educational needs to the public so that the schools gain public understanding and support. But, it was declared, the schools hesitate to go to the public for anything other than budget items.

One of the educators maintained that they do give sympathetic attention to the public. Eventually, he said, the educators will revolt against undue pressures. Still, he felt, there is much more public participation at present in school policy decisions than ever before. Very few school bond issues, he noted, are defeated in his part of the country.

The public actually should take many of the decisions out of the hands of the professional educators, another school official declared. One conferee believed that current interest in the schools did not grow so much out of an interest in education, but developed because the schools are now spending more money than ever before.

Is it not the educators' job, a participant asked, to tell the public what the schools need? Should they not stop being subservient to public pressures? One of the educators claimed that they do tell the community when something is wrong, but he conceded that many educators allow materials into the curriculum that they would prefer to exclude. One of the discussants declared that there are few attacks on educators where there is active community participation in school affairs. When the two groups keep their distance, sniping is heaviest. When the public actually sees how the schools work, it usually finds them operated far better than they had been led to believe.

THE SECONDARY SCHOOLS AND INDUSTRY

While nominally concerned with how secondary education could contribute to improved work skills, much of the discussion was related only indirectly to this specific subject. The participants were concerned with improving the quality of secondary education, not so much for its direct bearing on the development of industrially valuable skills as for the general preparation young people would receive in order to fit themselves for their future lives in general and, indirectly, for their future working lives in particular. A part of the discussion, however, dealt specifically with the direct relationship between the offerings of the secondary schools and the development of work skills.

Employers often use the high school diploma itself as a screening device, it was noted. It is considered to be both a sign of accomplishment and an indication of desirable motivations. One of the conferees pointed out that many capable people lack high school diplomas while many students complete high school simply by staying in school and drifting along. Better standards of selection than graduation from high school could be utilized, it was claimed.

In considering the type of high school graduate desired, the participants from industry generally agreed they were not seeking young job applicants who had been trained in specific skills. Rather, they were interested in young men and women whose school preparation makes them eligible for intensive skill-training. They want the schools to provide young people with a solid background in the fundamentals of mathematics and science, the capacity to read instructions with full comprehension, and the self-discipline to accept training and carry assigned jobs through to completion. In India, it was pointed out, one can as easily train a worker in very narrow skills as in the United States. But, because of the difference in the educational base, it is far more difficult to train a broadly skilled worker there than in this country.

A participant from the armed forces stated that the services prefer a young man with citizenship training, a sense of responsibility, a broad background, and an open mind, to one who has been trained narrowly in a specific skill. Among the services, the Air Force in particular is interested in men with a solid grounding in mathematics and science, since 70 percent of Air Force jobs are in electrical, electronic, and mechanical fields.

Training for adaptability to changes in skill requirements is vital, several discussants declared. This means not only skill training that is broad enough to enable the individual to pick up new techniques with comparative ease as his changing jobs demand them, but the emotional adaptability to accommodate himself to the changes created by technological innovations, particularly if they come fairly late in a worker's life. The foundations of such adaptability, it was said, must be laid in the schools.

One of the key questions raised in this area of discussion was how to divide the responsibility for skill-training between the schools and industry. The general consensus was that basic skills should be taught in the schools. Skills that are specific for a particular industry should be taught by the industry itself. In addition, the methods taught in the schools must be in keeping with current industrial development.

One of the participants elaborated on these points. He noted that if the schools attempted to train students in the special skills required by railroads, the telephone company, and similar organiaztions, the graduates would be limited in their opportunities to those specific fields and the industries would have their selection of employees limited to those who had been especially trained. The schools, however, can provide training in such fields as machine-shop work, printing, metal-trades work, and others, where the skills learned are applicable in many fields. It was also pointed out that the cost of equipment necessary for training in certain skills makes it impossible for the schools to provide adequate training in these areas. In addition, in fields where technological change is rapid, the need for constant replacement of obsolete equipment makes the whole undertaking almost impossible for the schools.

There was some opposition to the schools doing any specialized skill training at all. One of the participants from industry declared that skill training has to be done on a job. As the jobs are created, he said, industry will train people to fill them. Skilled workers, therefore, will be trained by industry when they are needed.

Another participant from industry disagreed that industry could be self-sufficient in training skilled workers. He pointed out that shortages of skilled workers not only affect national security but also limit the efficiency of individual companies. In California, it was noted, Lockheed spends $2 million a year on its own training programs. But, in addition, four to five thousand of its employees take evening courses in the public schools. Without these public facilities, it was said, the company would face many severe problems. Another conferee pointed out that adult enrollment in evening trade extension courses is double the student enrollment in day session trade and industry courses. He emphasized that vocational education does not necessarily terminate with the end of secondary education but may continue throughout a good part of a worker's life.

One of the conferees raised the question of how to divide training responsibilities in apprenticeship programs when the schools offer courses related to apprenticeship training. He suggested that joint school-industry councils should provide the necessary coordination in deciding what should be taught in school and what should be taught on the job. One conferee suggested that in such training programs a logical division can be made between what should be taught in school and what should be taught on the job. In many registered apprenticeship courses, theoretical material that can be taught in the classroom, such as mathematics, is part of school training; applied techniques, such as welding, are taught in the plant.

A participant noted that, in Denver, advice as to whether to provide training in the school or in the plant is offered by an advisory committee. Despite the general agreement by conferees from industry that they want broadly trained youngsters rather than those with specific skills, one participant maintained that it was the youngster with a specific skill who seems to find employment most easily. In a state like Maine, another conferee pointed out, the sheer variety of local industries precludes specific vocational training in the schools.

One conferee protested that, while the participants from industry were saying that specialized vocational education should not begin until after high school, many industrial employers are actively influencing the high school curriculum by giving machinery to schools, and by subsidizing programs. The effect may be to draw students out of liberal arts courses into specialized vocational work. As examples, the printing trades and food trades schools in New York City were cited.

A participant maintained that such a situation has always existed but has been intensified during recent years. As more children remain in school, it was claimed, the pressure to expand vocational education in the schools grows stronger. Industry, labor, and educators were said to be supporting the movement for more intensive vocational preparation. Many parents were said to favor vocational education for their children because they expect it will help them get jobs. This preparation may help a youngster land his first job, a participant declared, but in the long run restricts his career opportunities. Vocational schools, it was declared, are often "dumping grounds" for disturbed and retarded students. Several conferees pointed out that while this may be true in some cases, vocational schools often maintain high standards and are quite selective about admissions.

Twenty years ago, one participant noted, his company had exerted a great deal of pressure on the school in its community to increase its specialized vocational offerings. Disappointed with the results, the company has changed its policy and now favors the type of broad education previously outlined. Another participant felt that vocational education may be economically necessary in certain areas. He cited Lawrence, Massachusetts, as a community where economic conditions have created strong pressure for increased vocational education.

Educators were warned by one conferee against offering training only in terms of opportunities currently open in any particular community or to any particular group. He cited as an example the experience of the Negro colleges. A number of years ago, most of them were offering training in accordance with the opportunities then available. The lowering of discriminatory barriers has since shown their programs of study to have been far too limited. Another participant added that vocational schools must choose between preparing students for specific employment within the locality or providing general training for an industry. He felt the schools have a broader responsibility than just to train labor for a local area.

The importance of active advisory committees was stressed, so that the schools can know what type of training the community needs and can utilize. Several conferees emphasized the importance of improved communications between educators, the business community, and the armed services. One complained that educators receive no indication from industry of the training it considers desirable, either for high school students or in adult education.

A participant compared the problem of school cooperation with industry and the armed services to the marketing problem in industry. Industry wants to know what the customer wants, but the customer never goes out of his way to describe his wants to industry. He must be asked. Similarly, educators should not expect the business world or the military to come to them with suggestions about the kind of graduates they would like. But, he maintained, if the schools take the lead in making inquiries, they will receive eager cooperation. This is a safer way for the schools, he felt, since it reduces the danger of the schools' being pressured or misinformed by special interests.

VI. THE SECONDARY EDUCATION OF GIRLS

The Council Staff

IN ITS STUDY OF *Womanpower*, the National Manpower Council declared: "Women constitute not only an essential, but also a distinctive part of our manpower resources. They are essential because without their presence in the labor force we could neither produce and distribute the goods nor provide the educational, health, and other social services which characterize American society. They constitute a distinctive manpower resource because the structure and the substance of the lives of most women are fundamentally determined by their functions as wives, mothers, and homemakers."

When that study was published in 1957, the 22 million women working outside the home comprised almost one third of the civilian labor force. The virtual revolution which had taken place in women's employment since the beginning of the twentieth century appeared not only in the number and proportion of women in the labor force, but also in their age and marital characteristics. At that time, 60 percent of the women employed outside the home were married and 50 percent of them were over 40 years of age.

In view of the new place which work had come to occupy and promised to hold in the lives of women, a fresh examination of the education of girls and young women was clearly in order. "The Secondary Education of Girls" is one of the two chapters in *Womanpower* directly devoted to this purpose.

> *"The Secondary Education of Girls" is reprinted with a number of editorial changes from the National Manpower Council's* Womanpower *(New York: Columbia University Press, 1957), in which it first appeared as Chapter 6, pp. 167–90.*

FROM the beginnings of American secondary education in the nineteenth century, high schools have enrolled and graduated more girls than boys. The principle of equality of opportunity in education for all was established in secondary education long before many barriers to the employment of women were surmounted or contemporary patterns of work outside the home began to emerge. Consequently, developments in the high school education of girls during the present century seem modest when they are measured against the more spectacular changes in the paid employment of women.

The value of having girls and boys share essentially the same educational experiences during their high school years has long been taken for granted in the United States. The differences in the behavior of boys and girls in high school with respect to attendance and graduation, curriculum and subject-matter choices, and grades are equally taken for granted—judging by the lack of interest in studying their significance. These differences are intimately bound up with dominant views concerning the distinctive interests and abilities of girls and boys, and with the characteristic responsibilities and activities which they are expected to assume in adult life.

GROWTH OF A COEDUCATIONAL SYSTEM

The rule of having separate schools for boys and girls, derived from the practice of the early academies, was followed when the first public high schools were established. As the number of public secondary schools grew, essentially as an extension of elementary education, coeducational schools became increasingly common. Before the end of the nineteenth century, coeducation was a distinguishing feature of American secondary education. By 1900, only 2 percent of the nation's 6,000 public high schools were separate schools for boys and girls. Twenty years later, less than one half of 1 percent of the more than 14,000 public high schools in the United States were not coeducational. Between 1900 and 1956, the number of students enrolled in public high schools increased from a little more than half a million to almost 6 million. During this period, the number of graduates from public high schools rose even more strikingly—from 61,000 to over 1.3 million

annually.[1] Before the opening of the present century, girls accounted for almost two thirds of all public high school graduates; now they constitute slightly more than half. As Table 1
shows, both the number and proportion of boys completing high
school have increased significantly during this period. Nevertheless, more girls still graduate from high school. Thus, in 1956, the
number of boy high school graduates represented 58 percent of
the seventeen-year-old boys in the population; the number of
girl high school graduates, however, was 68 percent of the seventeen-year-old girls in the population.[2]

When the issue of a coeducational system was debated in the
nineteenth century, the primary argument against it held that
girls and boys differed so greatly in nature, interest, and ability,
as well as in the functions they would perform when they grew
up, that coeducation could not adequately serve the needs of
either. Their close association during adolescence, it was maintained, was improper, if not injurious. To some who opposed a
coeducational system, it was clear that the boys would constitute
a "vicious" influence upon the girls. Others were troubled by the
possibility that corporal punishment—viewed as an indispensable
instrument for educating boys—would not be inflicted in the presence of girls. The difficulty of administering large coeducational
schools effectively and the lack of adequate facilities for girl students in existing school buildings—particularly in the Eastern
cities—were additional reasons set forth for maintaining a system
of separate instruction.

Coeducation, however, had the tremendous advantage of being less costly than a dual school system. Moreover, it was more
convenient for families to send their daughters and sons to the
same school. The proponents of coeducation firmly believed that
it was "natural" and, consequently, more beneficial for girls and
boys to associate with each other during their school years. The
"refinement" of the boys, it appeared to others, would be an inevitable consequence of the presence of girls in common classes.

Table 1. Secondary School Graduates from Public and Nonpublic Schools, by Sex, and as a Proportion of the Seventeen-Year-Old Population, 1890–1958 *

	Boys			Girls			Girl Graduates as Percent of All Public and Nonpublic Graduates	Girl Graduates as Percent of All Public Graduates
Year	Total Public and Nonpublic Graduates	Graduates as Percent of All Boys Aged 17 Years	Public Graduates as Percent of Total Graduates	Total Public and Nonpublic Graduates	Graduates as Percent of All Girls Aged 17 Years	Public Graduates as Percent of Total Graduates		
1958	729,200	60	89	778,400	66	89	52	51
1956	634,300	58	90	735,300	65	88	52	52
1954	612,500	56	89	663,600	62	88	52	52
1952	569,200	53	88	627,300	60	88	52	53
1950	570,700	54	89	629,000	61	89	52	53
1940	578,718	48	93	642,757	54	94	53	53
1930	300,376	26	89	366,528	32	89	55	55
1920	123,684	13	73	187,582	20	75	60	61
1910	63,676	7	69	92,753	10	73	59	61
1900	38,075	5	59	56,808	8	69	60	63
1890	18,549	3	41	25,182	4	56	58	65

Source: U. S. Office of Education.
* This table is a revision of Table 13, *Womanpower*, p. 169.

The victory of coeducation was won relatively quickly, but there have been few searching inquiries to appraise its consequences. One study of separate education, undertaken in 1906 in Englewood High School near Chicago, seemed to demonstrate that when the boys were in separate classes, their scholarship improved and their tendency to "show off" was lessened. The study also indicated that the boys could be more severely disciplined when they were in separate classes; that they performed better with male teachers in early adolescence; and that more of them were motivated to continue their schooling. Finally, the study appeared to support the conclusion that, when boys and girls were taught in separate classes, the school work could be better adapted to the needs, interests, and the character traits of each. These findings did little to prompt further investigation of the advantages and disadvantages of a system of separate instruction. Compelling considerations of economy and the strong belief of educators that students should not be segregated on the basis of sex assured the continued growth of a coeducational public high school system. Coeducational instruction has been growing among the nonpublic secondary schools of the country, but separate schools for boys and girls still remain a distinguishing feature of the private high schools. Only a little more than one fifth of the independent day and boarding schools are coeducational, and they account for less than 30 percent of all students enrolled in such schools. Of the Catholic high schools—which enroll over 85 percent of all nonpublic secondary school students—about half are coeducational.

CHANGING PURPOSES OF SECONDARY EDUCATION

Up to the middle of the nineteenth century, private academies and seminaries provided a secondary education for girls which was essentially "practical" and terminal. These schools emphasized reading, writing, and arithmetic, and sought to train girls in the social graces considered appropriate for women and to prepare them for homemaking duties. Girls were sometimes accepted by private schools offering courses designed to equip young men for the fields of commerce and industry. In addition, some of the private academies offering a choice of either a classical course, which was college preparatory, or one known as the "English" curriculum, which was considered more "practical," also accepted girls.

Public demand for schools that would provide "practical" education of a terminal nature, and the growing demand for more equal educational opportunities, prepared the ground for the appearance of publicly supported secondary schools. By the middle of the nineteenth century, the principle of public education had won wide acceptance. By this time, too, the value of providing some form of "practical" schooling for girls was also generally recognized, and the movement for women's rights had been launched. In the free public high schools which subsequently developed, girls were included almost as a matter of course. Indeed, in 1890, the public schools accounted for almost 60 percent of all girl high school graduates, in comparison with about 40 percent among the boys.

Although the public high school developed in part to provide a terminal education, its curriculum was for many years essentially academic and college preparatory. The majority of boys who graduated from high school did in fact go on to college at the close of the last century. Girls accounted for well over half of the public high school graduates, but only a small number of them attended college.

Around the turn of the century, the college preparatory character of the high school curriculum began to be modified as a result of the introduction of such subjects as industrial arts, home economics, physical training, and commercial education. During the first decade of the century, the growing strength of the movement for a distinctly "practical" secondary education was manifested in the founding of the National Society for the Promotion of Industrial Education in 1906. In the same year, the National Education Association called for publicly supported trade and industrial schools. By the close of the second decade of the century, the content of the high school curriculum was no longer so clearly determined by college entrance requirements. Under the pressure of expanding enrollments, the high schools were compelled to respond to the needs of the overwhelming majority of their students who would not be going on to college or professional schools. This development was epitomized by the influential report, *Seven Cardinal Principles of Secondary Education,* issued in 1918 by the Commission on Reorganization of Secondary Education. It stated the aims of secondary education as "health, command of fundamental processes, worthy home membership, vocational efficiency, civic participation, worthy use of leisure time, and ethical character."

The passage of the Smith-Hughes Act in 1917, by which Federal funds were made available for programs of vocational education,[3] was another clear indication that the high schools were expected to help prepare their students, particularly the boys, for immediate entrance into gainful employment. In the eyes of the Congress, as well as of the public at large, vocational education for girls was viewed essentially as training in homemaking skills. The Act, consequently, made Federal funds available to encourage and develop home economics programs. In addition, the Act provided for reimbursement to the states for the training of girls in wage-earning occupations in trade, technical, and industrial pursuits under the trade and industrial programs.

The establishment of Federal support of vocational education at the secondary school level helped encourage the introduction of business education courses into the public high schools. The first comprehensive report on enrollments in these courses showed that in 1922 bookkeeping and typing courses each enrolled 13 percent and shorthand 9 percent of all students. Although the ratio of girls to boys among the students in these fields is not known, girls were probably in the vast majority.

During the 1930's, the objectives of the public high school, and, therefore, the scope of its curriculum, underwent further redefinition. Course offerings were added which were not required —and, indeed, often not accepted—for admission to college, and which had no direct relevance for preparing students for work. This is seen in the rapid growth of courses in social living, group guidance, personal problems, human relations, social adjustment, consumer buying, safety education, driver education, home management, and still other subjects. This development reflected the growing conviction that the secondary school had some responsibility for preparing students for life, as well as work, by contributing to their capacities for individual and social adjustment and for effective citizenship.

A report by the United States Office of Education shows that, between 1934 and 1949, enrollments rose in introductory survey courses in science and mathematics, but declined in specialized and advanced courses in these fields. The largest increases in enrollments occurred in courses in physical education and United States history (which increasingly became "required" courses), and in typing and general mathematics. The largest decreases took place in Latin and French courses. There were also substantial rises in enrollments in home economics and industrial arts courses. These changes were accompanied by modifications in teaching methods and practices and by the influence of what is known as the core curriculum approach, which emphasizes the relationships among different subjects and their common application to particular problem areas.

CURRICULUM AND SUBJECT-MATTER CHOICES OF GIRLS

The explosive growth of enrollment over the past half century has been accompanied by a transformation in the purposes of secondary education, as the high schools have sought to fulfill the needs and respond to the problems of all youth. This effort has led, in turn, to a preoccupation with those problems and needs common to all young people. A quite unintended byproduct of this development has been the paucity of statistical data about differences between girls and boys in curricula and subject-matter choices and in other aspects of their school behavior.

Significant new information has become available, however, as a result of a study of the educational and occupational plans of secondary school students. Undertaken early in 1955 by the Educational Testing Service for the National Science Foundation, this study, the first of its kind based on a large national sample, provides comparative data about public high school senior students in 1954–55. Further knowledge about differences between boys and girls as high school students has also been provided by the replies to a questionnaire circulated by the National Manpower Council in 1955 and 1956. Twenty-nine school systems, located in cities or counties in different parts of the country and of varying size, and five State Departments of Education generously supplied comparative information on curriculum and subject-matter choices, motivation, grades, graduation, guidance, and extracurricular activities.

The ETS study, as Table 2 shows, found that 35 percent of the girls were pursuing a commercial program, and another 6 percent were enrolled in what is described as a vocational curriculum. Not all of the girls in the last group, however, were actually receiving training for employment. Yet, it is safe to assert, about two out of five girls in the senior year of high school, in contrast to approximately one out of four boys, were enrolled in 1954 in courses of study where the primary emphasis was upon the development of skills qualifying them for employment immediately upon graduation. Among boys, 14 percent were enrolled in a curriculum identified as vocational in the ETS study, and 9 percent were in a curriculum identified as commercial. Among girls not going on to college, it appears that nearly one-half were enrolled in a commercial curriculum, nearly one-tenth in a vocational curriculum, and one-third in academic and general curricula. Of the boys graduating from high school but not going on

Table 2. Percentage Distribution of Girls and Boys in the Senior Class in Public High Schools, by Type of Curriculum, Region, and Ability Level, 1954

Type of Curriculum	United States		Northeast		N. Central		South		West		Students with Ability to Do College Work [a]	
	Girls	Boys	Girls	Boys	Girls	Boys	Girls	Boys	Girls	Boys	Girls	Boys
Total	100	100	100	100	100	100	100	100	100	100	100	100
Academic	29	38	36	45	26	34	23	29	36	45	54	66
General	19	28	12	22	23	33	24	29	16	24	13	18
Commercial	35	9	38	11	38	7	33	12	29	7		
Vocational	6	14	5	12	5	14	8	16	6	13	33	16
Other	7	7	7	7	6	8	7	7	9	7		
No response	4	4	3	3	3	4	5	7	5	4		

[a] Includes the top 30 percent of all senior students, as measured by a special intelligence test administered by the Educational Testing Service.

Source: Educational Testing Service study.

to college, nearly one-fifth followed a commercial curriculum, over one-fourth a vocational curriculum, and over one-third an academic or general curriculum.

Comprehensive and statistically reliable information about the subject-matter choices of girls enrolled in the vocational and commercial curricula is, unfortunately, lacking. Data are available for students in the Federally-aided vocational education programs. These programs currently involve more than 1.6 million full-time day students, but they represent only part of what the schools are doing by way of vocational preparation. Girls constitute 58 percent of these full-time day students. Almost all of them, however, are enrolled in the home economics program, which is designed to provide training for homemaking rather than for paid employment. Of the total number of full-time day students enrolled in trade and industry courses, the girls constitute only about 16 percent. Only 40,000 girls are full-time students in Federal-aided vocational trade and industry courses, and most of these are studying practical nursing, cosmetology, dressmaking, the operation of sewing machines, and food preparation or handling. These subjects are obviously related to occupational fields in which women workers predominate.

The Federally-aided vocational education program also enrolls more than 1.75 million evening and part-time students. Among these about two out of five are girls or women, most of whom are in homemaking classes. Less then 10 percent of the part-time and evening girl and women students are in the trade and industry programs, and about 15 percent are in the distributive education program, which provides part-time and evening training for selling and marketing jobs for persons employed in the field. Girls represent slightly more than half of all students in distributive education.

Replies to the National Manpower Council's questionnaire indicate that girls and boys in the commercial curriculum differ in their subject-matter choices. The girls show a distinct preference for typing, shorthand, and general business courses. Boys following a commercial curriculum, on the other hand, display a preference for courses in bookkeeping, commercial law, and selling.

The preference among high school girls for courses of study which promise to equip them for jobs immediately after graduation is also indicated by the fact that relatively few of them enroll in an academic curriculum. However, some educators report that a number of girls decide against a college preparatory program simply because the subject matter of many courses in other curricula is easier to master, and not because of occupational considerations. In any case, as Table 2 shows, about three out of ten senior year girls, compared to almost four out of ten boys, were enrolled in an academic, or college preparatory, curriculum in 1954. Among the senior year students who ranked in the top 30 percent on a special intelligence test, and were, therefore, presumed to possess the ability to do college level work successfully, a significantly smaller proportion of the girls than of the boys were pursuing an academic program. A larger proportion of boys than of girls with the ability to do college work were enrolled in the "general" curriculum, which may also serve to prepare students for college entrance. Relatively few students who pursue the other curricula go on to college.

The ETS study also shows that boys and girls are not equally prepared for college entrance with respect to science and mathematics courses. Thus, of senior year students, almost half of the boys, but less than a tenth of the girls, would have had more than six semesters of mathematics by the time they graduated. Almost a tenth of the girls would have had no mathematics at all, and as many as a fourth would have had only one or two semesters by graduation. In science, the difference between boys and girls, while not so great, was still substantial. Three fourths of the boys and half of the girls would have completed three or more semesters of work in science before graduation. Interest in additional courses in both science and mathematics was more pronounced among boys than girls, but almost 40 percent of the girls indicated that they wished they had taken more courses in both these fields.

A recent study by the U.S. Office of Education substantiates the finding that boys receive far more preparation than girls in mathematics and science. In 1954, almost as many girls as boys were enrolled in elementary mathematics courses in high schools. Boys made up about 60 percent of enrollments in plane geometry and intermediate algebra, however, and about 80 percent of enrollments in trigonometry and solid geometry. Girls outnumbered boys in biology courses by a narrow margin. But in chemistry classes three fifths, and in physics classes four fifths, of the students were boys.

The National Manpower Council's questionnaire returns also showed that, among the students in the college preparatory curriculum, a greater proportion of boys than of girls are interested in advanced courses in mathematics and physics. Judging from enrollments, there is a marked preference among girls for advanced courses in foreign languages. A number of school systems reported high interest among girls in courses in biology, chemistry, world problems, economics, social studies, history, English, and literature. All these subjects, however, turned up among the fields in which boys in other school systems showed interest.

Curricula and subject-matter choices in high school are related in part to what students expect, or consciously plan, to do after graduation. The ETS study shows that anticipation of college attendance is far stronger among boys than among girls. Of those students in 1954–55 high school graduating classes with the ability to do college work, 62 percent of the girls, in contrast to 78 percent of the boys, planned to enter college in the fall of 1955 or at some later date. Table 3 also shows that more girls than boys were not interested in going to college, or, even when interested, had made no plans to do so. Even among the students of marked ability—the top 10 percent—a significantly smaller proportion of

Table 3. Estimated Percentage Distribution of Senior Students in Public High Schools by College-Going Plans and Aptitude Test Scores, 1954–55 Graduating Classes

College-Going Plans	High Scorers [a]		Very High Scorers [b]	
	Girls	Boys	Girls	Boys
Total	100	100	100	100
With college plans	62	78	75	88
Going now [c]	42	47	58	59
Going later	20	31	22	29
Interest, but no plans	8	4	6	2
No interest, no plans	17	10	10	5
Miscellaneous	13	8	9	5

[a] The top 30 percent of all senior students in public schools, as measured by the mental ability test administered by the Educational Testing Service.

[b] The top 10 percent of all senior students, as measured by the Educational Testing Service.

[c] In the fall of 1955.

Source: Educational Testing Service study.

girls than of boys planned to attend. In this group, one out of ten girls, but only one of twenty boys, had neither interest in nor plans to go to college.

The gross differences between girls and boys in high school curricula and subject-matter preferences are the products of several factors related to fundamental differences in the lives they expect—and are expected—to lead as adults. The proportions of girls following an academic program in high school, and for whom college attendance is a goal, are strongly affected by family influences and by their expectations of marriage. The ETS study revealed, for example, that among the girls for whom college attendance was not a goal, half specifically indicated that it was not a goal because they would "rather get married."

For many girls still in high school the anticipation of becoming wives, mothers, and homemakers appears to be strong enough to turn them away from investing in more education. Marriage expectations or plans were apparently not part of the conscious thinking of the boys for whom going to college was not a goal. The major reasons they offered were that their occupational objectives were not yet defined, or that a college education is not required to fulfill their job aspirations. Economic considerations, as will be seen, also play a role in the decision not to go to college, as do certain social characteristics of the family.

The wives and the mothers who work outside the home are now familiar and accepted figures. Yet, most teen-age girls appear to take it for granted that their future lives will be centered chiefly, if not exclusively, around homemaking responsibilities. Although this expectation fits more closely the life of an earlier generation than the actual behavior of many women during the last decade and a half, it exercises a strong influence on the educational objectives of many girls in high school and encourages them to prepare for jobs which will be open to them immediately after graduation. Such jobs are overwhelmingly in fields already employing many women, and the curriculum and subject-matter choices of high school girls thus tend to respond to existing patterns of women's employment. It is not surprising, therefore, that more than one third of the girls in high school are enrolled in a commercial curriculum.

According to the ETS study, more than one fourth of all girl seniors named office or clerical work as the kind they would be most interested in having after graduation. Even among students of high ability, almost half of the girls who expressed a preference for jobs in office or clerical work indicated that they had no interest in further education and training at the college level. Only one fourth of the boys of high ability who preferred clerical work were not interested in pursuing a college course.

The ETS study sought to discover the fields of college study and subsequent employment which interested high school seniors with the ability to do college work. Among boys, the strongest preferences among fields of study were, in order of descending popularity, engineering, physical science, business, liberal arts, and the health professions. Among girls, the health professions ranked first and were followed by education, business, liberal arts, and fine arts. Among those who wanted to study one of the health professions, the boys were primarily interested in medicine and the girls in nursing and technicians' occupations. When asked to name in what occupation they wanted to be engaged fifteen years hence, on the assumption that with hard work they could be successful, about half the girls chose education, office or clerical jobs, nursing, or medical technicians' work. About half of the boys, on the other hand, chose engineering, business, science and mathematics, or medicine.

The findings on field of study and occupational preference once again suggest that marriage is a central concern among high school girls and that their occupational leanings reflect the existing distribution of women in the labor market. Their occupational preferences seem to be reinforced rather than altered by the vocational guidance and counseling available at the high school level. The replies to the National Manpower Council's questionnaire indicated that the opportunities for guidance and counseling are approximately the same for boys and girls. At the same time, most of the school systems indicated that their students were counseled in terms of the existing differences between boys and girls in education, work interests, and employment opportunities.

There is evidence that boys as well as girls are likely to express educational and occupational preferences which reflect more their acceptance of adult judgments, voiced both at home and at school, than their own positive interests. In some cases, the adult judgment provides an educational or career objective when youngsters lack positive interests. The ETS study showed that a fifth of the girls named education as their probable field of study, but it also revealed that only a tenth indicated that this was their field of greatest interest. Similarly, although two fifths of the boys listed engineering as their probable field of study, only a fourth indicated that it was the field in which they were most interested.

Most girls in high school assume that they will have some experience working outside the home after they complete their formal education. But they also take it for granted that paid employment will not constitute the central focus of their lives. Moreover, they see their future job opportunities largely in terms of a relatively restricted range of occupations growing out of existing patterns of women's employment. These are overwhelmingly in clerical and sales work, and in fields associated with the traditional functions of women—the care of the sick, the training of children, the handling or preparation of food, the manufacture of clothing. Even among girls in high school who have an interest in and plans for going to college, educational and occupational aspirations tend to be concentrated in traditional women's occupations or in new fields in which women predominate.

SCHOOL PERFORMANCE

It is not clear why girls achieve, on the average, better grades in high school than boys. But, on the basis of the measures used, there is no question that they do. Up to college, girls outdistance boys in the number of years of schooling achieved. Table 4 shows the differences in educational attainments for 1958.

Table 4. Estimated Percentages of Young Men and Women Completing Specified Amounts of Education, 1958 [a]

Educational Attainment	Young Men	Young Women
Less than high school	11	8
Some high school	29	26
High school graduation	24	43
Some college [b]	14	12
College graduation	15	8
Some graduate work	2	
Master's degree	4	3
Doctorate	1	
	100	100

[a] These estimates are designed to indicate the educational attainments of young men and women at the time their formal schooling terminates.

[b] The majority of this group pursue a baccalaureate college program, but an unknown number enroll in technical institutes, vocationally oriented junior college programs, and other post-high school educational or training programs.

Source: Based on data from U. S. Bureau of the Census and the U. S. Office of Education.

Those who replied to the National Manpower Council's questionnaire also reported that girls earn better grades than boys; that a smaller proportion fail; that they constitute a majority of the honor roll and scholarship society students; and that their grades, in relation to their intellectual ability, are higher than is the case with boys. About two thirds of the school systems reporting indicated that girls remain in high school on a full-time basis longer than boys, regardless of the curriculum they are studying.

The recently developed National Merit Scholarship testing program also indicates that girls, on the average, do better than boys in high school. The first step in the program involved the screening of students in all the high schools of the nation in order to select those qualified to compete for a National Merit Scholarship. On the basis of the standards used—grades and class standing—girls made up 55 percent of the total selected to compete. Boys, however, accounted for 69 percent of all of the scholarships awarded on the basis of a special test. The results of the College Entrance Board Examinations tell a similar story: boys make up a larger proportion of the students who qualify for college entrance or scholarship aid on the basis of tests measuring ability to do college work.

It is generally agreed that the reasons for the superior performance of girls in high school, or for the better record achieved by boys in college entrance examinations and scholarship competitions, do not lie in differences in native ability between the sexes. The results of tests of intelligence show that highly developed ability is more or less equally distributed between boys and girls. The distribution of intelligence test scores among the senior high school students covered in the ETS study, however, reveals slight, but still significant, differences. The scores in this test ranged from zero to twenty, and a score of eleven or less designated an intelligence level below the ability to perform college work. The median score for boys was 8.2, compared with

7.9 for girls. The same proportions of boys and girls—just about one third—scored below 6. One half of the girls, in contrast to 45 percent of the boys, scored between 7 and 13. More important is the fact that 20 percent of the boys, but only 16 percent of the girls, scored between 14 and 20. Other studies point up the fact that boys do somewhat better than girls with respect to intelligence test scores toward the close of their high school experience, even though girls achieve, on the average, a superior grade record.

THE PROBLEM OF MOTIVATION

Several explanations have been offered of the differences between boys and girls in high school performance and college entrance and scholarship examination results. In one way or another these explanations point to differences in the motivations of boys and girls during their high school years. Some educators hold that the better grades which girls achieve reflect in part the less demanding commercial and vocational courses many of them select. The evidence supporting this contention has been very much disputed. Although many girls do distinguish themselves intellectually in high school, it is also asserted that a majority are reluctant to appear outstanding for fear that they will be less sought after by boys. The report of the Commission on the Education of Women, *How Fare American Women?* cites recent investigations which indicate "that the intelligence quotients and grades of girls in high school become lower when they consider that successful academic work militates against their popularity or feminity."

The point has been made that the tests used in selecting candidates for admission to college and for scholarship aid merely reveal the poorer preparation of girls in mathematics and the sciences, a reflection of their curriculum choices. Most tests involve both verbal and mathematical components, and girls score less well than boys primarily because of their weakness in the latter. This may indicate that boys are better prepared in mathematics, but it may also suggest differences in mathematical aptitude. It is commonly assumed that boys are better endowed than girls, on the average, in mathematical aptitude. However, the ways in which this aptitude has been measured have been questioned, and doubts, consequently, have been raised about the asserted superiority of boys. It has been argued that an adjustment in the relative weights of the verbal and mathematical test components, in favor of the first, would result in better average scores for girls, who presumably excel in verbal aptitude.

Replies to the National Manpower Council's questionnaire frequently asserted that, although girls, on the average, are better students in high school than boys, the range from low to high in the performance of boys is greater than among girls. One school system in a large city presented data showing that "while more boys than girls earn very low or failing grades, more boys than girls are likely to rank within the top 5 percent of their graduating class." Educators and school administrators report that girls are, by and large, better motivated than boys with respect to learning, and suggest that this accounts for their superior record of performance in high school. Many respondents to the Council's questionnaire described the girls as being more curious about the subject matter of their courses, more conscientious in applying themselves to their work, and more concerned with high marks and academic achievement. They were said to take more pride in high grades. However, many also asserted that girls are much more likely than boys to conform to the requirements of the school situation and to measure up to the standards set by those in authority.

Just why this pattern of conforming behavior should be characteristic of girls is far from clear. It has been suggested that one reason is to be found in the influences which shape the personality of girls during their formative years. These, it is claimed, condition them to place a higher value than boys do upon conforming to the norms of social behavior. Meeting the standards of approved student conduct is, according to this contention, merely one expression of a basic orientation toward all social behavior. The point has also been made that the high school experience is much more likely to be regarded by girls than by boys as an end in itself. Boys, as they approach maturity, tend to view and evaluate their schooling as a means for realizing other objectives, such as further education or long range vocational goals. Girls, on the other hand, are more inclined to respond to the educational situation on its own terms and, consequently, to conduct themselves in ways which win approval by school standards, one of which is "good" marks. The predominance of women teachers, particularly in the lower grades, is another reason offered to explain why girls apparently display a marked impulse to measure up to the idea of being "good" students in high school. Differences in school performance are also traced to the fact that girls mature earlier than boys, and this is alleged to result in a more adult attitude toward grades and in a more realistic sense of the consequences of indifferent or poor school performance.

Such explanations, it may be remarked, themselves raise many questions, and some of them merely restate the assertion that girls generally exhibit conforming behavior. Moreover, it is important to bear in mind that little is known about the interplay of factors affecting motivation. All large-scale generalizations about differences in motivation are subject to almost endless qualification, and any representation of such differences in black and white is bound to be misleading. There is considerable evidence that differences among students enrolled in various high school curricula are greater than differences between girls and boys pursuing the same program of study. Students in the college preparatory program, for example, are said to be generally "better motivated" than those in the commercial or general curricula. While credited, on the average, with being better motivated in school, girls are more heavily represented than boys in the latter curricula. Within the academic curriculum, educators assert that boys whose educational or occupational goals are fairly well defined are certainly no less interested in learning than are girls.

Experienced teachers and school administrators remain convinced, however, that girls as a group are more responsive than boys to social pressures to do well in school, and are more disposed to measure up to the standards of conduct which the school sets. These characteristics, they believe, help to explain the differences between girls and boys in high school performance. Boys are reported to be more responsive to social pressure to excel in sports, while girls, according to some educators, are more likely to strive for academic achievement and recognition.

One respondent wrote in answer to the National Manpower Council's questionnaire that "The attitude of boys changes from one of calloused indifference to real concern about grades between the first and last years of their high school experience, whereas the attitude of girls remains about the same throughout, namely one of sensitivity and concern with the matter of grades." Although such a change in attitude can be related to the emergence and clarification of vocational or career objectives among the boys, it still remains true that the pattern of curriculum and subject-choices among girls points to a relatively high concern with short-run employment considerations. This is particularly noticeable, as a number of respondents pointed out, among students in the commerical curricula, who are aware that employment opportunities often depend heavily upon the record of their performance in high school.

If the vocational goals of girls tend to be secondary to the expectation of marriage and to be defined in terms of the jobs they are likely to hold immediately after completing high school, it is understandable why most of them do not view their educational experience as a means of preparing themselves for a lifetime of activity in paid employment. Replies to the National Manpower Council's questionnaire strongly suggest that the occupational and career objectives of boys, particularly in the later years of high school, are likely to be more sharply delineated than among girls, to be long-run rather than short-run in outlook, and to be more ambitious than those of girls.

PLANS FOR GOING TO COLLEGE

While in high school, girls and boys look with different eyes upon continuing their education in college. Just as there are gross differences between boys and girls with respect to curricula, subject matter choices, and performance, so there are significant variations between their plans to attend college. Ability, vocational objectives, and level of high school performance all affect these plans. At the same time, it is clear that family circumstances can be particularly influential in the decisions of boys and girls alike to go or not to go to college.

Thus, wanting to go to college is closely related to the educational and occupational level attained by the student's father. The positive leaning toward college attendance is markedly stronger among boys than among girls. But the ETS study shows that it is true of girls, as well as of boys, that the higher the educational attainment of the father, the more likely it is that his children will want to attend college. If the father's education was the equivalent of high school or less, the proportion of girls planning to go to college was substantially below that of boys. However, where the father's education reached graduate or professional school level, about the same proportion of girls as of boys planned to attend college.

Roughly the same situation is found when the father's occupation is correlated with children's plans for going to college. According to the ETS study, the higher the father stood on the occupational ladder, the more the girls' pattern approximated that of the boys. Among the sons of businessmen, 85 to 91 percent planned to go to college, depending upon the specific occupational status of the father. Among the daughters of businessmen, somewhat smaller proportions—70 to 74 percent—planned to go to college. From 90 to 95 percent of the sons of professional men were planning to go to college, and the proportions of college-oriented daughters of professional men ranged from 79 percent, for those whose fathers were in scientific occupations, to 94 percent, for those whose fathers were physicians. At the lower end of the parental occupational scale, the proportions of boys planning to go to college were considerably larger than among girls.

Levels of education and occupation are associated with income, and these findings point to the significance of the economic resources of the family as a determinant of college attendance. Among the high school seniors in the ETS study who did not plan to go to college, half of both the boys and the girls stated that the cost involved was one of the important reasons. Further evidence of the influence exercised by economic resources appears in the ETS finding that the chances of college attendance are reduced for both the able boys and girls as the number of children in the family rises. The proportion planning to go to college sometime in the future, rather than immediately after graduation, was also higher in larger than in smaller families.

The ETS study throws no direct light on whether parents are more inclined to make the effort to send sons rather than daughters to college, when expenses are a major consideration. The study did find, however, that a much higher proportion of boys than girls in wage-earning families plan to go to college. It is, therefore, reasonable to assume that among lower-income families parents are more likely to make sacrifices to send sons, rather than daughters, to college simply because the latter are expected to be supported by the men they will eventually marry.

Different career and economic objectives also help to explain why more boys than girls go on to college. Thus, the ETS study revealed that among senior high school students who planned to attend college, 59 percent of the boys, compared with 47 percent of the girls, planned to go to college because a degree was required for the work they wanted to do, or because of the higher earnings which would result from a college education.

The differences between boys and girls in high school are reflected in how they respond to the opportunities which the educational system offers them. These responses, in turn, help to determine whether or not they go on to college.

VII. ISSUES IN VOCATIONAL EDUCATION

The Council Staff

IT IS GENERALLY AGREED that one of the objectives of secondary education is to prepare boys and girls for the world of work. Yet, both the character of vocational education and its place within the structure of secondary education remain far from settled. This is made clear by "Issues in Vocational Education," which, in addition to sketching the development of vocational education and the growth and operations of Federally aided vocational education, also sets forth the views of its advocates and its critics.

The major contribution made by vocational education at the high school level to the development of skilled workers and technicians is by way of providing a foundation for subsequent skill acquisition. A *Policy for Skilled Manpower* showed that "Almost all vocational school graduates who later become skilled workers do so through apprenticeship, informal training, or on-the-job experience." Only a very small number of the graduates from vocational high schools are equipped to be considered for skilled jobs when they first enter the labor market. Fairly substantial numbers, however, do secure employment in the fields in which they pursued their vocational studies.

"Issues in Vocational Education" is reprinted with editorial changes from A Policy for Skilled Manpower, *in which it first appeared as Chapter 6, pp. 159–78.*

IN most industrial countries there is only one route through which young men become skilled workers. The route is well marked, highly formal, and begins at an early age, usually fourteen or earlier, when the youth who is destined for a trade is separated from the small minority of his schoolfellows who enter a course of study which prepares them for higher education. The future craftsman may continue in school briefly, but by fifteen or sixteen he enters apprenticeship, which lasts for four or five years, sometimes supplemented by evening courses in school. Then, as he approaches his majority, he is formally accepted as a journeyman. If he misses one of the turning points, there are no detours likely to bring him to this destination.

By contrast, there are many ways of becoming a skilled worker in the United States. The potential skilled worker is likely to graduate from high school before he begins work, and in school the chances are that he followed a course of study not unlike that of his fellows who go on to college. In any case, he is likely to remain in the common educational stream at least until sixteen.[1]

In addition to the variety of its forms, the process of becoming a skilled workman in this country is distinguished by the unusual role played by formal education. There is no European country in which a substantial proportion of potential skilled workers remain full-time students until they are eighteen or older. And there is none in which the student may pursue a program designed to provide him simultaneously with a secondary education and the skills of a trade.

It would be a mistake, however, to assume that the exclusive, or even principal, reason for lengthening the school attendance of the potential worker has been to provide him with training for his work. Indeed, the extension of full secondary education to more and more young people has not even been conceived as a lengthening of school attendance for the future worker—although that is largely what it amounts to. It has been viewed, rather, as the extension of the values of education to all American youth, whatever their occupational destination. This is seen in the fact that vocational curricula for high school students are never devoted exclusively to teaching trade skills and knowledge, but always include a substantial number of general courses. It is seen even more obviously in the fact that the majority of young people who become wage earners do not pursue vocational courses in high school; they could not, even if they would, because the facilities are lacking. In short, in so far as the problem of schooling for future workers has been faced as a distinct problem by American educators, it has generally been posed in the following terms: How can young people who may (or may not) become wage earners be best educated? The question of how the schools can provide future workers with the skills they will need at work has been seen as only a part—though often a major part—of this larger problem.

FORMS OF VOCATIONAL EDUCATION

It has often been pointed out that all education is vocational education, since all the things taught in schools have some applicability to work. In contrast to the past, many employers now believe that the most important subjects the schools can teach as preparation for work are reading, writing, and arithmetic. The schools, of course, may also teach skills that are useful only in certain specific occupations. Although the extent to which they should do so is a lively issue, it has been widely accepted in the United States for several decades that the schools, especially the high schools, should provide some specific occupational instruction.

The term vocational education is generally confined to instruction aimed at specific preparation for occupations not classified as professional. Most such instruction takes place in the secondary schools, though, as will be seen, an increasing amount is being provided in post-high school institutions. Whatever the level of the institution in which it takes place, formal school instruction in skills and knowledge applicable to nonprofessional occupations is the subject of this chapter and the next.

Vocational education occupies a unique place in the American educational structure, for much of it is financed in part by Federal funds, and when so aided, subject to Federal standards. Federal funds are channeled into the public schools for a variety of purposes, but the program of aid for vocational education is the only instance in which Federal money is available to all public school systems, contingent upon its use for teaching certain categories of subjects under certain conditions.

The aid program is based on the Smith-Hughes Act of 1917 and on subsequent supplementary legislation, primarily the George-Barden Act of 1946. Under the terms of this legislation, about $25 million has been made available to the states annually in recent years for financing instruction in four broad fields: trade and industrial occupations, agriculture, home economics, and distributive occupations. For the fiscal year 1955, Congress appropriated about $30 million.[2] Skilled worker and technician training is provided under the first of these categories. Education in distributive occupations—marketing and selling—is provided only on a part-time and evening basis for persons employed in the field, but in each of the other subject areas, instruction is also provided on an all-day basis for regular high school students. Home economics instruction is part of the same system, but since its aim is primarily the education of future housewives, and not training for gainful employment, it is not considered in this chapter. Courses designed to prepare for employment in dressmaking, cooking, and other skills that are also taught in home economics courses for home use are given as part of the trade and industrial program.

Although the term vocational education is frequently used to apply exclusively to the Federal-state program just outlined, a great deal of vocational education occurs outside of it. An unknown amount of training in the four fields subsidized by the Federal government takes place through courses for which Federal funds are not available because local school systems choose not to operate under Federal standards. Moreover, commercial and business education in the high schools—typing, shorthand, accounting, bookkeeping, office procedures, and similar courses— is not subsidized by the Federal government. Over half of all high school students take some commercial courses. Preparation for technician occupations in the public secondary schools takes place both within and without the Federal-state program. To be eligible for Federal aid, a technical high school program must meet the standards contained in the trade and industry section of Federal legislation.

One other aspect of secondary education that is closely related to vocational education, but is not part of the Federal-state program, is "industrial arts." In educational theory there is a clear distinction between industrial arts and vocational education. The latter is distinguished by the fact that its major aim is to provide effective preparation for employment in a specific occupation. It is intended only for students who expect to enter that occupation. Industrial arts, the outgrowth of what was once known as manual training, is intended to provide elementary knowledge of basic tools and processes for all students. In practice, however, the distinction between the two often seems to depend more on the goals of the student and on his over-all program of study than on the content of any given course. Over one million public high school students are enrolled in industrial arts subjects, compared to only about 225,000 full-time students in Federal-state trade and industrial occupations courses.[3]

In addition to the public secondary schools, public institutions of higher education are also increasingly involved in vocational education. These institutions, variously designated as junior colleges, community colleges, city colleges, and technical institutes, also offer specific instruction for occupations below the professional level. Generally, they tend to emphasize preparation for technician occupations and for the more technical of the skilled fields, such as electricity or television. Many of them, however, also teach the traditional skilled trades. Federal vocational education funds are available only for instruction at less-than-college level. Nevertheless, some junior colleges accept Federal funds and thereby limit themselves in part to instruction at this level.

Finally, vocational courses are taught in a wide variety of

private schools, both proprietary and endowed. These schools are especially well developed in the commercial and technical-industrial fields, and in such health fields as dental and medical assistant, physical therapy, etc. Usually, they concentrate on intensive, practical occupational training and ignore general and cultural subjects. Private correspondence schools perform similar functions for students who cannot or prefer not to attend a school in person. Some large enterprises, including manufacturing firms, retail stores, and hospitals, combine on-the-job training for skilled workers and technicians with formal, classroom instruction.

TRADE AND INDUSTRIAL EDUCATION FOR HIGH SCHOOL STUDENTS

Although a few states and localities had begun to provide vocational courses before World War I, the widespread development of vocational education for high school students stems from the passage of the Smith-Hughes Act of 1917. Since 1948, aid to the states under the Smith-Hughes law and supplementary legislation has amounted to about $25 million annually.[4] Allotted to the states on the basis of various population ratios, this money must be matched by at least an equal amount of state and local money spent according to the provisions of the law and the administrative regulations of the United States Office of Education. For many years most states have spent far more than the required minimum. In 1953, Federal expenditures were only about one sixth of the total of $146 million spent on vocational education under the terms of Federal legislation.[5] This sum, moreover, does not represent the full cost of even the Federal-state program of vocational education, much less of all vocational education, since it includes only money spent for purposes specified in the law. These include instruction and counseling; teacher, supervisor, and counselor training; and some administrative activities. Only a small part of the costs of equipment and supplies and no expenditures for building construction or maintenance are represented in the figure.

In the last few years, the $25 million annual Federal contribution has been divided among the four fields of study roughly as follows: $10 million for agriculture, $8.5 million for trade and industrial courses, $6 million for home economics, and less than $500,000 for distributive occupations.[6] To obtain Federal money a state must draw up a detailed vocational education plan which becomes a contract between the state and the Federal government. Federal money may be used only for instruction in public schools and for courses designed to fit persons over fourteen for useful employment in the field of study.

In 1953, about 190,000 boys and 35,000 girls were enrolled in all-day high school courses for trades and industrial occupations under the Federal-state program.[7] This represents about 10 percent of the boys and less than 2 percent of the girls enrolled in grades ten through twelve of the public secondary schools, during which most vocational education is given. There are some 20,000 public high schools in the country (excluding junior high schools), of which about 5,500 are in urban localities. About 2,000 high schools offer trade and industrial programs. Of these, about 400 are schools operated primarily for vocational education. The remainder are general high schools with vocational departments. Since average enrollment in the vocational schools is much larger than in the vocational departments of general high schools, the majority of students are found in separate vocational schools.

Most trade and industrial courses are confined to the eleventh and twelfth grades, but there are still many three-year, and even a few four-year programs, especially in the older vocational schools of the Northeast. Because these schools are large, probably the majority of trade and industry students are in three- and four-year programs. In the Western states vocational courses are rarely offered before the eleventh grade. In some California cities the great majority of students are in the thirteenth and fourteenth grades (junior college), and in North Dakota nearly all trade and industry students are high school graduates.

The term trade and industry has been very broadly interpreted by the U. S. Office of Education. It embraces any occupation directly involved in the design, manufacture, servicing, or repair of any manufactured product; any service occupation not classified as agricultural, business, or professional; and the technical occupations. Altogether, scores of different occupations are taught, some of them in only a single high school, ranging from janitor and waitress to industrial designer and tool and die maker. The trade and industrial program in at least one high school includes the performing arts: music, drama, and the dance.

Unfortunately, there is no current information on the numbers of students preparing for different occupations. A rough indication of the magnitude of training and the extent of facilities for each occupation is provided by a list of the states and cities in which various occupations are taught. There are now fourteen occupations or groups of occupations which may be studied in over 100 towns and cities. Two occupations are by far the most popular: machine shop and automobile repair courses. These are given in the high schools of almost every state, and, respectively, in over 700 and over 600 cities. Three groups of occupations are taught in almost all states and in over 300 towns and cities: electrician and electrial repair; cabinet and furniture making and wood working; and carpentry. Other occupations taught in at least 20 states and 100 cities are: printing trades, drafting, radio and television, welding, sheet metal, practical nursing, building construction mechanic, bricklaying, and barbering and beauty culture.[8]

In addition to full-time trade and industry students, there are other young people who have passed the age of compulsory full-time attendance and who have gone to work, but are continuing their secondary vocational schooling on a part-time basis. Many of these students are in cooperative programs, in which they spend half their total work-school time at paid work, receiving on-the-job training in a trade or industrial occupation. The other half is spent in school studying trade-related and general subjects. The size of this group cannot be determined from the data available.[9] Almost 10 percent of the graduates of trade and industrial programs in the North Atlantic region in 1953 were cooperative students.[10] Trade and industrial education for adults and for young people who have left school is considered in the following chapter.

THE BEGINNINGS OF VOCATIONAL EDUCATION

The permeation of the high school curriculum by vocational subjects, as has been seen, has not won unanimous approval from American educators. Indeed, the role of vocational education has been shaped by continuing conflict between vocational and general educators. The terms of the controversy began to take shape as early as the period following the Civil War, when proposals for adapting the schools to the requirements of an industrial economy and a changing school population received growing support. Manual training, advanced early in the nineteenth century as a means of broadening the cultural experiences of young people, received increasing support on the ground that it could provide students with general principles of craftsmanship which could then be applied to whatever specific vocations they entered. Vehement opposition, however, was expressed by those who believed that manual training represented a dangerous anti-intellectual trend in education.

Up to the close of the nineteenth century the idea that specific vocational preparation should be a part of "education" made little progress. The purpose of the schools, it was almost universally agreed, was to provide intellectual discipline, moral values, and a common body of culture. This was the task of the "common schools" at the elementary level, and it was therefore inconceivable that the elementary schools should undertake vocational training. Even if educators had wished to introduce vocational training into the high schools, the students who might have benefited were not there.

The real beginnings of the present programs of vocational education came in the first two decades of this century. The growth of professional schools in the universities and agricultural training in the land-grant colleges, and the founding of technical institutes helped to change the climate of educational opinion. The idea of free electives was beginning to modify the uniform classical curriculum in the high schools as well as the colleges. Most important was the spread of high school education, for this forced serious consideration of a secondary curriculum suitable for those who would become wage earners. By 1900, over 6 percent, and by 1920, 17 percent, of the nation's young people were graduating from high school. This expansion was in part the cause, and in part, no doubt, the result of the fact that the secondary curriculum, which had always been somewhat more "practical" than in Europe, became even more so. Courses were added in clerical skills, homemaking, civic intelligence, mechanical drawing, and sometimes handicrafts, while training in the classical languages declined.

There were two main lines of argument in favor of specific vocational education in the high schools, one economic, the other based on democratic values. Economists and businessmen emphasized the decline of apprenticeship, the expansion and increasingly technological character of industry, the superiority of European institutions for training workmen and technicians, and America's need to improve its competitive position in world markets.

The second line of argument was advanced mainly by labor leaders, social reformers, and a few dissident educators, who maintained that the schools in a democratic society are obliged to prepare all children for their life's work. Why, it was asked, should the public pay for the preprofessional training of those who will attend college, but contribute nothing toward the occupational competence of the wage earner? Does not the emphasis of the traditional secondary school on "academic" subjects reflect an undemocratic conviction that manual work is less worthy than brain work? Should not familiarity with tools and with physical work be a part of the background of all young people? It was argued also that the competent, well-trained worker would somehow be a better citizen with better attitudes toward work. Some advocates of vocational education saw it as a panacea for the ills of a growing industrial economy.

In the early controversy over the role of vocational education, three main positions, each of which has continued to receive strong support, may be discerned. One viewed vocational education as a final period of specialized training following the general education received in the common elementary school. The regular high schools, according to this view, should continue their traditional function of preparation for college, but separate vocational high schools should be added to the system to provide specific occupational training for future wage earners who would otherwise not be in any school.

At the opposite extreme was the view that any form of vocational education would "contaminate" the schools. Its proponents held that the primary purpose of schooling is the traditional goal of training the intellect, and that the creation of separate courses of study or separate schools for future manual workers is essentially undemocratic. To provide cultural and intellectual advantages and the qualifications for higher education to some students, while denying them to others, they said, was clearly a way of introducing class distinctions into the schools. They agreed with the champions of vocational education, moreover, that there is not enough time in the high school course of study to provide both adequate occupational preparation and thorough intellectual and cultural training for the same students.

The third main position on vocational education held that it was wrong both to segregate vocational and academic students and to ignore the needs of the future worker and the educational values of manual work. Urging the extension of the "common school" approach into the high school, its advocates also wanted to modify somewhat the nature of the common educational experience. They believed that general education should be continued for all students throughout the high school years; that all students should also receive some manual training; and that those students who wanted and could profit from specific vocational training should be given enough to prepare them effectively for work. This position reflected an effort on the part of general educators to compromise with the growing pressure for specific and separate vocational education as well as changes in educational philosophy which emphasized practical knowledge and the education of "the whole man."

By 1910 the efforts of those who favored some form of specific vocational education were beginning to bear fruit. The National Society for the Promotion of Industrial Education had been founded four years earlier. This organization, the nucleus of the present American Vocational Association, played a significant role in the passage of the Smith-Hughes Act of 1917. Also by 1910, Massachusetts had passed the first act for state aid to local vocational education; high schools were teaching stenography, "typewriting," and other commercial skills; evening schools were offering specific trade training; and the first proposal for Federal aid had been presented to Congress.

THE SMITH-HUGHES ACT

Support for the Smith-Hughes bill came from business, farm, reform, and labor groups, with the active aid of a few educators who had espoused the cause of vocational training. The debates in Congress were not concerned with educational policy but with states' rights, Federal control, and the costs of the proposed program. One of the reasons for the bill's success was that World

War I was then demonstrating the dependence of national security upon industrial supremacy and thus re-enforcing the arguments of those who urged the necessity of raising the skills of American workers.

The Smith-Hughes Act proved critical in the growth of vocational education. The states were eager to take advantage of Federal aid. Few educators had any knowledge of, experience or interest in, vocational education. The Federal agency set up to administer the act was equipped with a paid staff of devoted vocational educators and had broad powers to assist the states in setting up their programs and to administer the expenditure of Federal money. The states, moreover, were required to draw up a fairly detailed vocational education plan which had to be approved by the Federal agency before the states were eligible for aid. The circumstances, in short, were highly favorable to the development of strong Federal influence. While the Federal government did not dictate the forms and content of vocational education, its influence gave this field more uniformity than any other aspect of public education.

The provisions of the act and the circumstances of the time encouraged the creation of a vocational education system largely separate from the regular high schools. Vocational specialists, convinced that most general educators were basically opposed to any vocational education, saw a separate system as the only possibility. Many general educators, on the other hand, were quite content to see this alien growth take place outside of their province. An important factor was the provision in the act for a completely independent Federal Board for Vocational Education responsible directly to Congress and consisting, not of educators, but of the Secretaries of Agriculture, Commerce, and Labor, the Commissioner of Education, and one representative each of business, farm, and labor groups. The functions of the Board were transferred to the U. S. Office of Education in 1933, but by then the Board had already left its imprint. Some states set up independent boards for vocational education, paralleling the Federal Board. Federal funds were made available only to help pay for instruction designed to fit young people for useful employment. The use of Federal funds to provide the supplementary general courses necessary for a well-rounded education was specifically forbidden. Day school trade and industrial programs were required to include three consecutive hours each day of "practical work on a useful and productive basis," which has usually meant shopwork.

CONFLICTING TRENDS

While these circumstances were pushing vocational education in one direction, a number of developments set up contrary pressures. By 1930, 30 percent, and by 1940, one half of the nation's young people were graduating from high school. As high school enrollment increased, the proportion of graduates who entered college declined. Although vocational enrollment increased rapidly, it still accounted for only a small fraction of the total. Those who had forecast a dual high school system, with one part preparing some students for college and the other preparing a much larger number for work, were proved wrong.

It was becoming clear that most students were using high school neither as preparation for college nor as specific preparation for work. Vocational educators urged, with considerable reason, that specific vocational training be made available for this growing group. At the same time, however, it was becoming difficult to retain the conception of vocational education as a period of primarily occupational preparation between general education and work. As attendance became more nearly universal, the high school was increasingly viewed, both by the general public and by educators, as a continuation of the common elementary school with an obligation to provide all students with certain minimum cultural and intellectual advantages.

The expansion of college attendance introduced further difficulties. If, at first, potential vocational school students were forced to choose between vocational school and no high school, it did not matter if the vocational graduate could not enter college. Once it became apparent that many students were being forced to choose at an early age between vocational school and a chance to attend college in later years, educators saw an additional reason for expanding the general education provided for vocational students. As one result, specific vocational training was delayed until the last three, and then the last two, years of high school, and even until junior college. Some schools gave vocational students the opportunity to qualify for college entrance by taking elective courses.

The gap between vocational and general high school education was also narrowed by increasing the occupational elements in general programs. Obviously, if the concept of public schooling as a common experience for all young people was to be honored, and if some students were to receive vocational education, then all students had to receive some similar exposure. In addition, the trend toward practical "life-experience" education continued strong.

As a result of these developments, some communities have abandoned separate vocational and general high schools and are conducting all high school education in "comprehensive" schools which provide all students with both the traditional academic courses and more or less specific skill training; the precise mixture depending on the needs and abilities of the individual student. Industrial arts has become an important means of providing some exposure to skilled work for nonvocational students.

Elsewhere almost completely separate systems continue. As noted above, most trade and industry students are in separate vocational schools, especially in communities which are large enough to support several high schools. In three states the chief policy-making and administrative authorities for vocational education are completely independent of those who are responsible for the rest of the public school system. In fourteen other states, vocational education has some degree of independence at the highest state level. In some states, where vocational education is not independent at the state level, it is organized on a county or area basis, independently of the local school districts which run the other schools, in part simply because of the high cost of providing specialized vocational facilities in each district.

Each of the three major positions taken in the vocational education controversy a half century ago can claim some measure of success today. In some high schools the course of study is still primarily academic and college preparatory. On the other hand, a quarter of a million young people [11] are officially designated as vocational trade and industry students, are enrolled in vocational schools or formally distinct vocational departments, and spend most of their time learning an occupation. Finally, in the majority of high schools there is a substantial measure of compromise between these extreme features of the educational scene. Even among the minority of schools which have no courses of study under the Federal-state program, there are very few in which some vocational elements have not entered the curriculum. In the vocational schools and vocational departments, increasing attention is being given to keeping the route to college open to all and to reducing the formal separation of vocational students from other students.

The extent to which the line between vocational and general education has been blurred, however, should not be exaggerated. Current educational theory emphasizes the common goals of secondary education for all youth, but in practice, whenever a school system offers a Federally subsidized trade and industrial program, the vocational student is distinguished from other students in several respects. He stays in school six hours a day, an hour longer than most other students, and he spends at least half this time in a shop learning a trade or industrial skill. Generally, he spends about four and one-half hours a day in vocational classes from which nonvocational students are excluded by law.

Together with the growth of high school attendance and the spread of vocational education, the separate status of vocational programs has led to a struggle over the assignment of students. As long as the vocational schools offered trade courses for a few students who would not otherwise be in school at all, the problem of selecting students for vocational courses was unimportant. The schools could offer training in the most common trades, and those young people who chose to, could enroll. But as enrollment in high school became nearly universal in most urban areas, selection and assignment became major problems.

Most vocational educators tend to regard their schools primarily as a means of producing potential craftsmen. As vocational enrollment has increased, they have sometimes sought to protect this function by imposing high admission requirements and raising standards of school performance. Convinced that only those of average or above average intelligence are capable of becoming skilled craftsmen, they have sought to attract a larger proportion of the more able students.

Many general educators continue to feel, on the other hand, that the proper place for the able student is the academic program. In addition, faced with the necessity of doing something with many students who lack the ability or the desire to do well in high school, they have looked upon vocational courses as one means of providing course work commensurate with the ability of the less able students. Most vocational educators accept a responsibility for this group of students. At the same time, however, they protest when the vocational schools are used as the dumping ground of the general high schools and insist that they receive a reasonable share of students at all levels of academic ability. Frequently, in fact, there is a tug of war for the more able students and a battle of wits to avoid acceptance of the least able.

THE CONTINUING DEBATE

The Smith-Hughes and George-Barden Acts represent one answer to the still open question of how future workers can best be educated. For trade and industry students, the law declares, in effect, that the best education is that which is devoted primarily to training in the skills and knowledge of a specific occupation. The program which has been developed on this premise, it has been charged, inevitably involves some sacrifice of democratic values. The nonvocational courses taken by vocational students are rarely comparable in scope and quality to those available to other students. Usually, the trade and industry student has not been able to move from secondary school into college; frequently he has been segregated with other students who came from deprived economic backgrounds and lacked the ability or the motivation to succeed in academic work.

If the vocational program for trade and industrial education is vulnerable to the charge that it is "class education," it may also be questioned on other grounds. Even among vocational educators, few maintain that the full-time school is the ideal place for producing fully skilled workers. Vocational education is built on the premise that the student learns best by doing, by exercising the skills he needs under the same conditions he will encounter in a real job. At best, therefore, there are many things that cannot be taught as well in a school shop as in a well organized on-the-job training program.

The trade and industrial program has not enjoyed the continuous support of those interests which are most directly concerned with the training of skilled workers—industry and the unions. Business and labor groups supported the Smith-Hughes bill in 1917, but in later years there were few indications that major segments of industry or labor regarded the program as essential. At Congressional hearings on vocational education legislation and appropriations, farm groups have backed the agricultural education program, retailers have supported the part-time distributive program, and specialized educational groups endorsed the whole program; but industry and labor testimony was generally conspicuous by its absence. In the House and Senate major support has come from Southern legislators rather than from legislators of the more heavily industrialized areas of the nation. The National Association of Manufacturers and the U. S. Chamber of Commerce support vocational education but are opposed in principle to Federal grants-in-aid. The CIO and AFL, both before and after these labor organizations merged, have given strong official support to the Federal-state program. Nevertheless, there are still signs that many employers and local union representatives view the program without great enthusiasm.

Why then, the vocational trade and industrial program? What is its justification? Defenders of vocational education present a number of cogent arguments for preserving and expanding specific occupational training in the high schools. Proceeding from the premise that, with few exceptions, everyone should have the advantage of high school, they argue that while the potential worker is in school, he should learn something that will be directly useful to him in his later work. There is no reason, they maintain, why manual skill should not have as honorable a place in the schools as intellectual skill—except for the prejudices of educators. Vocational education is represented as a healthy corrective to the ivory tower atmosphere of the schools. In earlier and simpler days when every child learned about work by watching and participating in the work of his parents and neighbors there was some justification for the schools' confining themselves to booklearning, then a rare and valuable asset. Now that work has been removed from the home and direct participation in work is often postponed until eighteen or later, the schools have an obligation not to turn young people loose in the world of work and adult economic responsibility without prior preparation.

Second, vocational educators argue that no one learns without interest. Many young people of high school age—particularly those who do not do well in the academic subjects—are primarily interested in going to work and earning money. Some have already developed an interest in a particular occupation, or in activities related to an occupation. When students come from a family and neighborhood background in which books and intellectual activities have a small role, it is often impossible for the schools to capture their interest through the traditional curriculum. For all of these reasons, it is argued, the school can best enlist the enthusiasm of many students by centering their studies about an occupational goal. Only in this way will it be possible for the high schools to hold the two-fifths of all students who now drop out before graduation. Moreover, once the student's interest in purely occupational training has been captured, it is then possible to extend his motivation into related courses such as mathematics and science, and sometimes into general education courses which had formerly seemed to have no connection with life.

Third, it is maintained, the high schools must provide systematic skill training because apprenticeship and other organized on-the-job training programs are not sufficiently developed to take care of the nation's needs. In view of the large number of skilled workers who pick up their abilities haphazardly and by chance, the contribution of the vocational schools to the nation's skilled labor force takes on added significance. For the high schools to neglect systematic preparation in the fundamentals of industrial work, it is asserted, would not be fair to the worker, wise for the economy, nor safe for the national interest.

Finally, according to vocational educators, the values of vocational education cannot be achieved through superficial shop courses. It is impossible to generate sincere interest or to teach useful skills by having students make book ends or ash trays, and to pretend that it is possible is a fraud on both the student and the taxpayer. Learning by doing is the most effective method of learning. The vocational program, its champions insist, presents the schools with their best opportunity to teach through activity, but only if the activity is an honest, useful piece of work. If these requirements can be met only at the cost of setting the vocational student somewhat apart from other students, it is argued, then the cost is worth paying.

VIII. TYPES OF VOCATIONAL SCHOOLING

The Council Staff

"TYPES OF VOCATIONAL SCHOOLING" fills in the picture sketched in the preceding chapter. While it deals chiefly with education for skilled trades and industrial occupations conducted under Federal legislation, it also treats with other forms of vocational education and training, excepting those offered by the armed services and private industry. The armed services, of course, have educational and training facilities and opportunities on an enormous scale and of great diversity so far as skilled workers and technicians are concerned; and private industry has sharply increased its investment in education and training in recent years.

One major point made in this and the preceding chapter is the richness and the variety of means available in the United States for the development of skilled workers and technicians. A second is the degree to which controversies still surround the question of the responsibilities which the secondary schools should assume for the various kinds of vocational education.

> *"Types of Vocational Education" is reprinted with editorial changes from* A Policy for Skilled Manpower, *in which it first appeared as Chapter 7, pp. 179–207.*

ALTHOUGH Federal law has fixed the broad outlines of trade and industrial education in the high schools, state and local school systems have been free to fill in the details much as they choose. In describing trade and industrial education today, therefore, it is frequently impossible to do more than indicate the wide diversity of conditions and approaches in different communities.

Seeking current, specific information on the vocational programs in a representative group of communities, the National

Manpower Council reviewed published materials and sent a questionnaire to thirty school officials in communities all over the country. In addition, the Council staff interviewed or corresponded with school authorities and other educators in states as widely separated as New York and California, Michigan and Georgia.[1]

THE NUMBER OF FULL-TIME TRADE AND INDUSTRY STUDENTS

The great differences in trade and industrial programs are suggested by a comparison of the percentages of students enrolled. In most localities surveyed by the Council, the percentage of high school boys in trade and industrial programs is near the national average, about 10 percent. In such heavily industrialized areas as Gary and Providence, less than 5 percent are in such programs. In other communities over half the boys are enrolled.

These differences in enrollment are caused only in part by differences in the size, quality, and variety of shop facilities. Sometimes excellent, modern facilities are not fully used because not enough students apply. A 1952 survey showed that the vocational shops in Massachusetts were operating at only three fourths of capacity, with twelve vocational schools enrolling only two fifths as many students as they could handle. Surveys of high school students usually find that far more students plan to enter professional and managerial employment than can possibly get jobs in these fields. Many of them will later become industrial workers, but since they are aiming at white collar work they are not interested in the trade and industrial program in high school.

The vocational school has often been the "dumping ground" for students whom the regular high schools did not want. Even where this is no longer true, some teachers and parents urge young people to avoid the vocational school because they are not aware of the change. Where, for one reason or another, the schools and employers do not work closely together, there may be few channels through which potential vocational students can learn about and become interested in opportunities for employment as skilled workers.

The experience of communities like Allentown, Pa., where 60 percent of the public high school boys are in trade and industrial courses, indicates that this situation can be overcome. To do so, however, requires a combination of good shop facilities and teachers, school officials who are interested in vocational education, close cooperation with local employers and labor, and, above all, a guidance program which succeeds in attracting qualified young people to preparation for skilled work.

VOCATIONAL GUIDANCE AND VOCATIONAL EDUCATION

Vocational educators sometimes feel that the major role of guidance is to attract capable students into vocational programs.[2] It is not necessary to accept this view to admit that guidance activities in many school systems do not provide the student who is about to choose a high school program with adequate information about training and employment in skilled work. The teachers and counselors who are responsible for guidance are generally academically trained and often have little knowledge of industrial conditions. One common solution to this problem is to make sure that before the student has to make a final choice of high school program, he spends an exploratory year which gives him information about occupations and permits him to experience a variety of shop activities. This is one of the purposes of industrial arts courses.

The need for vocational guidance does not end when the student chooses a trade and industrial program. Changes in interests or mistaken estimates of ability and aptitudes may require a shift to another vocational course or to a nonvocational program. Some vocational educators, however, have little sympathy with guidance activities in high school. As one of them put it recently, "little real vocational guidance is needed after the boy has entered the vocational school. If the guidance is functioning properly in the junior high schools it is fair to assume that the boy was given all the necessary and available tests which pointed to the fact that he had mechanical aptitude and should go to a vocational school." This attitude is by no means universal. Many vocational schools do provide a continuous counseling program which includes a year of trial accompanied by various forms of guidance before requiring the final choice of a trade.

The methods, extent, and quality of guidance vary enormously. It is significant, however, that even in communities where guidance is highly developed, school officials are often dubious about its success. Federal aid, available for many vocational guidance activities under the terms of the George-Barden Act of 1946, does not strongly encourage the development of guidance.[3] The states are not required to use any part of their Federal allotments for this purpose, and most of them spend enough on other phases of vocational education to obtain their full allotment without expanding guidance activities.

FITTING STUDENTS AND CURRICULA

One of the most difficult tasks in vocational education is the guidance of students with varying degrees of ability into the courses from which they can benefit most. The extent to which vocational schools and departments face the special problems of dealing with very good and very poor students varies considerably, even within the same community. Among the twenty-six vocational schools of New York City in 1949, the I.Q. distribution of new students was about normal in one school, while in another the average was only 72. In the latter school, one fourth of the new students were below 62, and only one fourth were above 80. The appalling difficulty of operating a school with such a student body is indicated by the fact that persons with I.Q.'s of 70 to 80 are generally considered to be on the border line of mental deficiency, while a score below 70 is usually a clear indication of feeble-mindedness. In most of the communities surveyed by the Council, the average I.Q. of vocational students was about the same as, or slightly lower than, that of the whole population. Generally the most intelligent students were attracted only to vocational programs that offered preparation for technician occupations. But, unlike those in New York City, most vocational programs had succeeded in excluding the least intelligent students, occasionally through admission requirements, but generally through informal procedures.

Students of low ability have often been assigned to vocational programs because they are incapable of mastering the academic program and therefore, it is said, might as well spend their time learning a few simple manual skills which will be useful when they go to work. The protests of vocational officials against this policy seem to have contributed considerably toward raising the average ability of vocational students. Because of compulsory attendance laws, the vocational schools still cannot avoid entirely the problem of dealing with students of low ability. Generally the problem is met by providing courses in jobs such as janitor or in the simple, repetitive skills of mass production industries. Sometimes a student is admitted to a course for automobile mechanics and taught only the simplest jobs—changing a tire, filling a gas tank, and lubricating a car.

Some school do not provide special curricula for such students. In Chicago, the aim of the vocational schools is limited mainly to "the development of future skilled workers in the fields of design, tooling, maintenance, servicing, and sales engineering." The average I.Q. of the students, however, is quite low. As a result, one third to one half of them are incapable of completing their courses of study successfully. Some who should not be graduated manage to squeeze by, but the schools cannot recommend them to employers.

If average or above average intelligence is required to become a skilled worker, then it follows that a high proportion of those who can complete a rigorous vocational course of study could also succeed in the academic program and in college. A student who enrolls in a vocational course in the ninth grade may later demonstrate ability and interest in academic studies. Transfer to an academic program, however, is sometimes impeded by lack of academic credits in the early high school years, by inadequate guidance, and by the various barriers between vocational and general education already described.

Another way to prevent the vocational program from becoming a dead end with respect to higher education is to permit the vocational student to earn enough academic credits for college entrance, perhaps with the aid of a few courses taken after graduation.

Expanding the general and elective courses for vocational students, however, means taking time from skill training, and vocational educators feel that adequate skill training cannot be given unless most of the school day is devoted to it. Traditionally, vocational programs devote only about one fourth of the school day to "general" courses, usually English, physical education, and social studies. Some vocational educators resent any effort to merge vocational and academic preparation. They argue that by the time the student gets to the ninth, tenth, or eleventh grade, he should already have most of the general education he needs. Some maintain that vocational subjects are just as good, just as "cultural," just as challenging as academic subjects. Consequently, they say, there is no special need to worry about the general courses offered to vocational students.

On the other hand, expansion of academic studies is facilitated by the tendency to confine vocational programs to the last two years of high school, by the fact that the vocational school day is often an hour longer than the usual school day, and by the fact that it is frequently possible to combine "related" instruction with the required three hours of shop work so that the remaining three hours are free for academic courses. Many communities, including Chicago and Canton, Ohio, permit the able vocational student to pursue this combination of courses, and in Canton about 5 percent of the vocational graduates do enter college. In *The Double Purpose High School,* Franklin J. Keller describes twelve schools which seek to do this by eliminating wasted time and unessential courses from the curriculum.

The quality of general courses is just as important as the quantity, but in schools where most students are below average in intelligence the level of instruction is necessarily adjusted to the ability of the majority. Also, good academic teachers are reluctant to teach in vocational schools in which the enrollment includes a preponderance of problem students, the range of general courses is narrow, and the academic teachers are assigned second-class status. Until recently, New York City provided an extreme example of this problem. At the beginning of each school year, "substitute" academic teachers without tenure were hired for the vocational schools. Because many students dropped out before the beginning of the spring term, some of the substitutes were then released and some academic classes were turned over to shop teachers. This was done because it was known that at the beginning of the next year it would be much easier to hire new academic teachers than new shop teachers. Where the vocational courses are conducted on the same campus as academic courses, the problem of providing high quality academic instruction is often solved by combining vocational and nonvocational students in the same classes for academic subjects.

Another group of students who constitute a special problem for the vocational schools are those who have done poorly in school, not because of lack of ability, but because they are simply not interested. Studies have shown that this group is very large. Of the roughly 40 percent of young people who do not graduate from high school, many drop out not because of lack of ability or economic pressure, but because they do not like school or would rather work.[4] Some vocational educators are convinced that vocational programs are uniquely suited to developing school motivation and therefore urge the extension to almost all students of occupationally centered education. The data available, however, do not bear out these claims. Generally, the vocational schools lose at least as many students before graduation as do other schools.

VOCATIONAL EDUCATION AND THE EMPLOYER

Although the principal obligation of the vocational school is to the student, it is plain that unless he receives training useful to an employer the student's time is being wasted. Vocational programs employ a variety of means to keep their instruction in line with the current needs of employers, including advisory committees, "coordinators" who serve as liaison between industry and the school, surveys of local job opportunities, and informal contacts with industry.

The U. S. Office of Education strongly recommends the organization of advisory committees that include representatives of both employers and labor by all school units with trade and industrial programs. The extent to which this policy is followed in the country as a whole is not clear. Some large cities—San Diego is one example—maintain an elaborate network of active advisory committees, one for each of the trades taught. On the other hand, it has been charged that vocational educators frequently do not appreciate the importance of employer and labor cooperation and that, especially where vocational programs have been established for many years, officials sometimes view the vocational schools as their private preserve to be guarded jealously against outside influences.

However effectively the vocational school is geared to employers' needs, it cannot meet their requirements fully. The trade and industry graduate is seldom ready to step directly into a skilled job. At best he has a head start for apprenticeship or other on-the-job training. There is not enough time in high school to train a skilled worker. The shopwork per year of full-time school is the equivalent in hours of only about three and one-half months on a full-time job.

There are also many things a school cannot do because it is a school and not a factory. It cannot duplicate the specific requirements of each of the many jobs found in most localities, the pressures of production for profit, or the problems of getting along with other workers and the foreman in a real job situation. Vocational educators maintain that most schools do approximate real work situations closely enough to fit the graduate for a beginner's job in a skilled occupation. Some schools simulate work conditions by having the students produce goods or provide services on a commercial basis. This, however, is very expensive unless the products are sold, and some educators believe that, for both practical and ethical reasons, the schools should not become engaged in marketing operations. Also, labor unions and employers frequently object when goods made by unpaid students are placed on the market.

Vocational educators agree almost unanimously that the best answer to this problem is to be found in cooperative programs in which the advanced student spends half of his weekdays in school, studying trade-related and general courses, and the other half at paid work getting actual experience in the same occupation. Nevertheless, enrollment in cooperative trade and industrial programs has always been small, largely because it is difficult to interest employers in a program supervised by school officials and devoted to systematic training of the student. Newton, Mass., Allentown, Pa., Detroit, and other communities have demonstrated that when school officials make a concerted effort to enlist employer support, it is possible to run an extensive and successful cooperative program. Only the better students are usually admitted to such programs in order to encourage employer participation.

The fact that the vocational school does not duplicate factory conditions offers advantages as well as disadvantages. Because it is not concerned with production for profit in a changing market, the school is in a better position than the factory to concentrate on systematic, comprehensive training given in the proper sequence. While the vocational graduate may be no better prepared for the tasks of a specific job than the worker who is trained exclusively on the job, vocational educators assert that he is less likely to be totally ignorant about large areas of his trade, and, therefore, that he is in a better position to get another job or to win promotion.

The extent to which the vocational program meets the needs of the employer is a problem of policy as well as of method. The school must provide training which looks forward to placing most graduates in appropriate positions in local industry. Yet, if the school is tied too closely to the needs of local employers, it may become a publicly supported adjunct of local business, neglecting the student in favor of the employer. Should the school base its curriculum on the expressed wishes of students or on the needs of employers? Should it concentrate on fitting students for the local labor market if this means reducing their opportunity to take jobs in other localities? In selecting occupations to be taught, should it give greatest weight to the cost of equipment, to the availability of good teachers, or to the local occupational pattern?

These considerations do not necessarily conflict—but they may. A school's specific problems depend largely on whether vocational education is separated from or closely integrated with the rest of the school system and on whether the school is located in a large city, a town dominated by one or two employers, or a diversified manufacturing community. These problems are rarely discussed but are reflected in the contrast between vocational programs that go their own way with little contact with employers, and others that are closely geared to the needs of a few major enterprises.

Relatively few school systems have undertaken surveys to find out how employers evaluate the graduates of vocational programs. Even fewer conduct systematic follow-up studies to see how well their graduates are doing after several years of employment. Consequently, most of the evidence on employer evaluations of vocational education is indirect, fragmentary, and inconclusive.

The National Manpower Council's survey found that in most communities there is a sizable group of employers who cooperate closely with the vocational schools. They help plan curricula, are eager to hire vocational graduates, support the program in the community, participate in cooperative work-study programs, and even contribute machinery and equipment. The Canton, Ohio, vocational school was built and equipped in 1940 with a $1,350,-000 grant from the Timken Roller Bearing Company. Evidence that vocational education is valued by employers is also found in the fact that most vocational graduates today are placed in appropriate positions shortly after graduation. On the other hand, the excellent placement records of recent years are partly a reflection of continuing prosperity and abundance of jobs. There is considerable evidence that employers are frequently much less interested in specific vocational training than in good general background and in favorable attitudes toward work.

It is not surprising that employers differ on the merits of vocational education. Where vocational education is a neglected part of the school system or where school officials have not sought to enlist employer cooperation, employers are not likely to feel much concern. Large firms with well-developed training programs and a high degree of work specialization are likely to feel less need for specific training provided in school than are small firms. Because of financial considerations a vocational school system has to concentrate on training in a relatively narrow range of skills for which there is a steady and substantial demand. Since there are always many jobs for which vocational graduates are not prepared, many employers cannot have a vital interest in vocational education.

THE QUALITY OF VOCATIONAL EDUCATION

How well a vocational program accomplishes its goals depends in large part on the quality of its teachers, the suitability of its buildings, and the extent to which its equipment is kept up to date. Like public education as a whole, vocational education is often handicapped by the fact that its financial resources are inadequate to perform the tasks assigned to it by the community. The financial problems of the vocational schools are intensified by the relatively high cost of the required buildings and equipment. In addition, in seeking shop teachers the school must compete directly with industry which can pay more for workers with the broad skill and long experience desirable in a teacher.

Most of the communities surveyed by the Council reported increasing difficulty in securing good shop teachers. In one large city with a high salary scale, several courses had been discontinued because qualified teachers were not available. On the other hand, a substantial minority reported that getting qualified teachers is not a serious problem. The degree of difficulty encountered in finding teachers reflects great variation in both the standards of qualification for shop teachers and the salaries paid. Some communities require a few years of practical experience and very limited classroom training in teaching methods. Others require many years of experience plus college training in vocational education. All communities place primary emphasis on trade experience rather than on formal education.

About half of the communities reported that all their vocational school equipment is thoroughly up-to-date, in a few cases, more modern than in local industry. The other half have some obsolete equipment and varying degrees of difficulty in getting money to replace it. Providence reported that nearly all its vocational school machinery is obsolete.

Keeping facilities up to date seems to be less of a problem than providing training facilities for a variety of occupations. In the large metropolitan areas, trade and industrial enrollment is usually sufficient to justify the cost of training in a large number of occupations—frequently in specialized schools, each devoted to one group of occupations. New York City has thirty-one vocational schools offering training in over seventy occupations. In smaller communities, the schools usually provide instruction in only a few major occupations. Nassau County, Long Island, has a population of about one million,[5] many of whom work in New York City industries or in the rapidly expanding industries of the county itself. Yet in the many independent school districts in the county, only four high schools offer trade and industrial courses in a total of only seven occupations. Sparsely settled rural school districts can rarely afford to offer trade and industry courses, even though many of their young people will eventually find industrial employment in the cities.

One result of the difficulty of expanding the number of occupations taught is that the traditional skilled trades receive strong emphasis while many newer, rapidly expanding occupations are neglected. It is possible to study cabinet or furniture making in the high schools of over three hundred communities, located in almost every state. On the other hand, courses for typewriter and office machine repairmen are given in only twelve communities, and for industrial laboratory technicians in only three.

To meet these problems, some states are beginning to develop centralized vocational schools to serve an entire county, an even larger area, or, as in Connecticut, a whole state.[6] In addition to creating transportation or housing problems, however, this solution divorces the vocational schools from the normal administrative structure and intensifies the problem of coordinating vocational programs with other secondary education.

In the South, where segregated schools have been maintained, vocational education facilities, like all school facilities, are much less adequate for Negro than for white students. This remains true in spite of substantial progress in recent years. In 1952, in fourteen states for which data were available, Negroes constituted 20 percent of the population, but only 10 percent of the enrollment in trade and industrial programs. Even more important, opportunities for vocational education are limited mainly to those occupations in which Negroes have traditionally been employed and those in which Negroes can gain employment providing services for other Negroes. Almost 30 percent of the Negro trade and industry students were preparing for work in the building trades. Another 40 percent were in five other nonindustrial occupations: auto repair, barbering and beauty culture, domestic service, practical nursing, and sewing and tailoring. Machinist and draftsman, respectively, are the most commonly taught of the skilled and the technical occupations. Yet, in these fourteen states, there were only 263 Negro students in machine shop courses, and only 80 studying drafting.

Vocational educators in the South maintain that they cannot devote their limited resources to training Negroes for occupations in which they have little chance of gaining employment. Negro leaders respond that unless Negroes are trained for these occupations it will be impossible to break down the barriers which now keep them out. They add that Southern Negroes who cannot make use of their skills in the South can, and frequently do, migrate to the North.

These problems are not confined to the South. A survey [7] by the Connecticut Commission on Civil Rights found that although Negroes constituted about the same proportion of vocational graduates as they did of the population of the state, the distribution of students among occupations showed the same pattern as in the South. "Negroes were represented proportionately less than whites in the electrical, machine, and drafting trades, and proportionately more than whites in auto repairing, dressmaking, and practical nursing. . . . No Negroes had ever attended private vocational schools specializing in tool and machine design."

AGRICULTURAL EDUCATION IN THE HIGH SCHOOLS

Most of the literature about, and most of the controversies over, vocational education have centered about the trade and industrial program. Meanwhile, agricultural training under the Federal-state structure has inconspicuously won a major place in the rural high schools of the country. Nearly half the high schools in the country offer vocational agriculture courses. About 430,000 high school students are enrolled in full-time agricultural programs in 10,000 high schools. The agricultural program involves about twice as many full-time students and about five times as many schools as the trade and industrial program. The number of all-day students in trade and industrial courses has remained relatively stable since the close of World War II at a level almost one-third lower than the peak year of 1942. Even though the agricultural labor force has been declining, enrollment of full-time agricultural students is now nearly a third higher than in 1942.[8] Most experts agree that the agricultural program has made an important contribution to the skills of the agricultural labor force and to the great increases in agricultural productivity.

Perhaps the outstanding contrast between the trade and industrial and the agricultural programs is the much closer integration of agricultural education with other parts of secondary education and with the outside experiences of students. Vocational agriculture courses are rarely conducted in separate schools. Enrollment in rural areas is generally not large enough to justify the creation of specialized schools. Since many of the practical aspects of agricultural schooling are conducted on the farm rather than in the school, it is not necessary to build and equip extensive shops.

In agricultural programs, moreover, Federal law and administrative regulations do not separate vocational students from other students to the extent they do in trade and industrial programs. While the trade and industry student must spend half of every school day—and generally spends three fourths—in classes from which other students are legally excluded, the student of farming is required to devote a minimum of only about seven hours a week to agricultural courses.

By its nature as well as by design agricultural instruction is also more closely linked with the student's outside learning opportunities and experiences. The problem of coordinating theoretical instruction with realistic practical experience—which is so difficult in trade and industrial programs—is relatively easy. Most students would be getting practical experience on family farms in any case. In addition, Federal regulations require the student to carry out actual farming projects under the year-round supervision of the teacher.

After he graduates, the young farmer finds well-developed public facilities for extending his training. If he enrolls in an evening vocational agriculture class, he can continue to take advantage of the individualized guidance of the teacher. The extension service, run by the Department of Agriculture and the state land-grant college, is equipped to help him in the continual development of the specific skills he needs on his farm. A relatively small proportion of vocational agriculture graduates, however, go into farming. Some critics have maintained, therefore, that rural high schools should place more emphasis on college preparation and on training for nonagricultural occupations.

Agricultural education in the high schools is likely to be part of a lifelong process of skill development consisting of formal instruction closely coordinated with practical needs and experience. Trade and industrial education is more likely to be the only contact of the individual with formal instruction and less likely to be as closely related to his job needs and experience.

VOCATIONAL EDUCATION FOR ADULTS

Recognizing both the difficulty of and the need for closely coordinating trade and industrial education with the needs and experiences of the skilled worker on the job, many vocational educators feel that evening and part-time courses for employed workers are the most effective part of the trade and industrial program. The importance of such instruction is reflected in the provisions of Federal law requiring that at least one third of the funds supplied by the Federal government, and of the matching funds supplied by the states, must be used for part-time classes. Originally, one of the purposes of these provisions was to encourage the part-time continuation of the general secondary education of young people who had started to work. Part-time general continuation courses, however, are rapidly disappearing. Almost all evening and part-time courses are now devoted to extending the skills of employed workers.

Part-time and evening courses of the "trade extension" type in the Federal-state program now enroll over half a million students, more than twice as many [9] as are enrolled in all-day trade and industrial courses for high school students. Several years ago a survey of adult education facilities found that more school districts offered evening courses in industrial subjects than in any field except recreation. In cities of over 50,000 population, 80 percent of the school districts offered evening industrial courses. Of the more than half a million "trade extension" students, about 120,000 are apprentices receiving related instruction in vocational schools as a regular part of their apprenticeship training. The U. S. Bureau of Apprenticeship recommends that apprentices receive at least 144 hours a year of related instruction in a vocational school. About two thirds of all apprentices in programs registered with the Bureau do so.

Most of the remaining "trade extension" students are young workers attending classes on their own time to help them to improve their skills in their present jobs or to qualify for promotion. Evening classes generally meet for two hours an evening two evenings a week for a period determined by the needs of the students. They may meet during the day for workers employed at night. Recently, there has been a trend toward greater emphasis on theoretical and technical instruction and toward greater reliance on on-the-job experience and training for development of manual skills. About 20,000 workers are enrolled in courses for foremen and supervisors.

Because evening students attend on their own time and because many evening instructors are employed during the day as skilled industrial workers or foremen, most evening courses are closely related to job needs. Special classes are sometimes set up primarily for employees in a particular plant, and instruction may be provided by a foreman from the same company. It is even possible to hold Federally-aided classes within the plant provided certain stringent Federal requirements are observed to insure that the primary purpose is the training of the students rather than the profit of the employer.

During World War II the Federal-state vocational system became the main instrument for government assistance in training of workers for war industries. The program's success in rapidly preparing large numbers of inexperienced men for semi-skilled production jobs led to the conviction that a similar program would be useful for reconverting war workers to peacetime pursuits. Consequently, when the George-Barden Act was passed in 1946, it provided for pre-employment trade and industrial training for unemployed workers.

Like the war-time program, these courses are designed to prepare men in the shortest possible time for a beginner's job in a new field of work. Frequently the sessions last eight hours a day, with the majority of the time spent in shopwork and with no time devoted to general education courses. In some states they have been used to retrain people on relief rolls. In New England these courses have been used to train unemployed textile workers for work in the electronics industry and other light manufacturing plants. How many workers are enrolled in such courses is not known.

DISTRIBUTIVE AND COMMERCIAL EDUCATION

All distributive education is conducted in evening and part-time classes for students employed in the field. The merchandising program began in 1938 and expanded steadily, except for the war years, until 1950. Then, heavy cuts in Federal funds led to a sharp reduction in enrollments. These cuts occurred for several reasons, including Congress' desire to reduce unessential expenditures during the Korean war and evidence that Federal money was poorly spent. The increased appropriation for Federal aid to vocational education for 1955 restored half of the previous cuts. Several considerations were involved—fear of recession, which served to emphasize the importance of salesmanship, improvement in the administration of vocational aid funds, and continuing protests from retailing organizations.

In the peak enrollment year of 1950 about two thirds of the distributive students were in evening classes on their own time. Less than 10 percent, about 30,000, were high school students in cooperative work-study programs. The remaining one fourth were employees given time off, usually with pay, to attend part-time courses closely coordinated with their work.[10]

One of the goals of the distributive program is to reduce the rate of failure among small retailing establishments. A high proportion of enrollments have consisted of the owners and employees of such businesses. In 1950, slightly less than half of the students were enrolled in courses for store personnel—sales clerks, stock clerks, cashiers, etc. Less than a fifth were in managerial courses, including courses in finance, sales promotion, merchandising, etc. The remainder were in courses centering about the distribution of specific commodities or services, most of them in the restaurant and food fields. Recently more than half of the students have been women.

Although high school courses in business or commercial subjects are closely related to the distributive program, they are considered separately because general business courses are not aided by Federal funds. The main reason for this seems to be that Congress has felt that business courses are sufficiently developed not to require special encouragement. Bookkeeping and typing were among the earliest occupational subjects introduced into the high schools. At present, over half of all high school students take at least one business course.

This does not mean, however, that the majority of students are preparing for work in office occupations. First-year typing courses enroll the largest number of students, most of whom acquire some typing skill for personal use and do not take a second year of typing. Bookkeeping and shorthand courses rank next to typing in number of students. Most evening high schools also give business courses.

Like the trade and industrial program, business education in the high schools seeks to produce graduates with the skill needed to begin employment rather than fully skilled workers. Some of the graduates enter public or private post-high school institutions to develop their skills further, but the majority go right to work and learn whatever else they need on the job.

The precise number of students enrolled in post-high school courses in office occupations is not known, but is very large. These institutions range all the way from schools offering one or two years of instruction in typing and shorthand to four-year colleges which grant degrees in accounting and business administration. There are about 1,500 private business schools. Nearly 500 give courses of at least twenty-five hours a week for thirty-six weeks and otherwise meet the standards of the National Association and

Council of Business Schools. Few of this group have less than 100 students and some have several thousand.

In the last few years enrollment in private business schools has decreased substantially. This is partly because few World War II veterans studying under the GI bill are still in school. In addition some employers have lowered their minimum hiring standards because of shortages of office help.

The Accrediting Commission of Business Schools has approved seventeen business schools which offer at least two-year programs at the collegiate level.[11] These schools emphasize a broad understanding of business methods and problems rather than the stenographic and clerical skills, and devote at least one fourth of their programs to academic subjects. Many colleges and junior colleges that do not specialize in business courses also have large enrollments in these subjects.

TECHNICAL EDUCATION

The term "technical education" covers a variety of educational programs and institutions. Unlike vocational education for the skilled trades and collegiate training for the professional engineer, technical education has not yet evolved a substantial body of common theory and practice.

Perhaps the most important reason for this situation is the difficulty of separating the technical occupations from the skilled and professional occupations. In listing the occupations for which their graduates are trained, technical schools sometimes include jobs ranging all the way from semi-skilled equipment assembler to professional engineering consultant. Actually, a single graduate may pass through this range of jobs in the course of his career. Because many companies follow a policy of promoting from within to fill all positions below the professional level, the technical school must often prepare its students not only for their ultimate technical occupation, but for the semiskilled and skilled jobs they may hold on the way up. Recently, however, a growing number of companies have been placing graduates directly in technician positions, in part because of shortages of engineers.

A second reason for the great variations in technical education is that the widespread development of educational programs designed specifically to prepare students for technician occupations is very recent. Most technical education takes place in institutions designated as "post-high school" but "noncollegiate." Their functions are not yet as clearly established as those of the elementary school, high school, college, and university, nor have they won the same degree of public understanding and support.

A substantial number of high school students are enrolled in technical high schools or departments.[12] Some high school technical education is conducted within the framework of general or academic high schools. Such programs range all the way from traditional college preparatory courses with some extra work in shopwork and drawing to that of Brooklyn Technical High School, which offers such intensive technical training that many of its students are accepted into engineering colleges with advanced standing. Especially when they impose high admission standards, technical high school programs within the academic structure frequently tend to serve as prep schools for engineering colleges.

Since World War II, increased emphasis has been placed on technical courses of study within the Federal-state trade and industrial program in the high schools. Such courses are designated as "vocational-technical." This new emphasis is the result not only of the changing character of industrial operations, but also of an increase in the average age and intelligence of vocational students, which has enabled more of them to complete the necessary mathematics and science courses. Because of their close association with education for skilled work, vocational-technical programs often emphasize manual skills rather than theoretical knowledge. Some vocational educators feel that technicians cannot validly be distinguished from skilled workers, nor technician training from skill training. From their viewpoint, vocational programs should simply seek to match industry's increasing need for skilled workers who have broad theoretical backgrounds.

In the West and Midwest, junior colleges represent another important effort to provide technician training within institutions originally designed for other purposes. Many of the junior colleges were established to provide the first two years of the liberal arts college program. However, they have generally been closer to community needs than other colleges and less bound by traditional curricula. As the demand for technical workers increased, the junior college was the logical institution to fill the need in areas where there were few technical institutes. Technical training in the junior colleges also seemed the best way to meet the needs of the growing number of high school graduates who did not intend to go to college and had not prepared for any particular job.

More than half of all junior college students are in California. The philosophy that every young person should receive as much education as he can benefit from has been widely accepted there. Reinforced by the difficulties of coordinating vocational and general education in the high schools, this viewpoint has led to the conclusion that most vocational instruction should be moved from the high school into the junior college. The high school orientation of junior college vocational and technical education in California is increased by the fact that it is aided by Federal vocational funds. These funds are available only for instruction of less than college grade and many vocational and technical courses duplicate trade and industrial training in the high schools, except that they are adapted to take advantage of the greater maturity of junior college students. On the other hand, some of the junior colleges in California and elsewhere have made pioneering advances in the development of formal instruction for technical occupations.

Junior college enrollment is now about 570,000.[13] Three

fourths of the students are in the West and Midwest. More than 85 percent of the students are in publicly supported institutions, most of them locally controlled. About 35,000 of the students are preparing for jobs as engineering, science, or health technicians or as skilled workers. Another 56,000 are preparing for wholesale and retail distribution, and less than 20,000 each for agriculture and home economics. The junior colleges also offer part-time and evening courses. Most of them now admit non-high school graduates who can profit from the instruction, and about two thirds of all students are adults or special students.

Technical institutes, unlike junior colleges, concentrate exclusively on occupational training. The first technical institutes were founded in the United States over a century ago, but most of the early schools evolved into degree-granting engineering schools. The development of today's institutes stems mainly from the years after World War I. Almost all technical institute students are found in four types of schools, as shown in Table 5.

Table 5. Students in Technical Institutes, January, 1954 [14]

	Day	*Part-time and Evening*	*Total*
State and municipal	10,200	7,900	18,100
Privately endowed	2,800	7,800	10,600
Extension divisions of colleges and universities	3,000	9,800	12,800
Proprietary	5,800	3,400	9,200
Total	21,800	28,900	50,700

Source: "Annual Survey of Technical Institutes for 1953–4," prepared by Leo F. Smith, Dean of Instruction, Rochester Institute of Technology, *Technical Education News,* August, 1954.

Of the twenty-two state and municipal technical institutes, thirteen are in New York State.[15] The latter enroll about five sixths of the students. Six of the other nine are in the North Atlantic region, as are most of the twelve privately endowed institutes. The thirteen extension divisions and the twenty-four proprietary institutes are scattered across the nation. Between 1950 and 1954, enrollment in publicly supported institutions increased substantially. Enrollment in the endowed schools remained stable.[16] The proprietary schools, private schools run for profit, have lost substantial ground as World War II veterans have completed training under the GI bill. In business and technical education and in other fields, the GI bill led to rapid expansion of enrollments and to the hasty establishment of many new proprietary schools. Within a few years the sharp decline in veteran enrollments not only put many of the new schools out of business, but also endangered the financial positions of some old and reputable institutions.

The schools covered by the survey summarized in table 5 graduated over 6,200 engineering and science technicians in 1953. The largest number, about 2,400, were electrical technology graduates. About 1,400 were in various mechanical fields, including drafting, machine and tool design, instrumentation, steam and diesel engines, and welding. Over 600 were graduates of aeronautical courses, and about the same number, of architectural, building, and civil technology courses.[17]

These figures do not accurately represent the extent of technical institute education. They include only schools which concentrate primarily on industrial technology. They exclude not only junior colleges, but also medical technician and business schools. Perhaps one fourth of the listed enrollments, however, are in such nonindustrial fields as agriculture, business, graphic arts, health services, and home economics. Some schools listed by the survey failed to supply enrollment data.

The figures for proprietary technical institutes are particularly incomplete. Some refuse to cooperate in the annual survey, and others are excluded because the survey is confined to schools of the type accredited by the Engineers Council for Professional Development and the National Council of Technical Schools. Scores of other private schools offering some technical training range from those which could almost qualify as approved technical institutes to trade schools with low standards. A directory issued in 1953 listed almost 4,000 private, non-degree granting schools, accredited or approved in one way or another, offering some form of occupational instruction.

Even among approved schools technical institute programs vary considerably, in part because they must be closely coordinated with the changing needs of industry. The students, many of whom are experienced workers paying substantial tuition fees in order to qualify for better jobs, know what they want. The private schools tend to concentrate on a single occupational field, such as electronics or aeronautical technology, while most of the public institutions offer courses in a number of fields. In any case, the student is likely to be prepared for a group of related jobs. Thus the graduate of a mechanical technician course might, with some experience, qualify as a laboratory assistant, a time-study man, a power plant operator, a tool designer, or a production supervisor.

Technical institute programs run from about one year to three and sometimes even four years, though the most usual length is two years. They are often arranged so that the student can drop out at the end of any semester with training which he can put to immediate use. By staying an additional term he can qualify for a more responsible position or a wider range of jobs. All accredited institutes require high school graduation or its equivalent for admission.

Curricula invariably include courses in mathematics and science, in the theory of the specific field, and in the practical application of general principles to specific problems in laboratory or shop. The relative emphasis on manual skills as opposed to theoretical knowledge varies considerably depending on the school and the field of study, but accredited schools place primary emphasis on mathematics and science. A few technical institutes offer cooperative work-study programs.

The role of general education is now a lively issue in the technical institute field, just as it is in the vocational high school and the engineering college. Originally, most institutes offered little or no general education. Many of the private schools still offer nothing in this area beyond a few courses in technical English. Students are generally not eager to devote their time and their money to courses which do not have an obvious relationship to their intended jobs. Some technical institute educators maintain that in such fields as electronics and aviation, qualified technicians cannot be trained in two years unless at least 80 or 90 percent of the curriculum is devoted to specialized courses. There is, however, a trend in the other direction. In the New York State institutes, one fifth of the curriculum is devoted to general courses.

The primary intent of all technical institutes is to provide practical, terminal training. Yet, since many of their students have the ability to complete engineering courses, the institutes have had to concern themselves with the needs of those who decide that they want to go on for a bachelor's degree. This has meant further changes in curricula, together with efforts to persuade the colleges to grant for institute work at least some credit toward a degree.

Because of these and other developments, technical institute programs have assumed many of the characteristics of junior colleges. At the same time, technical curricula in the junior colleges have assumed some of the features of technical institutes. The original differences between the two kinds of schools, reflecting the primarily academic orientation of the one and the industrial training orientation of the other, have been growing less pronounced. Admission requirements have become more formal in the institutes, less so in many junior colleges. The junior colleges have given increasing attention to specific occupational training, and less to general scientific background, academic education, and college preparation. The technical institutes have moved from training for single jobs to broad training for groups of related jobs. They have given growing attention to scientific background and general education. The five new institutes established in New York in 1946 are now legally designated as community colleges. Little distinguishes them from the junior colleges elsewhere except that they still concentrate mainly on occupational training.

Training for one group of technical occupations, health technicians, is concentrated in hospitals and in university schools of dentistry and medicine. Many of the hospitals combine in-school and on-the-job training programs. The number of students enrolled and the number graduated in 1951 from schools approved by the American Medical and Dental Associations is shown in Table 6.

Table 6. Enrollment and Graduation of Health Technicians, 1951 [18]

	Enrollment	Graduation
Occupational therapists	1,971	411
Physical therapists	723 *	585
Medical record librarians	176 *	58
Medical technicians	3,518	2,220
X-ray technicians	1,907 *	1,080
Practical nurses	6,711	n.a.
Dental hygienists	1,454	632

    n.a. = not available.
    * Capacity rather than actual enrollment.
    Source: *A Report to the President of the President's Commission on the Health Needs of the Nation*, 1952, Vol. 3, and *Journal of the American Medical Association*, Hospital Number, May 10, 1952.

Many schools not accredited by these associations, including some of the public technical institutes as well as private schools, also train health technicians. The term "technician," like the term "skilled worker," includes occupations with widely different minimum training requirements. Thus, occupational and physical therapists are usually college graduates with several years of postgraduate training. On the other hand, practical nurses are often trained through high school or correspondence courses. Practical nursing is taught as part of the vocational trade and industrial program in the high schools of 158 communities in 41 states.[19]

CORRESPONDENCE SCHOOLS

For many years, a significant amount of technical instruction has been provided by correspondence schools. There are now some 300 private correspondence schools with an estimated enrollment of about one million. Another 175,000 students are enrolled in correspondence courses given by university extension divisions. The forty-two schools accredited by the National Home Study Council account for about 80 percent of enrollment in private schools. Probably about 300,000 of these students are taking courses in the skilled and technician occupations.[20]

Correspondence instruction, because of its nature, must concentrate on technical information even in courses for skilled workers. The vocational and technical correspondence courses serve the same types of people who enroll in parallel evening courses—young ambitious workers seeking knowledge to qualify for promotion or to keep a new job. About 5,000 companies have contracts through which their employees may take at company expense either regular correspondence courses or specially developed courses. Because the larger schools have very large enrollments scattered all over the country, they are able to offer a great variety of courses, many not available in the residence schools of most localities.

A typical vocational-technical course, in radio or television repair, for instance, consists of 75 to 100 lessons, each based on a booklet of more than fifty pages and requiring about fifteen hours of work by the student. To pass the course the student must complete a written assignment on each lesson, which is sent to the school for grading and comment. The graduates of reputable schools seem to have considerable ambition and self-discipline, and the ability to read with understanding and to express themselves clearly in writing.

VOCATIONAL EDUCATION AND DEVELOPMENT OF SKILLED WORKERS

Vocational education for skilled workers and technicians embraces a great variety of public and private efforts. The total cost of the vocational training provided in the public high schools, junior colleges, and technical institutes has never been calculated but runs to many millions of dollars annually. The national importance of training for skilled and technical work is suggested by the extent to which the Federal government has become involved in it. Federally-sponsored and supported training activities during World War II were directed mainly toward training workers, technicians, and foremen. Most of the enormous school structure of the armed forces today is devoted to training for skilled and technical positions. Federal law and Federal funds have made vocational education in the public high schools the closest approach to a uniform system of education that exists in the United States. Although the Federal government is deeply involved in vocational education, it does not have a comprehensive policy that relates its vocational education activities to its other educational programs, to its policies for skilled and technical manpower, or to the multiplicity of other institutions which contribute to the development of skilled workers.

Partly because it is, in some respects, a national system, the Federal-state program has dominated most discussions of vocational education problems. Each year, however, hundreds of thousands of people receive formal vocational instruction in other schools. High school education which is not specifically vocational also constitutes important preparation for work. The largest part of the skills and distinctive abilities of the country's skilled workers and technicians, moreover, is acquired on the job rather than in school.

Improving the means through which skilled workers are developed therefore requires careful consideration of all these institutions—of how they can be better used together for increasing the opportunities of individuals and the quality of the nation's labor force.

Part Three

VOCATIONAL GUIDANCE

IX. VOCATIONAL GUIDANCE AND COUNSELING

The Council Staff

A MAJOR TASK faced by secondary education is to help youngsters learn enough about their abilities and interests, the educational opportunities and choices open to them, and about the world of work, so that they may make informed and sound, rather than ill-founded and haphazard, decisions about their own futures. The importance of guidance as an aspect of secondary education has been expressed in a host of current studies, reports, and proposals for reform. Establishment of a satisfactory educational and vocational guidance system, for example, leads the list of twenty-one recommendations designed to improve secondary education made by Dr. James B. Conant in his *The American High School Today.*

The sharper stress of recent years upon the need to improve the availability and the quality of vocational guidance at the secondary level has in large part been stimulated by a growing concern with reducing the extent to which potential abilities are wasted, with shortages of scientific, engineering, and other professional personnel, and with the growing scientific, technological, and military advances of the Soviet Union. These considerations have not so much supplanted as they have complemented the more traditional and fundamental concern with the realization of individual potentialities and aspirations by rendering the educational and occupational choices of youngsters as genuinely free and well-founded as possible. "Vocational Guidance and Counseling" delineates the manner in which vocational guidance is provided in the public high schools, and identifies its strengths and shortcomings. In addition, it sketches the resources for vocational guidance outside the secondary school structure and indicates the differences in approach to guidance functions and problems found among professional guidance personnel. Finally, it argues, in view of the fact that present resources of trained personnel are not adequate to provide all the kinds of guidance and counseling needed by high school students, that concentrating upon the target of improving vocational guidance is preferrable to the pursuit of other objectives even more difficult to realize with the personnel either now or likely to be available in the near future.

"Vocational Guidance and Counseling" is reprinted with editorial changes from A Policy for Skilled Manpower, *in which it first appeared as Chapter X, pp. 266–82.*

I**N** this country freedom of opportunity is an article of national faith. The vast majority of Americans believe that every American youngster should be free to enter any occupation for which he can qualify. When discriminatory practices restrict freedom of opportunity, they arouse nation-wide controversy.

Yet freedom of opportunity is restricted by a condition far more widespread and far less obvious than discrimination—the general ignorance among youngsters, and almost equally among their elders, of the myriad types of trained personnel required by our complex society. Ignorance of available vocational opportunities can as effectively prevent access to them as restrictions rooted in racial, ethnic, or religious discrimination.

Although a youngster often reads about different kinds of work with which he can have no firsthand experience, when he thinks about choosing a field of work he is likely to be most influenced by the occupations he has actually encountered. Generally, these occupations are limited to the principal professions and the services and trades he becomes acquainted with in the course of his daily life. Consequently, the average youngster becomes familiar with only a tiny fraction of the many different types of work which exist.

As our economy has grown, so has the number of occupations that support it. As our technology has become more specialized, so have the kinds of jobs that maintain it. The 1951 *Occupational Outlook Handbook* of the U. S. Department of Labor describes 433 occupations. The U. S. Employment Service's *Dictionary of Occupational Titles* describes 22,028 different jobs—that is, the specific duties performed by individuals in their work.[1]

Casual familiarity with an occupation may leave one ignorant of its actual diversity and requirements. For example, the *Dictionary of Occupational Titles* lists about 60 different job categories under the main title of carpenter. To name only a few, there are acoustical carpenters, foundry carpenters, stage carpenters, ship carpenters, and refrigerator carpenters. The much newer occupation of draftsman is similarly subdivided. The latter is an example of an occupation in which even the specializations have become subspecialized. Not only does the *Dictionary* list approximately 30 different kinds of draftsmen, it also, for example, details 7 different kinds of marine draftsmen.[2]

GUIDANCE IN THE SCHOOLS

With such an enormous diversity of job opportunities open to the qualified, it is obviously desirable that some systematic procedure exist through which a youngster is informed about the occupations for which he might qualify and told how he can prepare for them properly. Such assistance becomes critically important at the time the young person is ready to enter secondary school. No longer can he simply accept an assigned curriculum as he did in elementary school. He has reached the point where he must begin to make choices. Shall he take a general, college preparatory, or vocational course? Does he expect to graduate from high school or does he anticipate leaving early? Does he show signs of any special aptitudes or interests, and, if so, how can they best be developed? What vocational goals is he beginning to set for himself?

While in secondary school, the individual is going through a period during which he should be making a tentative occupational choice. Occupational choice is a gradual process in which a compromise is eventually reached between a person's abilities, interests, and values, and the realistic necessities presented by his actual opportunities for preparation and employment. Although knowledge of the world of work is clearly not the only element needed to make sound decisions about one's high school education, it is highly valuable. Unless deliberate steps are taken to supply such knowledge, most young people will be handicapped in attempting to make sound educational plans.

Learning about the relationship between education and occupational opportunity is important to youngsters for a second reason. As they move into their teens, they often become less willing to attend school and take it seriously unless they understand the advantages of doing so. The realization of how their education helps determine the work they can later do will help motivate youngsters to take full advantage of their educational opportunities.

If youngsters understand that their early selection of courses of study may restrict their freedom to make subsequent educational and occupational choices, if they can perceive the importance of their schooling in preparing them for the work they might want to do—in short, if they are shown the relationship between education and their future vocational opportunities, most of them would probably be far more interested in their education. The inability to understand the function of education as preparation for work often causes youngsters to leave high school early or to become recalcitrant students who merely go through the motions of attending school until they reach the legal age at which they can withdraw.

As an institution, the secondary school has come to occupy the most effective position for giving a youngster the guidance he will need to prepare himself for work. The schools have access to most teenagers in this country, since the great majority enter high school. The school must acquaint incoming students with its curriculum and in the process can indicate the value of education as a whole and the specific usefulness of different parts of the curriculum in terms of the individual's aptitudes and interests. The school is able to draw on government and industry for vocational data and information so that students can have a better idea of how their preparation will affect their chances when they look for a job. For all these reasons, vocational guidance and counseling have a critical role to play in secondary education.

A survey covering the school year 1952-53 revealed that there were slightly over 18,000 persons in the junior and senior high schools of the nation who are doing counseling. The study does not differentiate those who are primarily concerned with vocational guidance. Although the results are not strictly comparable to those of a survey made in 1946, it is apparent that the number of counselors has risen sharply from the older figure of a little over 8,000. There is now approximately one counselor for every 453 school pupils. But less than half of these 18,000 counselors devote as much as half of their time to counseling.[3]

At the present time, thirty-nine states employ state supervisors of guidance.[4] There is still, however, a wide variation in the scope of guidance programs. California has over 1,200 counselors who devote at least half their time to counseling, while New York and Massachusetts have 700 and 530 respectively. At the other extreme North Dakota has 4, and Alabama has 9.

In the fiscal year 1952 about $400,000 in Federal funds were expended under the George-Barden Act to help states with their guidance programs. The states reported the expenditure of a little over $1 million in order to qualify for the Federal contribution. Much more money was expended by states and localities other than that reported under the Act. Massachusetts, for example, reported that local school committees spent just under $2 million for guidance in the fiscal year 1952. Responding to the same 1952-1953 survey noted above, Washington reported over $1 million; Texas, about $850,000; and Georgia, $450,000.[5]

OTHER VOCATIONAL GUIDANCE FACILITIES

Institutions other than public schools also provide vocational guidance. Among these are various social agencies. Of outstanding importance has been the work of the Young Men's Christian Association. B'nai B'rith has pioneered in group guidance methods, and facilities are provided in a number of cities by Jewish Vocational Service agencies. The Catholic Youth Organization and various service clubs, such as the Rotary and Kiwanis, have long been interested and active in the field of vocational guidance.

In many communities throughout the United States, vocational guidance services are provided either by an independent agency, such as the Vocational Advisory Service in New York City, or in connection with the placement work which is undertaken by various social and religious groups. Since these placement efforts are usually directed towards helping special groups, a careful investigation of vocational aspirations, abilities, and interests is required.

A directory compiled by the American Personnel and Guidance Association, which was formed in 1951 by the amalgamation of the National Vocational Guidance Association and several other societies, lists the vocational counseling services approved by the Association. In 1953, there were slightly over 150 such services. More than 40 percent of these operate as part of a college or university, but are also open to the public. Another large proportion consists of services provided by such organizations as the Y.M.C.A. or Jewish Vocational Service agencies. A small number are private agencies or individual guidance counselors in private practice. These approved counseling services are concentrated in the larger cities and more industrialized states. About one fifth of them are located in two cities, New York and Chicago, and many important cities do not have a single approved service. Twenty-two states lack approved services of any kind.[6]

The Federal government, as has been seen, contributes to the training of counselors and to the payment of guidance supervisors' salaries at the state level under the George-Barden Act. During recent years, in connection with its large-scale educational and training program, the Veterans Administration has become deeply involved in advisory programs that are primarily focused on vocational guidance. About 600,000 disabled veterans who sought benefits under Public Law 16 were required to secure guidance. Millions of other veterans who pursued training or education under Public Law 346 were entitled, and in some cases required, to use these guidance services. The Veterans Administration estimated that it spent $26 million on counseling services during the first six years after World War II.[7]

Guidance functions have also been part of the work of Federal and state employment services. The state agencies affiliated with the U. S. Employment Service placed considerable emphasis on counseling during the 1930's. Guidance was particularly important during the depression because the many people seeking employment possessed a wide variety of qualifications. Counseling was de-emphasized under the federalized U.S.E.S. during World War II, when there was a shortage of workers and the need was to fill job openings as quickly as possible. Since the war, efforts have been made to rebuild the guidance and counseling aspects of the employment services. These efforts have been handicapped by the lack of trained personnel.

The Bureau of Vocational Rehabilitation, located in the U. S. Department of Health, Education, and Welfare, seeks through its affiliated state agencies to appraise and counsel clients, as well as support them through the period of necessary training and initial employment. This service is intended for any handicapped person, but insufficient funds have limited the Division's aid to a relatively small number. Recently, Congress has enacted legislation which will progressively increase the funds available over the next five years to nearly triple the 1953 appropriation.[8] The use of some of these funds for the training of additional counselors and for research is also authorized.

Every young man who enters the armed services takes a battery of comprehensive tests. Their purpose is to discover his present skills and his potential for acquiring new ones. The kind of training he will receive largely depends on his test scores and his civilian background. This has the effect of introducing many young men to new fields they might otherwise never have considered. During the demobilization after World War II, the services operated extensive counseling programs designed to assist men in their return to civilian life.

The Federal government also contributes to vocational guidance through its various information services. The U. S. Department of Labor, in cooperation with the Veterans Administration, has developed an *Occupational Outlook Handbook*, which carries the subtitle "Employment Information on Major Occupations for Use in Guidance." Within two brief pages [9] for each occupation it attempts to provide the following information: a summary of the prospects for employment throughout the next five or ten years; a short description of the nature of the work; training and other qualifications required for employment; a more detailed analysis of the factors affecting the demand for and supply of workers which have been noted in the outlook summary; some statistical information about earnings and the range of earnings in different parts of the country; finally, where to go for more information.

Several divisions of the Department of Labor, particularly the Bureau of Employment Security, have also been engaged in the compilation of occupational information. Basic to the collection and effective utilization of such information was the development of the *Dictionary of Occupational Titles,* first published in 1939, which introduced a system of job classification and shows the relationships that exist within job groupings. The Bureau of Employment Security has also contributed to guidance by developing tests and job analyses, and by doing some counselor training.

A good deal of the existing literature on occupations and vocational opportunities is sponsored by trade associations and professional societies. Much of it is designed, however, to attract entrants into particular fields. A number of private publishers have also tried to meet the sizable market that exists for up-to-date and usable information about the world of work.

Tests, which play so important a role in current guidance, received great impetus from their extensive use and development in the armed services. Even more extensive use of tests is made by the public schools. Tests are now available that are intended to reveal an individual's general intelligence, special aptitudes, present achievements, interests, values, and personality—nearly all the psychological factors considered important for vocational guidance. One current textbook for students of guidance devotes eleven pages of small type just to list available achievement tests.

THE DEVELOPMENT OF VOCATIONAL GUIDANCE

Professor John M. Brewer of Harvard University, the historian of vocational guidance in the United States, offered six reasons for the rise of the movement. First, the removal of work from the home, which meant that most children were no longer in intimate contact with the world of work. Second, the increasing complexity of technology, which multiplied the types of work available. Third, the failure of many who had undertaken vocational training for which they were not suited. Fourth, the difficulty of finding appropriate employment in a world of increasing technical specialization. Fifth, the transformation of secondary schools from specialized institutions serving the minority of youngsters preparing for college to common schools serving most adolescents. Finally, Brewer stressed the importance in a democratic society of insuring that vocational choice is not only free but based on sound knowledge.

The vocational guidance movement was started in the United States by Frank W. Parsons. In 1908 he established a vocational bureau in Boston which he called the "Breadwinner's Institute." During the same period E. M. Weaver, a teacher in the public schools of New York City, was pioneering in attempts to find the right vocations for young people when they graduated from high school. Parsons was convinced that, "Society is very shortsighted as yet in its attitude toward the development of its human resources. It trains its horses better as a rule than its men. It spends unlimited money to perfect the inanimate machinery of production, but pays very little attention to the business of perfecting human machinery, though it is by far the most important in production."

In his book, *Choosing a Vocation,* Parsons presented three conditions necessary for wise vocational choice:

1. A clear understanding of yourself, your aptitudes, abilities, interests, ambitions, resources, limitations, and their causes; 2. A knowledge of the requirements and conditions of success, advantages and disadvantages, compensation, opportunities, and prospects of different lines of work; 3. True reasoning on the relationship of these two groups of facts.

Every young person needs help on all three of these points. He needs all the information and assistance he can get. He needs a vocational counselor. He needs careful and systematic help by experienced minds in making this greatest decision of his life.

Parsons further stressed the evil of unbalanced specialization and argued that children require broad culture and experience if they are to develop properly.

Parsons' methods included all the elements of present vocational guidance, from aptitude tests to occupational forecasts. Subsequent developments in psychology and psychiatry have caused the guidance movement to concentrate at different times on specialized aspects of guidance and to broaden enormously the original goals of counseling.

Psychological testing on a large scale was introduced by the Army during World War I. In the next decade, business and industry began to use tests on a large scale. Educators were introducing them into the public schools during this period, and testing has since been adopted by almost every school system in the country. Psychological measurement is now an important tool of guidance.

In the 1940's and the 1950's, the whole guidance movement became increasingly concerned with personality problems. This concern had always been felt by some within the field of vocational guidance. It had already been expressed in the 1920's when the National Vocational Guidance Association drew up a statement of principles and practice. In it, the point is made that, "Problems of adjustment to health, religion, recreation, to family and friends, to school and work, may be included under the general term 'guidance.'" Counselors have always been aware that some individuals who repeatedly seek occupational counseling often do this as a substitute for counseling on their deep-seated psychological problems.

Recently, furthermore, many preparing to become counselors have been doing graduate work in psychology. Such preparation makes them interested in over-all problems of adjustment in addition to the narrower problems of occupational guidance. This broadened emphasis has resulted in the emergence of a new psychological specialty, "counseling psychology." Another indication of how the field has expanded far beyond Parsons' original goals is the four areas into which guidance problems are divided in a recent textbook for students of guidance. These areas are: vocational pursuits; vocational activities; activities concerned with maintaining mental and physical health; and social and civic interests. The term "guidance" clearly encompasses much more than vocational guidance. Vocational guidance has become one facet of a larger movement. The importance of vocational guidance within the whole guidance movement appears to be constantly declining.

APPRAISALS OF VOCATIONAL GUIDANCE

Many who are enthusiastic about the potentialities of vocational guidance admit that its achievements have so far been modest. Improvement, it is often felt, will come about through the training of a large number of competent guidance counselors, in securing improved occupational information, and in improved methods of individual appraisal and counseling.

Vocational guidance has been handicapped by the fact that the educational and training program recommended for guidance personnel has not been adopted by all states and school systems. School superintendents have been free to appoint almost anyone in the school system to be a guidance counselor. Recently, however, many states have adopted certification requirements. The most recent survey [10] shows that twenty-one states and the District of Columbia now have mandatory certification. Eighteen states either have optional standards or are working on certification plans. All these states require a certificate to teach and several years teaching experience. Most require also a period of work experience and courses of particular relevance to guidance and counseling. Nine states still have no plans for certification nor are they preparing any.

Another handicap has been the lack of occupational outlook materials that local guidance counselors can apply to their particular problems. At present, good occupational outlook data usually deal with national situations. But individuals involved in preparing themselves for work need, if not local, at least regional information. Some communities are now making special and successful efforts to provide the essential local information.

Although some guidance workers believe that more emphasis on psychological testing would improve the effectiveness of vocational guidance, many leaders in the field do not believe that such efforts will result in much improvement unless guidance is first strengthened in other ways. After making a special review of the guidance movement, Dr. Nicholas Hobbs of George Peabody College for Teachers declared in his paper entitled *The Social Scientist and the Field of Guidance* that the movement, which "started in the interest of the fullest human development," seems to have become a vast technology, almost completely absorbed in its own operations, rather vaguely concerned about the nature of the individual it proposes to serve, and seemingly oblivious to the demands of the society in which the individual must work out his destiny. I came away from this experience feeling that we in guidance have been captured by our methodologies and that we have lost sight of the meaning of what we are doing. In our preoccupation with how to do things, we seem to have lost interest in why we do them.

After a careful review of ten of the leading textbooks in the field, Dr. Hobbs concluded that, "The texts are skimpy on discussion of the nature of the child and young person, and almost completely barren of any discussion of the society in which the effectiveness of guidance efforts will be validated."

Elaborate special aptitude tests, to which so much effort has been devoted, do not enable one to predict with high accuracy performance on most jobs. The important determinants of success in many occupations are: higher general intelligence than that of others in the same job; competence in the basic skills—reading, writing, and computation—and willingness to learn and to work hard. Although guidance people tend to exaggerate the importance of psychological testing, it does have many valuable applications. One, for example, is in discovering exceptional aptitude which would otherwise not be revealed.

The effectiveness of vocational guidance would no doubt be increased by improving the training of those becoming counselors, by providing better forecasting materials, and by the wiser use of psychological tests. But one other factor continues to hamper vocational guidance. This is the ever-growing emphasis in the guidance movement on counseling for over-all adjustment.

Even if vocational guidance were to restrict itself to helping individuals prepare for work, it would still have to provide an imposing array of services. Most experts have agreed that a well-organized public school vocational guidance program should provide the following: (1) a vocational information service, which collects occupational information; (2) a personal data collecting service, which obtains information about the individual; (3) a counseling service, in which the individual is helped to study himself, his occupational opportunities, and his occupational goals and plans; (4) a placement service, which helps the individual get into contact with job opportunities and work out a job-getting program; (5) a follow-up and research service, designed both to evaluate the program and to help the individual make job adjustments.

How far guidance has attempted to go beyond even these ambitious goals is illustrated by "The Illinois Secondary School Curriculum Program," specifically the part dealing with guidance services. The study is oriented toward a set of guidance objectives that go far beyond the vocational area. Questions are raised, for example, asking how those responsible for guidance can help the student overcome difficulties in personal relations, choose companions wisely, and develop attitudes that will lead to a happy marriage and satisfying family life.

In theory there is no reason why young people cannot be provided with broad counseling for life adjustment in addition to more restricted vocational guidance. In practical terms, however, school systems have a limited amount of money, personnel, and time to devote to guidance and counseling activities. The newer emphasis on dealing with the pupil's adjustment problems may compete with vocational guidance for the available resources. Or, counselors now concerning themselves primarily with vocational guidance may turn their attention to other areas of counseling. It seems likely that the increasingly broad goals of guidance may work against more effective vocational guidance.

THE NEED FOR EFFECTIVE GUIDANCE

Unless the vocational guidance services provided for young people during the period they are in school are performed effectively, the most important contribution guidance and counseling could make to individual satisfaction and to economic and social efficiency will be lost. Effective vocational guidance could encourage many young people to derive more value from their education.

Perhaps the most important reason many adolescents derive little value from their schooling is that they cannot see the relevance of their current education to their future lives. They drift along within the school system, more or less doing the required work and choosing courses they consider easy or that their friends are taking. Not only students with limited intellectual ability act this way, but even some gifted children show a lack of interest in school work after they enter high school.

The second reason many young people fail to get as much from their secondary schooling as they might is that their occupational objective is too modest. Many who have the ability to go through college never consider doing so because they are unaware of the possibilities for financial assistance. Most American families, even those in the lowest income level, are able to maintain their children in high school. But a considerable number do not have the financial resources to support their children's education after high school, especially if they have to study away from home. Yet there are many opportunities for young persons with limited financial resources to secure either a college education or some type of specialized training. Many young persons needing financial aid fail to learn about scholarship opportunities for which they might qualify.

Many young people do not foresee the jobs that would be open to them if they received a solid education. They are not made aware of the enlarged opportunities for training or employment that may be open to them in communities in other parts of the country or in the armed services. It has already been pointed out that the armed services offer the young man with a good high school background opportunities for technical training. Moreover, he can also take advantage of educational benefits after his discharge. The restricted employment opportunities of rural areas or one-industry towns may give young people a limited picture of the world of work. They fail to consider that they are likely to migrate to other parts of the country. Such ignorance of possible future opportunities is undoubtedly an important reason why approximately 40 percent of young Americans terminate their education before they graduate from high school.[11]

Making sound vocational plans is not easy for a young person under even the most favorable circumstances. He must take into account his abilities and interests, the advanced education and training he can hope to secure, occupational prospects, and other goals such as marriage and raising a family. Ideally, sound vocational planning requires a youngster to make tentative vocational commitments that help to give him a sense of direction and purpose as he goes through school. But he must also maintain sufficient flexibility to shift his plans as he matures, his interests stabilize, and his knowledge expands. This requires that he does not make the type of premature choice of courses or schooling that can prevent him from later changing his plans.

Occupational choice is made during adolescence, that period when a youngster is being transformed from a child into an adult. A process involving such a radical transformation is never smooth and easy. Further, the most insistent pressures of the period relate, not to occupational choice, but rather to emancipation from parents and adjustments to the opposite sex. In a period of such turmoil, even well-balanced individuals will make errors. Many will inevitably fail to make maximum use of their opportunities. They will delay making choices, or they will, for a long time, pursue the wrong choice.

OBJECTIVES OF IMPROVED VOCATIONAL GUIDANCE

In trying to reduce this waste, vocational guidance faces many difficulties. Yet even after acknowledging the scale of these difficulties, it is not unfair to assert that vocational guidance is far from effective. Because of the dangers to vocational guidance implicit in the ambitious goals of the total guidance movement, it becomes necessary to ask what are reasonable goals for vocational guidance.

The previous discussion has already implied what these objectives should be. A fundamental objective of vocational guidance must be to make young people aware of the need to give more deliberate thought to the problem of their occupational choice. A second objective should be to help young people avoid early acceptance of overly modest occupational goals. This is closely related to the third objective, keeping young people from committing themselves to curricula or courses that will prevent them from changing or raising their occupational sights later in their educational careers.

Next, vocational guidance needs to help a young person discover the range of occupational goals he can reasonably expect to attain, and the opportunities available to him for education and training. Lastly, the success of all of these objectives depends upon the vocational counselor's helping youngsters to learn the value of getting as much as they can out of their high school education.

Guidance counselors are already trying to meet three of these objectives—inducing awareness of the problem of occupational choice, providing information about jobs and educational and training opportunities, and emphasizing the value of high school education. The activities of some counselors, however, hinder the fulfillment of the other two objectives. Seeking to make sure the youngster will prepare himself for a specific occupation, the counselor may guide him into curricula or courses based upon too modest a goal. By following such a course, the youngster is often unable to later raise or revise his occupational objective.

A youngster's occupational choice and his preparation for work are molded by several powerful influences apart from the direct vocational guidance he may receive—for example, his family, friends, school experiences, and the prevailing economic situation. Formal vocational guidance may not be encountered until relatively late in the occupational choice process, when the youngster's direction may be firmly set.

Vocational guidance cannot be expected to act as the overriding factor in the occupational choice process. The occupational adjustment of the population does not depend upon vocational counselors any more than the mental health of the population depends upon psychiatrists. Yet just as psychiatrists have a contribution to make to raising the emotional health of the population, so there is much that guidance experts can contribute to vocational adjustment. The responsibility for contributing to sound occupational choices must be borne not only by the vocational expert, but by all the sectors of the community capable of making effective contributions—the family, teachers, industry, mass communications media, the armed services, and government at local, state, and Federal levels. A key task for the guidance movement is to stimulate these contributions and, by integrating them, encourage their effective use.

Even within the narrower confines of the school system, individual counseling by the guidance specialist is not the only, and probably not the major, factor in vocational guidance. Much of it must be accomplished by the teacher in the course of teaching. A good teacher knows how to show the implications of what he is teaching for the future lives and working careers of his pupils. He knows how to stimulate and encourage those of ability to set high goals for themselves. He also knows how to persuade a young person who has set his goals too high or in the wrong direction to alter his choice and to make it more realistic, without discouraging him. A competent guidance specialist assists the teaching staff to bring out the occupational implications of the subject matter presented to the students.

By the eighth grade, youngsters already need to be made aware of the considerations that must influence their early occupational decisions. The school system forces the youngster to make critical educational choices before he enters high school. For example, he must make a choice between courses that are either narrowly vocational or broadly academic. Postponing vocational guidance until the eleventh grade, as frequently happens, often limits its usefulness. By then, numerous students have already cut themselves off from many possible lines of development. Fortunately, a trend is developing to start vocational guidance activities as early as the elementary school.

The effectiveness of vocational guidance may be endangered by the increasingly ambitious goals of the guidance movement. These goals lead to programs which seek to counsel the youngster regarding all his adjustment problems. They may thus divert attention and effort from the specific objectives of vocational guidance. If attention were concentrated on the basic objectives of vocational guidance, more youngsters would derive greater benefit from their secondary education and a greater number would seek advanced education and training. This would be a significant contribution to the more effective development of the nation's human resources.

X. VOCATIONAL GUIDANCE AND THE SKILLS OF THE WORK FORCE

Charles E. Odell

"VOCATIONAL GUIDANCE AND THE SKILLS OF THE WORK FORCE" was originally commissioned as a working paper for the National Manpower Council's Arden House conference of 1955 on Improving the Work Skills of the Nation. One of its purposes was to submit to critical examination the Council's recommendations with respect to vocational guidance which had been made in *A Policy for Skilled Manpower*. It was also designed to indicate how improvements in the structure and outcome of vocational guidance could be brought about, and many of the suggestions made in it have since been fulfilled.

Mr. Odell, the author, was at that time Chief of the Division of Counseling, Selective Placement, and Testing of the Bureau of Employment Security. He is currently the Director of the Older and Retired Workers Department of the United Automobile Workers.

It should be noted that Mr. Odell's emphasis upon the need for more professionally trained personnel in the field of guidance is no less pertinent now than it was in 1955. The rapid growth of the secondary school population during the 1960's may well result in exacerbating the imbalance between the rising demands for trained and competent personnel and available supplies—a possibility to which Mr. Odell calls attention.

> "*Vocational Guidance and the Skills of the Work Force*" *is reprinted with editorial changes from* Improving the Work Skills of the Nation, *in which it first appeared as Chapter 4, pp. 36–57.*

IN its report, *A Policy for Skilled Manpower,* the National Manpower Council presented a series of recommendations on how best to employ vocational and educational guidance services to develop and maintain the skills of the work force. This paper explores ways and means of implementing these recommendations. In order to do this, the basic recommendations have been recast as a series of questions, each of which will be discussed in turn.

Question 1: What can be done to stimulate state and local governments and boards of education to recognize the importance of educational and vocational guidance services and to increase substantially and rapidly the funds and staff available for guidance and counseling purposes?

Basically the problem involves the whole financing of public education. With the tremendous increase in the school-age population, and with every expectation of its continuously rapid growth, school administrators and educational leaders are hard pressed to meet the elemental needs for physical facilities and teaching personnel. The problems of an inadequate tax base for school support, of inadequate teachers' salaries, and of overcrowding and split shifts are well known. The practical question is whether existing guidance personnel and resources in the nation's public schools can be maintained in the face of the tremendous pressure for funds for classrooms and subject matter teachers.

The majority of school officials accept guidance services as a necessary and important part of the educational process, and increasing numbers have done something about it. As the National Manpower Council study points out, in 1952–53 there were 18,000 persons providing some form of guidance service in the elementary, junior, and senior high schools of the nation. This is in marked contrast to a 1946 study which showed only 8,000 persons providing guidance services. But as late as 1952, less than half the persons reported as guidance counselors devoted even half time to guidance work. Also, most counselors were employed in the larger school systems. The predominantly agricultural and rural-industrial districts, in which a large proportion of out-migrant surplus population is located, have woefully inadequate guidance facilities and educational facilities only slightly less inadequate. For example, a 1952 study showed that guidance services were available in only about 17 percent of the nation's secondary schools, and that these schools served about 50 percent of the secondary school enrollment. There were no guidance services reported in the remaining 83 percent of the schools serving at least half of the school enrollment. The number of school counselors will probably continue to increase, but it is very doubtful that the increase will keep pace with the rapid increases in junior and senior high school enrollment. Furthermore, unless present trends are reversed, less and less of the guidance worker's time will be devoted to vocational and educational guidance services.[1]

Any real answer to the basic question raised by the National Manpower Council recommendation obviously depends on heroic action not only at the state and local level, but at the Federal level as well. Many people believe that some form of Federal aid to education, with a minimum of Federal standards and control, or even none, is essential. The Eisenhower administration has recognized this need in several ways: first, by appropriating money for, and stimulating a series of, state-sponsored conferences on educational problems, culminating in a national White House Conference on Education; second, by sponsoring a specific Federal aid bill which would aid school districts which cannot finance additional building facilities; and third, by passing legislation which provides Federal aid to areas which face school population problems brought on by the in-migration of Federal employees engaged in essential civilian and military work.

The first step should be to make sure that the need for vocational and educational guidance services is brought out dramatically in these state and national conferences on education. The American Personnel and Guidance Association and one of its divisions, the National Vocational Guidance Association, have been trying through state and local branches to bring guidance needs into focus at these conferences. The National Manpower

Council itself ought to bring this matter to the attention of the White House and the Department of Health, Education, and Welfare in order to insure that guidance needs are properly considered in these conferences.

Despite complaints about Federal interference in state affairs, most states follow the Federal government's lead in developing health, education, and welfare programs. In 1938, prior to the establishment of an Occupational Information and Guidance Service in the U. S. Office of Education, not a single state had a state guidance supervisor. Today, 39 states employ state supervisors of guidance.[2] The strengthening and maintenance of an effective and integrated Guidance Service in the U. S. Office of Education is essential to get greater emphasis on guidance in the states and localities. Fortunately, Federal funds are available for matching in the states in order to expand and improve guidance services under the provisions of the George-Barden Act.

Since the precedent has already been established in this field of Federal aid, it would also seem wise to ask the Office of Education and the state departments of education to review existing programs and to determine how, through the provisions of the George-Barden Act, additional funds could be made available to "increase substantially and rapidly" the vocational and educational guidance facilities and services of the public schools. This action might reverse a current trend toward using funds formerly allocated for guidance purposes for other phases of the vocational education program in the states.

The National Manpower Council should further prevail upon the President and the Cabinet to emphasize the importance of vocational and educational guidance in the manpower and defense planning of the nation and, specifically, in identifying, developing, and conserving the professional, technical, and skilled manpower potential of the nation's youth. Few school administrators and even fewer private citizens understand the urgency of this problem. As a people we have apparently not yet matured to the point where we can calmly and efficiently plan and prepare for national defense in the manpower field. The necessity for and the manpower implications of a standing military force, of a selective service system, of a ready reserve, and of a stand-by war production potential have apparently not been too well accepted or understood by the vast majority of school officials nor by the public. Until their continuing importance for our survival is made clear, and the relationship to them of vocational and educational guidance is established, there will continue to be psychological as well as financial obstacles to their proper establishment and maintenance.

One very important step in overcoming both the financial and the psychological barriers would be a forthright declaration of policy by the Federal authorities with sufficient explanation and implementation to insure public understanding and support for official action at appropriate levels. Such forthright action by the Federal government will not solve the problem of public and official lethargy and misunderstanding. This can only be overcome by action through groups who influence educational policy and programs at the state and local levels.

The National Manpower Council should therefore seek the support of citizens' groups in implementing its recommendations on this question. For example, the 1950 White House Conference on Children and Youth made strong recommendations for vocational and educational guidance paralleling those of the National Manpower Council. Each state established a council of public officials and private citizens to implement these and other recommendations. A few states, such as Pennsylvania, have had remarkable success in implementing the vocational and educational guidance recommendations. However, many other states have not taken aggressive action in this field and should be urged to do so.[3]

The National Manpower Council should also seek support for its recommendations from the many national organizations that maintain an active interest in vocational and educational guidance services. These include the service clubs and civic organizations; professional organizations in the field of guidance and education; the professional groups facing manpower shortages; and the many management groups, trade associations, and labor organizations directly affected by an inadequate or poorly trained supply of skilled workers and technicians.

Many of the above mentioned groups are already interested in vocational guidance to the limited extent of developing and furnishing occupational information for use in guidance and educational programs. Few of them, however, have really understood the limitations in the scope and effectiveness of guidance resources and services. Nor have they understood that their independent interests in attracting a better motivated and better trained labor supply are in a sense competitive and diversionary to an integrated training and guidance effort. Bringing them together into a coordinated effort to extend the base of educational facilities and of vocational guidance resources, and to insure that the world of work is presented objectively and comprehensively to all youth, would be a major achievement and a major step toward the goal implied in the question at hand.

Unless educational services are better financed, guidance services will diminish rather than expand. Influencing state and local officials to act on expansion will be difficult without Federal leadership and Federal financial aid. Guidance services and leadership in the U. S. Office of Education should be maintained and strengthened. Public awareness of the problems and needs should be stimulated through such existing machinery as the State and White House Conferences on Education. Public groups, service organizations, professional educational and guidance associations, trade associations, labor unions, and management groups should be asked to band together in bringing the message for the need of more adequate guidance services to the state and local groups. In all this, the National Manpower Council might well be in the best position to act as leader and coordinator. We appreciate its studies and recommendations. We will appreciate even more its leadership in implementing these recommendations.[4]

Question 2: What can be done to encourage school officials to use their guidance and counseling staffs primarily for vocational guidance purposes?

Partly, this is a problem of organizing and coordinating guidance services, and partly a problem of philosophy and policy in operating school guidance services. The National Manpower Council report emphasized the latter. It apparently felt that counselors are either directed by their superiors or influenced by their own training and interests to work primarily with personality adjustment problems rather than with vocational adjustment problems. It is true that the most recent thinking in the preparation of counselors stresses a clinical or therapeutic emphasis in guidance services. It is also increasingly apparent that vocational counselors, or any type of counselor, must be equipped professionally to deal with the "whole person." But it is doubtful if the majority of high school counselors think of themselves or try to act as if they were therapists in the field of emotional or personality maladjustment. Most authorities in the field would be happy if they felt that school counselors were capable of detecting and dealing with the relatively simple problems of the vast majority of individuals who fail to achieve their potentialities.

The diversion from vocational and educational guidance into other areas sometimes occurs because principals and teachers mistakenly unload on the counselor all the "problem" children in the school. Since some of these children are emotionally disturbed and present interesting but time-consuming problems, a small number of them can monopolize the counselor's time. This type of diversion can probably be best overcome by emphasizing in counselor training and in state and local administration that vocational and educational guidance services are intended basically to meet a normal need of normal people. In addition, it will probably be necessary to develop more adequate psychological and social services in the school system to which students with serious emotional problems can be referred for proper attention. Unfortunately, money for these services is frequently not available because of basic needs for classrooms and teachers.

The most common and serious reason vocational and educational counselors are diverted from guidance is the load of routine administrative and record-keeping duties in which they become involved. Some counselors become the school's attendance officer. Some counselors become the test administrator, scorer, and record custodian for the school, with little time left to use the tests intelligently in guidance. Some counselors are called upon to organize and advise all student activity programs such as student councils, student courts, extracurricular clubs, and social functions. Many counselors are known to spend most of their time on such routine clerical activities as keeping student records and furnishing transcripts to colleges. When such nonguidance functions are added up and related to the further complicating fact that so many counselors are also expected to maintain a part-time teaching load in regular subject matter areas, it is not difficult to see why guidance services have so little direct impact in so many schools. A study in the state of Ohio [5] showed that most counselors spend at least 50 percent of their time on administrative and record-keeping tasks that have only an indirect bearing on their professional responsibilities as guidance workers.

Another source of difficulty in getting proper administrative emphasis on vocational and educational guidance in so many school systems is the historical association, in the educator's mind, of vocational guidance and vocational education. This is reflected in much of the early literature in vocational guidance; also, in the administrative organization of guidance services in the U. S. Office of Education, in most states, and in many local school systems. It is also reflected in the controversy which has developed in the professional guidance movement and among counselors. The aversion to the word "vocational" in guidance is a widespread phenomenon. It is not due primarily to a feeling that vocational guidance is passe or unimportant. It is due primarily to a desire to break away from the old idea that vocational guidance is the handmaiden of vocational education rather than a basic service needed by all students regardless of their course of study. Within the guidance profession there are, of course, extreme points of view on both sides of this question. A few people on one side feel that every counselor must be in effect a clinical psychologist and a few on the other side feel that vocational guidance is really just a matter of giving occupational information. The great majority in the profession believe that the vocational counselor must be able to analyze and interpret personality data as well as occupational information and that his basic function is to help the individual in using the data to reach his own decisions.

The answer to Question 2 is therefore not simple. It involves not only administrative but philosophical considerations. From an administrative point of view, more adequate financing of public education is a big part of the underlying problem. As long as counselors are expected to carry classroom teaching, record keeping, attendance officer, student government, and volume testing responsibilities along with impossible student case loads, it is hard to see how either the quality or effectiveness of vocational and educational guidance services can be improved. More adequate financing would also permit the establishment of better services for the emotionally maladjusted and the retarded child. This would require better facilities for special education as well as more psychologists, psychometrists, social workers, attendance officers, visiting teachers, and other types of pupil personnel specialists ,who usually serve a whole school district instead of being attached to individual schools.

Even assuming adequately financed guidance services and broader pupil personnel services, there is the philosophical problem of the attitudes and approach of school administrators, teachers, and counselors to vocational guidance. In reorganizing guidance services, the U. S. Office of Education recognized this problem and as of July 1, 1955, the guidance service aided all levels of education and, organizationally, was a part of the general education program rather than the vocational program. Similar steps should be encouraged at state and local levels so that guidance is no longer identified as a servant of only the vocational education program.[6] To some readers this suggestion may seem to be at cross-purposes with the objective sought in Question 2. Actually, it is not. Proof of this lies in the reorganization of guidance services in New York and California. Both have resulted in broadening the scope and effectiveness of general pupil personnel services and strengthening the nature and extent of vocational and educational guidance in the schools.

The understanding and support of professional organizations in the fields of guidance and education should also be cultivated in overcoming this philosophical barrier to more effective vocational and educational guidance. This can probably be best accomplished not by insisting that vocational guidance be given a priority in the high school program, but by demonstrating that the nation's manpower requirements make greater vocational emphasis in guidance a necessary and desirable objective. Educators in general and guidance workers in particular badly need reassurance that vocational guidance is wanted and needed as a service in the schools. The reassurance can best be provided by showing how vocational and educational guidance services can help meet the needs of the individual student, of the community, and of the nation. In this effort, the same forces and groups mentioned as sources of support in answer to Question 1 should be called upon to join with the National Manpower Council in stimulating public support for more and better educational and vocational guidance services.

Question 3: What can be done to encourage school officials to make vocational guidance available no later than the ninth year and to have it continue through the high school course?

Generally speaking, authorities in the field of guidance would agree that vocational guidance should begin in the ninth year—if not earlier—and that it should continue through high school. Many school systems offer survey courses in occupations during the ninth year. Some offer such courses as early as the seventh year. Many others offer a so-called "unit" on occupations, usually associated with Social Studies, Civics, or Problems in Democracy, which lasts for about 6 weeks at ninth grade level. These school systems are also likely to have a more advanced course or unit on occupations at twelfth grade level. It is probable that a great many of the schools which claim to have formal guidance programs include units or courses of this type in their curricula. A 1948-50 survey [7] indicated that more than 3,500 school systems were offering courses or units in occupations along these lines. Usually, it is the larger school systems which offer such programs. Such courses are lacking in about 80 percent of the public high schools.

There should be a critical evaluation of the effectiveness of these courses in meeting the vocational guidance needs of students. Limited studies [8] show that students who are exposed to such courses do make sounder vocational decisions, earn relatively more money, and achieve a higher degree of job adjustment and job satisfaction than their "unexposed" fellows. Such studies, however, have not answered the basic question as to which methods and approaches are best.

Various other methods of introducing a vocational emphasis in guidance are being used. A study [9] of student evaluations of the most effective methods of presenting occupational information points out that more than half the students surveyed favored talks by people in different occupations as being most helpful. One-fourth favored reading of occupational information materials, about 10 percent favored movies on occupations, and the remaining students favored plant visits or other approaches. For the most part, talks on occupations are given in schools through the medium of "Career Days." Generally, they are presented once a year and are usually directed at the twelfth graders, although many schools permit lower classmen to attend. Valuable as they may be, career days are pretty much a "one-shot" affair.

Most schools maintain some type of occupational information library. These may vary from complete and carefully indexed materials—books, pamphlets, and articles—to a scattering of publications. Again, the best libraries and indexes of occupational literature tend to be in larger school systems. Plant or office visits are not likely to be a major and continuous source of occupational information in most school systems. Usually a few key establishments are visited, not primarily by interested students, but by whole classes who happen to be studying the particular industry.

Plant visits could be made a more meaningful source of occupational information through more systematic visits by students interested in employment in a particular occupation or industry. Communities like Youngstown, Ohio,[10] and Evansville, Indiana,[11] systematically acquaint high school students with the occupational opportunities in their own communities. These communities have also arranged for students to see workers in action on the job, to observe the total production process and the end products produced, and to discuss with workers, foremen, and employers the nature and conditions of the work. Youngstown runs an annual industrial exposition to which all high school students in the school district are invited. They are transported by school bus facilities. Here they can see the work and the workers and discuss jobs and job opportunities with those who know the work best. Both communities also have produced elaborate and effective occupational surveys of local occupations and industries.

All these methods supplement regular classroom teaching of occupations. Of course, this does not eliminate the need for individual counseling in the choice of vocation, the planning of an educational program, and the mapping of a job-winning campaign.

An unmet need which results in ineffective vocational and educational guidance programs is the lack of adequate counseling staffs to provide individual guidance to students in vocational and educational choices in the ninth or tenth grades or whenever it is needed. The National Manpower Council states that there "is now one counselor for every 453 school pupils." [12] This assumes that all so-called counselors have full time to spend on a case load of 453 students. This is certainly not the case. Further, the type of individual service recommended here calls for a case load of not more than 250 students a year for each counselor spending full time on counseling duties. Because of staff inadequacies in numbers and quality, individual counseling is not offered uniformly to all students to meet the "normal need" at ninth or tenth grade level in many schools. Instead, it is assumed that those who really need it will seek it, or will be "picked up" by classroom teachers. But true freedom of vocational (and educational) choice is impossible unless the individual student knows enough about himself and about the available opportunities so that he can make an intelligent decision and develop a workable educational and vocational plan. Further, this knowledge and insight establishes a basic frame of reference for meeting problems of vocational change and adjustment that may occur at later points in the school or work life of the individual.

The answer to Question 3 is at least partly related to the answers to Questions 1 and 2. Accomplishing this objective will require more adequate support and financing of educational services and greater emphasis on vocational and educational guidance in regard to both group methods of presenting occupational information and individual counseling services. School officials will institute individualized vocational and educational guidance services at the ninth grade or earlier and continue them through the twelfth when this is demanded of them by the community and when the community is willing to pay for such services.

Not all of the professional knowledge needed to carry out such an integrated guidance program is already at hand. Professional organizations in the guidance and personnel field need to study both group and individual methods of presenting the world of work. Some progress has been made in this field by the National Vocational Guidance Association, but much more must be done, particularly in evaluating media and methods. Professional groups also need to evaluate the adequacy and effectiveness of counselor training programs in colleges and universities.

Although most counselor training programs offer a course in occupational and educational information, most of the counselor training institutions need to develop a worthwhile training program for educational and vocational counselors patterned on the outline in the National Vocational Guidance Association Manual on Counselor Preparation. Another requirement is for practical training in the form of supervised work experience and internships for counselors in training. Revitalized Federal and state leadership through the Federal and state departments of education, using George-Barden funds to stimulate college and in-service training programs, is necessary if Question 3 is to be dealt with qualitatively as well as quantitatively.

Question 4: What can be done to stimulate the classroom teacher to assume increased responsibility for helping students to make sound educational and occupational decisions?

This question seems to imply that classroom teachers can and should assume increased responsibilities for individual counseling, for presentation of occupational information, for the teaching and demonstration of good work habits and basic working knowledge and skills, and for the detection of the student's needs for the services of the school's trained vocational and educational counselors. Because of teacher shortages, crowded classrooms, and the high proportion of partially qualified (uncertified) teachers, this becomes a very difficult question to answer in any positive manner. Like counselors, many teachers are bogged down with the clerical and record-keeping routines required by school boards and state departments. They are also expected to carry a heavy workload of extracurricular activities. In addition, many find it necessary to work after school hours and week ends at other jobs to augment their incomes. Finally, they are expected to take readiness courses on their own time in order to maintain their certificates or to advance their status. All these factors tend to limit their effectiveness as sources of sound vocational and educational guidance.

The classroom teacher, particularly the homeroom teacher, is admittedly in a better position than anyone else in the school to know the child as an individual. But there is a considerable gap between knowing the child as a student and providing him with meaningful vocational and educational guidance, even if we assume enough time is available for this purpose. If teachers are to assume more responsibility for guidance, they need counselor training. They also need to understand their own limitations as counselors or advisors in the field of educational and vocational choice. It is doubtful whether all or even a considerable number of teachers can or should be given intensive graduate level training in guidance unless they desire such training and seek it.

On the other hand, they should all be trained to understand and appreciate the purpose, functions, and limitations of the guidance service so that they can make intelligent use of it and so that the counseling staff can receive proper cooperation and communication with the teaching staff. This type of training or orientation is a responsibility of the principal or the supervisory staff of the school district and is essential to the intelligent use of the individual school's guidance resources. But it is doubtful whether principals and supervisors will provide such training until they are themselves oriented to a better understanding and acceptance of the teacher's role in the school's guidance services.

Schools of education should therefore offer "guidance apprecia-tion" courses to those who aspire to principalships and super-visory jobs.

Teachers should be trained how to use occupational informa-tion in their homeroom and classroom teaching. They should also be encouraged to think more constructively about developing in each child a sense of workmanship or achievement specifically and practically related to the world of work. The outstanding teacher frequently does this almost instinctively, but the average teacher fails to make these connections because of this lack of insight beyond the skills and knowledge required of his own profession.

As mentioned earlier, some attempt has been made in the past ten years to bring vocational guidance services down to the level of the classroom through courses in occupational informa-tion, community civics, group guidance, student services orienta-tion and psychology.[13] The total national enrollment in courses that might be described as "guidance oriented" in 1953 was as follows:

Community Civics (Grades 7, 8, or 9)	930,000
Occupations	158,000
Orientation	115,000
Psychology	46,000
Group Guidance	92,000
Student Services	8,800

This indicates that classroom teachers are assuming more direct interest and participation in the vocational aspects of guidance in the school. Still, not counting the high enrollment in community civics, long a required course in most junior high schools, much remains to be done in bringing guidance, and particularly occupa-tional information, into the classroom in an organized and system-atic way. This, of course, is also a problem of research, prepara-tion, and publication of occupational information for classroom use. Most commercial publishers of occupational information have faced serious problems in making it pay. The Federal and state governments have therefore had to play a large role in the publication of occupational information for use in guidance. Much of the Federal and state product is not geared to classroom use, and few teachers have either the time or inclination to make their own adaptations.

There is much to be done by the U. S. Office of Education, the Departments of Labor and Commerce and their state counterparts in order to develop and adapt occupational information for classroom use. Much also needs to be done at the local level to bring local labor market conditions into focus and to adapt national and state materials so that they present the local picture as it really exists. In this effort, local schools and local employment services ought to be working much more closely together.

In regard to Question 4, it is doubtful if classroom teachers can generally be expected to assume the principal responsibility for effective individualized educational and vocational guidance. With more adequate general financing of education and guidance services teachers can be expected to do much more in presenting occupational information, in detecting the need for individual counseling services, in teaching good work habits, basic work knowledge and skills, and in making students conscious of jobs and job requirements through better integration of such information in regular subject-matter teaching. All teachers, supervisors, and principals should receive some orientation in guidance in college preparation for teaching and administration, and also through in-service training courses. The guidance profession should study and evaluate methods of presenting occupational information more effectively in classroom situations. Occupational researchers should give more attention to the problem of presenting occupational information in the classroom. Finally, Federal, state, and local schools, employment services, labor statistics, and population experts should work together on the problems involved in making occupational information more meaningful and useful to teachers, counselors, and students.

Question 5: What can be done to stimulate school officials to take the lead in their communities in vigorous cooperative efforts to provide occupational information and other types of assistance essential for effective vocational guidance?

The largest and most extensive source of vocational guidance outside the schools is the nationwide system of public employment service offices. The employment service system has been providing aptitude testing, employment counseling, and job placement services for school graduates and dropouts for many years. It is estimated by officials of the Bureau of Employment Security that between 300,000 and 400,000 high school graduates benefited from these services in 1954.[14] The present program of school-employment service cooperation was developed in 1950 through a collaborative effort at Federal and state levels. It resulted in the joint release of a Statement of Principles Governing School-Employment Service Cooperation prepared by the U. S. Office of Education and the U. S. Bureau of Employment Security. It is a detailed and comprehensive document outlining the broad functions and responsibilities of both schools and employment services and setting forth the basis for the development in the community of a year-round program of school-employment service cooperation. The statement recognizes the school's primary responsibility for youth's vocational guidance and preparation and the employment service's primary responsibility for job counseling, placement, and follow-up of school graduates and dropouts. It also recognizes the different stages vocational guidance, training, and placement services have reached in different communities, and outlines a basis for cooperative agreements which maximizes the use of these resources and minimizes duplicated services and costs.

Many states have developed statewide programs following

these basic principles. Others have preferred to have cooperative programs develop from the "grass roots" or community level. As a result, schools and employment services are working effectively together in hundreds of communities all over the country to the mutual advantage of young people, employers, trade unions, schools, employment services, and the community.

Implementing these cooperative relationships on a year-round basis usually means that arrangements are made for employment service officials to contact seniors in the fall of the final year in high school. At this time the services of the employment office are explained, information is given concerning jobs and job opportunities on a group basis, and arrangements are made for aptitude testing, application taking, and employment counseling services. Usually this is done well in advance of graduation for all seniors who plan to go to work when they graduate. Then the employment service attempts to develop jobs and training opportunities, including apprenticeship and on-the-job training, so that each graduate has something definite lined up even before he leaves school. Special arrangements are also made in some communities for the referral of dropouts to the employment service so that similar services can be provided for them.

In many of the European guidance and training programs, the employment service has the primary and frequently the exclusive responsibility for the vocational guidance and placement of youth. All too frequently the guidance exposure is a "one-shot" proposition and the youth really doesn't make his own decisions or choices. This is done for him by the vocational guidance officer who is thinking primarily in terms of the country's manpower needs rather than the interests and potentialities of the child.

A few experts have wondered why the public employment service in the United States should not assume the primary or even the exclusive responsibility for vocational guidance. They argue that schools are not well equipped to provide vocational guidance since teachers and counselors do not know enough about the labor market. They also argue that school counselors and educators in general seem less and less interested in vocational guidance and more and more concerned with the day-to-day adjustment of the child in the school.

The Bureau of Employment Security and the Labor Department have opposed this point of view. As a matter of basic policy, the employment service has urged that school guidance services be strengthened and extended to reach all youth in all communities. The Department of Labor has contributed to school guidance programs by developing and stimulating the development of varied types of occupational information.

Some states, such as Michigan and Ohio, have made outstanding contributions by publishing guidance materials on a state and local basis. In many communities employment services have taken the leadership, or at least a very active part, in community occupational surveys, and area surveys of training needs.

Employment services do not wish to replace schools in the field of vocational guidance. The official view is that the better job the schools do in vocational guidance and preparation of youth, the easier will be the job of placement, long-term occupational adjustment, and stabilization of employment in the community. These have been the underlying objectives of the employment service in working with schools.

A simple and direct way for school officials to begin answering Question 5, therefore, would be to cooperate with local employment services in their communities. Too many school superintendents, supervisors, and principals are not well informed in this field, while others have been misled by their guidance and placement experts to regard the employment service with suspicion and distrust. Yet there are far too many instances of successful cooperation to justify these attitudes. No informed person can deny that the local employment service is actually and potentially the most extensive and fruitful source of information about local jobs and job opportunities. During a normal year, these offices make close to 2 million contacts with employers. They inquire not only about job orders, but about past, present, and future employment prospects by occupation, sex, age, color, etc. This information is recorded for use in local office planning and programming. It is also tabulated, analyzed, and published in varying forms, but primarily for internal administrative use. If school officials were really interested and concerned with getting such information for guidance, training, and curriculum planning purposes, and would make their needs in this connection known, they would receive a great deal of valuable information.

But neither the schools nor the employment services can go it alone, nor can the two agencies working together solve all the problems involved in community organization for vocational guidance. Of primary importance in creating community awareness and support for better guidance and training programs is the understanding and active cooperation of labor and management in the community. These groups are vocal in their criticism of the schools and other agencies for their inadequacies in preparing youth for work, but indicate little understanding of the importance of good vocational guidance services in overcoming these deficiencies. Usually complaints about the schools center on the "three R's" or "poor attitudes toward work" or some other generalized expression of adverse opinion. Concern with the need for better guidance services is a comparatively new development.

Therefore, school officials must seek out the cooperation of key employers and labor leaders on a systematic and organized basis. In 1940, the American Youth Commission published a book by Howard M. Bell called *Matching Youth and Jobs*. This book set forth the elements of a sound approach to a community occupational adjustment program. World War II and subsequent turmoil in the labor market have obscured the significance of this work. Bell called for the establishment of community occupational adjustment councils made up of representatives of labor and management and officials of public and private agencies to study youth employment and training needs, to advise and assist the agencies in working more harmoniously together, and to use their influence "to generate public interest and win public support." [15] It would now be appropriate to review Bell's findings, bring them up to date, and undertake positive efforts to implement some of his recommendations.

A major concern of such councils should be to see to it that available guidance resources and facilities are properly coordinated to insure a maximum of service at a minimum of cost. Much remains to be done in the field of administering and organizing guidance services, both within the educational system and in the community as a whole. In this connection, it might well be desirable for the National Manpower Council or a group established under its auspices to study desirable patterns of school and community organization for guidance services and to attempt to arrive at some desirable patterns which could be used to stimulate states and communities to re-examine existing programs, which are frequently poorly organized and coordinated. The Committee on Community Organization for Guidance of the American Personnel and Guidance Association is looking into this problem and has made recommendations concerning pilot programs in several areas. Unfortunately, sufficient funds are not available within the Association at this time to finance the type of exploration necessary to arrive at valid conclusions.

At present a young person may receive some form of professional guidance at six different points in his life. The process starts, or should start, in the schools. If the youth plans to work after graduation, he may be tested, counseled, and placed by the employment service. The employer usually has some type of testing and personnel evaluation procedure. Then if he is drafted or volunteers for military service, he starts on another round of testing, personnel classification, and assignment procedures. As a veteran he may be tested, counseled, and placed again by either the Veterans Administration or the employment service. If he goes to college before or after military service, he is exposed to another type of testing and counseling procedure, and so on.[16]

In the best interests of the individual something should be done to provide some continuity in all this personnel and guidance work. An individual is at least entitled to some consistency and uniformity of treatment. There are also other considerations. Each institution has its own methods, its own tests, its own records, its own institutional focus and purpose. It is possible that more people could be served better if a few were not being served over and over again. It is also possible that more of the available resources for test research, occupational research, and the preparation of useful guidance materials could be used to extend knowledge into new fields rather than duplicating work in old or overlapping ones.

For these and many other reasons, it would seem that some attempt should be made to transmit information about the individual as he moves from one level or setting to another. The best way to do this is by making sure that the individual knows and understands what has happened to him in each institutional setting. Theoretically, this is the end objective of all good counseling; actually, it doesn't happen as frequently as it should. It would therefore seem desirable to furnish the individual with some basic record that he can use, or not use, as he sees fit, in contacts with other agencies. This record would be initiated in the school and could be added to or modified at any other point.

Those familiar with the European system of "work books," which serves as a form of passport for the worker from one job to another, will probably object to this idea on the grounds that the record system would be, or could be, abused. The essential difference here is that the individual need not show the record if he does not so desire. However, if he feels that he has been helped and wants to save himself and the new agency time in exploring vocational interests, abilities, and goals, he has an official record he can use.

As an alternative, some form of record, reasonably well standardized, might be developed for exchange of information between agencies upon request. This is done frequently in social work without any adverse effect on the client. The basic point is that guidance and counseling resources will always be limited, and efforts should be made to conserve them by proper community organization and efficient procedures of communication.

Educators should probably take the lead in such efforts. Yet it is doubtful if they will unless the community demands it of them. In many ways the key to the problem of extending and improving guidance services depends upon our ability to stimulate and cultivate community understanding and support.

Perhaps the single most effective way of implementing the National Manpower Council's recommendations on both professional and scientific personnel and on skilled workers would be to convene a conference or series of conferences that would bring representatives of all the key groups mentioned in this paper together to discuss practical plans of action. The National Vocational Guidance Association and other professional groups in the guidance and personnel field would certainly join enthusiastically in sponsoring and organizing such a conference or conferences. To again quote Howard M. Bell:

> It is true that the kind of program here suggested demands a modest expansion of public funds for education, employment service, and research. It is equally true that such increases will be more than cancelled out by the personal, social, and material benefits which both employer and worker will enjoy.
>
> Adequate and effective programs of occupational adjustment assure returns in social and material dividends that are gratifyingly high. It is the author's conviction that no type of social program costs so little and yields so much. As adventures in human engineering, such programs, when properly understood, have the rare virtue of appealing to both humanitarianism and self-interest.

When this statement appeared in 1940, the term "human engineering" did not have some of the "directive" connotations now associated with it. Therefore, let it be said in closing that the interests and opportunities of the individual, in his quest for self-realization as a useful and productive citizen, should be the primary concern in any guidance and personnel program designed to improve the skills of the work force. Achievement of this goal requires, however, that we afford each individual not only the opportunity, but also the knowledge, both personal and environmental, on the basis of which he can make sound vocational decisions and plans. Guidance services, so oriented, will afford each individual with a frame of reference he can test and retest against the realities of the working world as he faces the necessity for initial and subsequent choices and adjustments in a dynamic and changing economy.

Part Four

HIGHER EDUCATION

XI. THE POTENTIAL FOR HIGHER EDUCATION

The Council Staff

THE GROWING DEMANDS for scientific and professional personnel and the realization that these demands would not be met unless the total supply of college and university graduates is substantially increased, prompted two concerns. One was with the extent to which potential high ability is wasted; the other was with the proportion of the population capable of successful undergraduate and graduate study.

Early in the 1950's, when the National Manpower Council undertook its study, *A Policy for Scientific and Professional Manpower,* some fears were expressed that the reservoir of total ability would be too shallow to provide all the persons needed for occupations and functions requiring bachelor's, first professional, or graduate degrees. These fears have since been largely allayed, but the concern with the large-scale waste of potential ability has been intensified.

"The Potential for Higher Education" maintains that there is a large hidden reserve of potential ability, in addition to that which can readily be identified, which, under more favorable developmental conditions, could be drawn upon to expand the intellectual resources of the nation.

"The Potential for Higher Education" is reprinted with editorial changes from A Policy for Scientific and Professional Manpower *(New York: Columbia University Press, 1953), in which it first appeared as Chapter IV, pp. 77–93.*

A CONCERN with the numbers and competence of the nation's scientists and professional persons raises important questions about the proportion of the population which has the high ability required for advanced training. Far more is known about the country's reserves of natural resources than about its reserves of intellectual resources. The possibility that reserves of essential materials such as oil and timber might be depleted has long been recognized, and means have been sought to guard against such an eventuality. Only recently, however, has an awareness developed that the nation's reserve of men and women capable of advanced training is also limited.

How large is this reserve? A precise numerical answer cannot be ventured until research develops the answers to a large number of problems about human resources. However, a beginning can be made in estimating the size of the reserve.

Today, most of the young people who enter scientific and professional occupations are college graduates or, at the very least, have completed part of a college education. A good deal is known about the distribution of mental ability among those entering and graduating from college and among the population as a whole. Consequently, one way of estimating the size of the reserve of individuals of high ability is to compare the number in the population who are capable of successfully pursuing a college education with the number who actually enter and graduate from college.

IDENTIFICATION OF COLLEGE ABILITY

Colleges conventionally use two methods for judging whether an individual has the mental ability to complete college. One is based on high school grades, which are highly correlated with scholastic performance in college. There are, however, great variations in the standards of high schools. This method, therefore, would not be useful for estimating the number in the nation as a whole capable of completing college, even if adequate data on grades were available. Colleges can employ high school grades as an aid in selecting freshman students only when they can judge from experience how the grades earned in a particular school are reflected in the scholastic performance of its graduates in college.

The second method relies on a variety of scholastic aptitude tests, the scores of which are also closely related to scholastic success in college. Moreover, the scores of individuals from different schools can be compared. These tests are similar to the Army General Classification Test (AGCT). While the AGCT measures approximately the same abilities as the college aptitude tests, it has not been used to predict success in college. Since the AGCT was given to many millions of young men during World War II, however, it provides a convenient tool for estimating the proportion of the college-age population with the mental ability to graduate from college. The AGCT is also closely related to intelligence tests, but its score is not the same as the much better known I.Q.

Figure 1 shows the distribution of AGCT scores for the population as a whole. The average score is 100, and most people

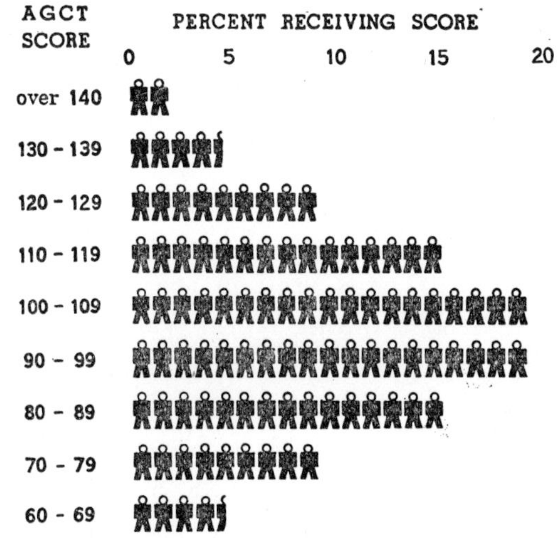

Figure 1. Distribution of Population by AGCT Score

achieve scores somewhere near this average. Sixty-eight percent of the population score between 80 and 120.

In order to estimate the number of people able to graduate from college, it is necessary to draw a line at some point in this distribution separating those deemed able to complete college from those who are not. Wherever this line is drawn, it will not distinguish with any high degree of accuracy those who will fail to graduate from college from those who will succeed. There is no sure way of predicting on any basis whether an individual will do well or poorly in college.

Some people who score fairly low on the AGCT succeed in graduating from college and go on to perform well in professional or scientific work. On the other hand, every college has repeated experience with individuals who despite high aptitude for college work fail to pass. The assertion that individuals who achieve a certain score are capable of completing college, therefore, only means that they are more likely to have the ability required for graduation than persons with lower scores.

An AGCT score of 120 is certainly high enough to justify using it as a minimum for estimating the number of individuals capable of college work. This score was used during World War II in deciding who should go to college under the Army Specialized Training Program. Scholastic aptitude equivalent to an AGCT score of 120 is now one of the criteria for determining whether a college student should be considered for deferment. A lower score (110) was used in selecting students for Officer Candidate Schools during World War II. It is known, moreover, that over 60 percent of those who enter college and half of those who graduate achieve scores on scholastic aptitude tests which are the equivalent of an AGCT score of less than 120. The facts indicate that a score of 120 on the AGCT is a high standard for determining how many persons are capable of graduating from college, and that its use will underestimate, rather than overestimate, the number with the requisite intellectual ability to pursue a college education with success.

THE RESERVE CAPABLE OF COLLEGE AND POST-GRADUATE EDUCATION

The distribution of AGCT scores (Figure 1) shows that about 16 percent of the population of college age has the mental ability needed to score 120 or higher. Figure 2 shows the percentages

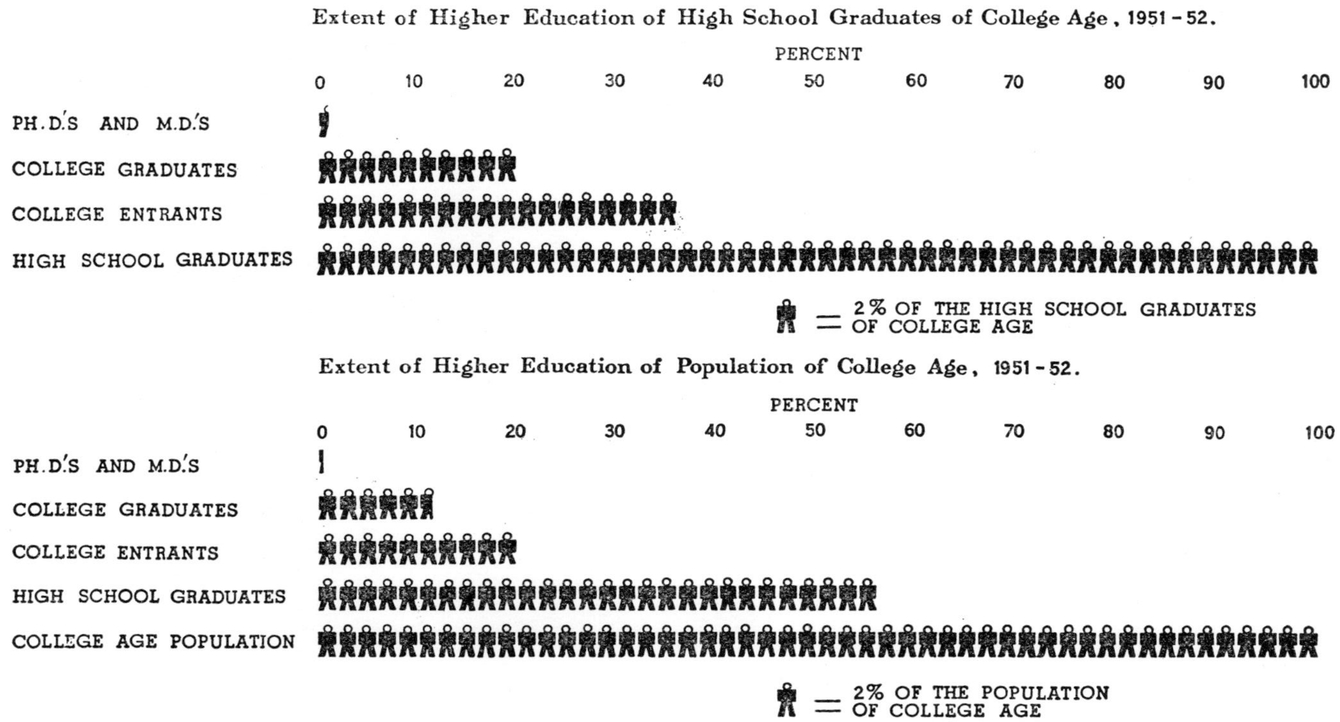

Extent of Higher Education of High School Graduates of College Age, 1951–52.

PERCENT

| 0 | 10 | 20 | 30 | 40 | 50 | 60 | 70 | 80 | 90 | 100 |

PH.D.'S AND M.D.'S

COLLEGE GRADUATES

COLLEGE ENTRANTS

HIGH SCHOOL GRADUATES

= 2% OF THE HIGH SCHOOL GRADUATES OF COLLEGE AGE

Extent of Higher Education of Population of College Age, 1951–52.

PERCENT

| 0 | 10 | 20 | 30 | 40 | 50 | 60 | 70 | 80 | 90 | 100 |

PH.D.'S AND M.D.'S

COLLEGE GRADUATES

COLLEGE ENTRANTS

HIGH SCHOOL GRADUATES

COLLEGE AGE POPULATION

= 2% OF THE POPULATION OF COLLEGE AGE

Figure 2. Higher Education in the Population of College Age, 1951–52

Based on data provided by The Commission on Human Resources and Advanced Training of the population of college age and of the high school graduates now completing various stages of higher education.[1] In recent years, the attendance of large numbers of veterans has caused college enrollment and graduation to fluctuate widely. When the figures are adjusted to eliminate this effect, it appears that about one out of five of the college-age group now starts college and about one out of nine graduates.[2] If almost 12 percent [3] graduates from college and 16 percent of the population scores 120 or above on the AGCT, it would appear that the reserve able to complete college but not doing so is about 4 percent of the population of college age. This figure, however, errs on the side of safety, for it substantially underestimates the side of the reserve. It has been seen that the majority of those entering college, as well as half of the graduates, have less ability than is represented by a score of 120 on the AGCT.

A better estimate of the size of the reserve can be developed from the data summarized in Figure 3, which shows the percentage of persons not entering college, entering college but not graduating, and graduating from college, for three ranges of scholastic ability. These figures indicate that the higher the mental ability of the group, the more likely are its members to graduate from college if they enter. While about two thirds of those with an AGCT of 100 or higher who enter college finally graduate, almost 84 percent of those with an AGCT of 130 or higher who enter college graduate. The higher the mental ability of the group, moreover, the greater is the percentage of persons entering college. Yet, half of the persons with an AGCT of 120 or higher do not enter college and only about one third of them graduate. The remaining two thirds are the reserve of persons with the necessary ability to graduate from college. Of the more than eight million people of college age, about 800,000, or 10 percent, have the ability to complete college but will not, under current conditions, graduate. Most of them will not even enter college.

Many professional and scientific careers call for further formal training after graduation from college, as in the case of medicine and research careers in physics, chemistry, and the social sciences. In scientific and scholarly fields a doctoral degree (usually the

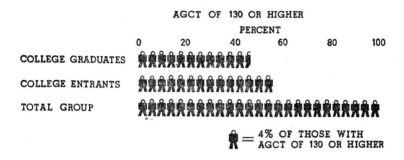

Figure 3. *Extent of Higher Education in the Population of College Age by AGCT Score, 1951–52*

Based on data provided by The Commission on Human Resources and Advanced Training

Ph.D.) has come to symbolize the completion of advanced formal training. As the next step in estimating the reserve capable of undertaking higher education, it is necessary to compare the number in the population deemed to have the required intellectual ability with the number that actually acquire postgraduate degrees. Again it is necessary to select an AGCT score representative of the ability necessary to obtain these degrees. Tests of mental ability indicate that an AGCT score of 130 is about average for persons who now receive doctoral degrees, including the M.D. This score, therefore, may safely be used to determine how many of the college-age population have the ability required for these degrees. The use of 130 will result in an underestimation of the reserve for graduate education, but makes it very likely that those in the estimated reserve possess the required mental ability. Since it is the average score, it matches the severe standard of 120 used above to estimate the reserve of undergraduate ability. Between 6 and 7 percent of the total population, as Figure 1 shows, have scholastic ability equivalent to an AGCT score of 130 or higher.

About 2 percent of the college graduates actually go on to earn doctoral degrees other than the M.D. About the same number receive the M.D. Since only about 12 percent [4] of all young people graduate from college, the number earning these degrees is less than half of one percent of the college-age population. The difference between the number who have the ability and the number who now acquire such advanced education is great, and points to a sizable reserve of individuals with high intellectual ability who are not receiving postgraduate training.

HIDDEN POTENTIAL

The reserve capable of graduating from college or obtaining advanced degrees consists of persons identified on the basis of standard tests. That reserve has been estimated very conservatively, for the AGCT scores of 120 and 130 which have been used represent relatively high standards. There is another reason for regarding the estimate of the reserve as conservative rather than optimistic. Scores on tests of mental ability do not measure inborn potential. They reflect differences in education and cultural opportunity. It is pointed out in *The Uneducated*, published in 1953, that "it is difficult, perhaps impossible, to devise a test which takes proper account of the cultural and environmental factors in the individual's background so that his response to questions reflects his intellectual ability and not his specific knowledge of certain words and circumstances." If more children attended school regularly, if they attended school longer, and if the schools they attended were better, then more than 16 percent would develop learning ability equivalent to a score of 120 or more on the present AGCT and more than 6 or 7 percent would be capable of scoring 130. There is, thus, a hidden reserve of persons whose intellectual potential for advanced training has not been adequately developed.

Obviously, those who comprise this hidden reserve are not using their ability in acquiring the education needed for scientific and professional work. Their capacities, moreover, have not been developed to the point where they would be revealed by national survey or testing programs. No one can say with confidence how significant an addition to the number of persons capable of undertaking college training could be obtained by developing this hidden reserve. There are indications, however, that it may be very great. This judgment is supported by recent studies of the performance of Negroes on scholastic aptitude tests. Most social scientists now believe that there are no inborn differences in intellectual potential between Negroes and the rest of the population, or that such differences, if they exist, are very small. Yet, a study of college freshmen showed that the average freshman in a Negro college scored only a little higher on aptitude tests than the lowest-ranking freshman in the average college.[5] This finding testifies both to the sensitivity of the test to prior educational experience and to the great differences between the educational opportunities of Negroes and whites.

Because this hidden reserve is not revealed by the usual scholastic aptitude tests, it has sometimes been contended that the tests are grossly unfair. This conclusion, however, misconceives the purpose of the tests, for they undertake to measure ability to do well in college, in Officer Candidate Schools, or in some other learning situation. They claim to measure not the amount of intellectual potential with which an individual is born, but the immediate readiness of individuals for advanced education. Individuals who have been educationally deprived and who do not perform well on these tests would not perform well in college either. Aided by intensive pre-college work they could probably better their test scores and improve their later college performance.

The improvement of elementary and secondary education, which would raise the percentage of the population with college ability, would not necessarily result in an increase in the percentage attending college. If applicants for admission had greater ability, colleges might raise their standards and thus keep the college population relatively stable. Even the mental tests might not reveal that the college ability of the population had risen, for ability tests are periodically revised and restandardized. The average score remains at some arbitrary figure, such as 100 AGCT. Scores on such tests reveal how an individual performs compared to others, and not how he measures up to some absolute standard. For these and other reasons, the tangible results of improvements in pre-college education, which would have the effect of increasing the mental ability of the population, might be obscured.

GROUP AND REGIONAL DIFFERENCES

The failure of a great many people of high mental ability to undertake or complete higher education is due to various economic and motivational factors. The members of different socio-economic groups in the population vary, not only in financial ability to secure higher education, but also in the interest they have in doing so. The lack of motivation among some groups is to some extent economically determined. Thus, the young man who has grown up in a home where making ends meet had been difficult may be determined to achieve economic independence early, even when his family is in a position to send him to college. Many who do not attend college because of economic reasons would be capable college students. Studies of veterans who would not have been able to go to college without the aid of the G.I. Bill show that they did at least as well as other students.

There are striking differences among states in the proportion of young people entering college, as Table 7 shows. The statistics upon which it is based are not completely reliable, but they adequately demonstrate the existence of great state variations. From all the Southern states except Florida the percentage enrolling in college in the fall of 1948 was below the national average. On the other hand, the percentage was very high in most of the Far Western states. South Carolina had the lowest percentage, under 10 percent, while Utah, with almost half of its young people entering college, had the highest. (The national average, shown in Table 7 as 24.6 percent, includes veterans and is, therefore, higher than the 20 percent figure previously used.)

These differences are accounted for in part by the proportion of the population completing high school and in part by the proportion of high school graduates entering college in the different states and regions, both of which are, in turn, closely related to variations in economic conditions. The percentage of young people graduating from high school in 1948 was below the national average in all but two of the Southern and Southwestern states. This was due in part to low average per capita income in these states, which, in spite of substantial increases since 1929, remained well below the national average. The high percentage of Negroes in the population of most of these states was also a significant factor. Even in Maryland and the District of Columbia, where per capita income was above the national average, high school graduation was low because of the pattern of Negro education.

It is significant that the percentage of high school graduates who went on to college was above average in several states, in-

Table 7. College Entrants as a Percentage of Eighteen-Year-Olds, 1948 [a]

Alabama	14.6	Nebraska	29.5
Arizona	25.4	Nevada	28.4
Arkansas	19.5	New Hampshire	24.7
California	32.8	New Jersey	28.8
Colorado	33.8	New Mexico	20.1
Connecticut	32.8	New York	33.7
Delaware	22.2	North Carolina	15.7
Dist. of Columbia	30.6	North Dakota	32.7
Florida	25.5	Ohio	24.8
Georgia	17.8	Oklahoma	31.4
Idaho	39.1	Oregon	34.9
Illinois	37.2	Pennsylvania	19.4
Indiana	25.7	Rhode Island	24.9
Iowa	28.5	South Carolina	9.7
Kansas	33.5	South Dakota	30.5
Kentucky	15.1	Tennessee	18.3
Louisiana	19.6	Texas	23.7
Maine	18.6	Utah	48.4
Maryland	23.3	Vermont	27.8
Massachusetts	28.4	Virginia	19.2
Michigan	22.3	Washington	34.3
Minnesota	29.7	West Virginia	17.8
Mississippi	18.5	Wisconsin	22.8
Missouri	26.8	Wyoming	29.4
Montana	32.5	U. S. Average	24.6

[a] Based on U. S. Census Reports and publications of the U. S. Office of Education. The figures represent the residents of each state entering college in any state.

cluding Georgia, Louisiana, and Tennessee, which ranked near the bottom both in per capita income and percentage of population graduating from high school. The explanation lies in the fact that high school graduation was far more the privilege of a small minority who expected to enter college in these states than it was elsewhere.

Eighteen states were above the national average both in percentage of population completing high school and percentage of high school graduates entering college. All but five of these states were above the national average in per capita income in 1948. These prosperous and well-educated states were not concentrated in any region, nor were they all highly urbanized. Among them were New York, Illinois, Wyoming, and California.

Economic considerations do not explain all the differences among the states. Utah, with the highest proportion of population entering college of any state, was below average in per capita income. Several other Western states also had a higher proportion entering college than one might anticipate solely from income data. The opposite was true of a number of states, especially Pennsylvania, where per capita income was high but the number entering college was low.

In short, much of the difference among states in college enrollment can be explained in terms of the ability to pay for higher education and of employment opportunities for college graduates. But this is not the whole story, for variations in the value placed upon education in different areas are also important. The same situation is found with respect to elementary and secondary schooling. Counties and states with approximately the same per capita income frequently differ widely in the quality of their school systems and the proportions of children enrolled in them.

PROBLEMS IN MAKING USE OF THE RESERVE

The conclusion that the United States has a large reserve of persons capable of graduating from college and of securing advanced degrees must be qualified in several important respects. Mental ability, as determined by a score on a test, has been used as the sole criterion of ability to pursue higher education, but it is clearly not the only factor which influences success in college or in later life. There may be other abilities not highly related to general scholastic aptitude which are vital for success in certain fields. Relatively little is known about such abilities or how to measure them, but that does not mean that they are insignificant. The important role of motivational factors has already been indicated. It is known that high scholastic aptitude cannot lead to college success and outstanding performance in later professional work unless the individual wants to succeed.

Even if it is assumed that all persons with a specified level of scholastic aptitude are capable of earning a particular degree, not every individual in the group can be counted on to secure it. As stated previously, although about 6 percent of the population possesses the mental ability assumed to be necessary, less than one-half of one percent now secures a doctoral degree or an M.D. This suggests a reserve of about 5½ percent of the population, half male and half female, that could be drawn upon to increase the numbers now obtaining these degrees. Actually, far more than half of this theoretical reserve is made up of women, because only a small fraction of the doctoral and M.D. degrees are currently granted to women. About 10 percent of the doctoral degrees given in the sciences, which account for about half of all doctoral degrees, for example, are received by women. The comparatively small number of women who receive doctoral degrees is obviously not due to any failure in the public school systems since more girls than boys graduate. Nor is it due to a lack of qualified women college graduates, for over 40 percent of nonveteran college students are women.[6]

Still other considerations impede the training of all of those who are apparently able to complete postgraduate education. Males with the mental ability represented by an AGCT score of 130 amount to about 3 percent of the total population. The entire 3 percent cannot, however, be considered as likely candidates for the doctoral or M.D. degrees, for some do not enter college, others do not graduate from college, and some of the graduates do not do well enough in college to warrant their continuing their studies.

Approximately one fifth of all the male college graduates who have the ability do receive either doctoral or M.D. degrees. The four fifths who do not go on with their education past the bachelor's or the master's degree may be estimated at about 40,000 college graduates a year. The significance of this figure can be appreciated when it is contrasted with the record high number of almost 14,000 students, counting women and veterans, who received doctoral degrees and M.D.'s in 1952.[7]

It cannot be concluded, however, that all of this reserve of 40,000 persons should receive doctoral degrees. Many in this reserve now enter employment which demands a high order of intelligence, but does not require an advanced degree. It is essential to draw upon the most intelligent 6 percent of the population for many occupations, both professional and nonprofessional. In short, unless the total number of college graduates was also increased, any substantial increase in the numbers acquiring doctoral or M.D. degrees might be made only at the expense of reducing the number of highly potential people entering other fields. A substantial increase in the number of college graduates who would go on to secure a doctoral degree would be difficult to achieve without expanding significantly the number of persons of high ability who enter and graduate from college.

The number of persons of high ability who graduate from college and who earn high degrees has, in fact, been continually increasing as a result of long-term occupational and social changes, such as rising national income, changing attitudes toward education, and the reduction of religious and racial inequalities in educational opportunity. It may be argued that these changes, even if accelerated, operate slowly, and if an appreciable addition to the number of scientists and professionals is desired, more direct measures to increase the number trained must be developed.

To proceed with confidence toward increasing the number of college graduates who receive higher degrees, firmer knowledge is essential in at least two areas. First, one must know what would happen to the work that the people with high ability but without advanced degrees are now engaged in. At present, there is little information available on the occupational distribution of able college graduates who do not complete postgraduate education. It is also necessary to know more about the reasons why such high potential persons terminate their formal education with a bachelor's degree. The failure of many to go on to graduate study or professional school is due, not to economic barriers, but to lack of motivation for further education. It is not known what incentives would be effective in inducing additional students to complete their studies and continue in the field for which they were trained. If these additional students were not strongly motivated to study and to work in particular fields, later occupational performance would be disappointing, among other reasons because many would probably leave the professional field for which they prepared themselves.

Another approach to the problem of stimulating an increase in the numbers securing advanced training is to raise the proportion of able persons who graduate from college. It has been pointed out that less than half of those whose AGCT score is 120 or over enter college, and that the majority of college students are below this standard. These facts have led certain experts to argue that it would be desirable to "exchange" college students with relatively low mental ability for abler people who do not now enter college. They contend that the quality of professional and scientific workers could be raised by concentrating educational efforts on the abler people rather than dissipating them on the less promising. Why should the doltish sons of the rich enter college while the brilliant but less affluent high school graduate works at the filling station?

If those who achieve low scores were exchanged for those who achieve high scores on a national test of scholastic aptitude, the results would be quite different from those intended. Because the score on such a test depends heavily on the quality of prior educational experience, the children in deprived groups, who now manage to get into college, would be the first to suffer from this reshuffling of the college population. It has been noted that students in Negro colleges do relatively poorly on scholastic aptitude tests. If college entrance were limited to those attaining high scores on a college aptitude test, the enrollment of Negroes would be greatly reduced. The same would be true, but to a lesser extent, of Southern whites as compared to Northern whites, rural residents as opposed to those who live in large cities, and children from poor families compared to the children of the well-to-do.

This, in turn, would impede the processes through which the position of such groups is being raised. Thus, teachers for the schools of the depressed rural areas are not recruited from among the well-prepared high school graduates in New York, Chicago, or Los Angeles who score high on tests of college ability. They come, rather, from the areas in which they teach and consequently, on the whole, score poorly on tests of scholastic aptitude.

There need be no fear that the nation is short of young persons with sufficient ability to complete advanced training. All of the approaches to the problem of increasing the number of persons who secure such training, however, will involve major difficulties.

XII. FACTORS INFLUENCING EDUCATION FOR SCIENTIFIC AND PROFESSIONAL OCCUPATIONS

The Council Staff

THE SUPPLY OF SCIENTIFIC and professional manpower is the product of a complex interplay involving individual abilities, interests, and motives, social values and aspirations, economic circumstances and considerations, and institutions. Both private and public policies and actions affect the outcome of the processes which shape the size and the quality of the supply of young men and women who are prepared for occupations in the society which require undergraduate or graduate study.

This chapter delineates the factors which determine the total flow of young people into institutions of higher education and the manner in which that stream comes to be distributed among the various scientific and professional occupations in a market economy.

"Factors Influencing Education for Scientific and Professional Occupations" is reprinted with editorial changes from A Policy for Scientific and Professional Manpower, *in which it first appeared as* "Training and Occupational Distribution," *Chapter III, pp. 62–76.*

AT the same time that deaths, retirements, and transfers to other fields of employment cut into the number of scientists and professionals actually available for work, the educational system continually provides a new supply. The size of each of the groups which comprise the total supply of scientists and professionals depends, in the first instance, on decisions made by individuals to train for and to choose employment in particular fields. Broadly speaking, the decisions to go to college, to specialize in a field, and, on the completion of training, to seek a particular kind of employment, determine the size and the distribution of the total supply of scientific and professional manpower.

The decisions that individuals make with respect to their training occur within the context of a continuing process of personal development and education. Decisions about schooling and work made at one period of time will have an influence on and may even determine decisions at a later date. A boy who fails to pursue an academic course in high school will find it difficult to obtain admission to college.

The number of students in college at any time is limited by the size of the college-age population who have completed high school, which, in turn, is a function of the number of births some sixteen to twenty years previously. The extent of college attendance also depends heavily upon prevailing attitudes toward the value of education, which are neither quickly nor easily modified. One measure of society's regard for formal schooling appears in the fact that high school attendance, once viewed as preparation for college, is now characteristic of three-fourths of the population in the appropriate age group. The democratic belief in equality of opportunity, as well as the demands of a technological and urbanized culture, have encouraged attitudes that favor more education for more people. Compulsory school attendance laws and larger educational budgets are tangible expression of the strength of these attitudes.

What were once "upper-" or "middle-class" aspirations for college study are now found in all social groups. The desire to improve one's status and to provide greater advantages for one's children is the natural legacy of a nation of immigrants. Increasing numbers of parents are willing to make sacrifies so that their children can secure the kind of education which will help them to have a better life.

ECONOMIC FACTORS AFFECTING COLLEGE EDUCATION

In addition to the birth rate and social attitudes towards education, three other factors are crucial in determining how many people actually seek a college education. These are the economic incentives in the society, the costs of education to the individual and his family, and the availability of educational and training facilities.

The economic incentives involve the difference between the anticipated earnings of people who are college-educated and of those who are not. The promise of higher earnings for college graduates acts as a magnet to pull people into the colleges. The costs of education—that is, the price one must pay to become educated—obviously limit the number of people who can afford a college education. The availability of training facilities affects not only the number who are college-educated, but also the numbers in different fields.

Education is an investment in the sense that money and effort must be spent to acquire it, and the decision about whether to make the investment depends on how people estimate the returns. Since the preparation for certain kinds of work which are well rewarded is largely made through college training, the college graduate is likely to occupy a preferred economic status. The available studies do in fact show that the incomes of college graduates in each age group are considerably above those of nongraduates, but this gap may reflect differences in the ability and opportunities of the two groups. Since income and social position tend to be closely related, college graduates are likely to have higher social status.

In recent decades, colleges have been the training grounds not only for scientific and professional work, but also for a growing range of positions in the business world. Today, business strongly prefers the college graduate to the person with less formal education. The college graduate may or may not perform better in business than the nongraduate, but the presumption is that he will. Even if there has been no notable difference in performance, once the practice of employing college men is established, it is likely to be continued. Because of the preference for college graduates, the young person with ambition is better armed in competing for advancement to managerial and executive jobs if he has a degree. Unemployment during the depression of the 1930's made it possible for the business community to set higher standards for employment, including higher educational attainment. Those who aspired to better industrial employment were quick to realize the desirability of college training. During World War II, the armed forces also played a part in the formation of attitudes favorable to college education. Education was a factor in granting direct commissions, in selection for officer candidate schools, and in promotion to responsible posts. A sample survey conducted in 1944, for example, revealed that over two-thirds of all army officers had attended or graduated from college.

This emphasis upon college education has been questioned on several counts. In *The Market for College Graduates,* Seymour Harris of Harvard University argued that, while the average income for college graduates is higher than that for other groups, the differential has been declining in recent decades. Ascribing this decline in large part to the great expansion in the number of college graduates, he warned of a potential oversupply of graduates in relation to employment opportunities. However, the economic incentive for college education need not be significantly weakened by a reduction in income differentials. As the number of college graduates rises, a college or even a postgraduate degree becomes more, rather than less, essential for high-salaried employment. Moreover, for those who seek economic and social advancement through education, the aim seems to be a relative improvement over the status of their parents, rather than an absolute increase. For the individual who achieves a relatively better economic and social status through college graduation rather than by some other path, his education, in spite of its cost, will probably prove worthwhile.

The second factor which influences the number who go to college is the cost of education, which includes living expenses and tuition. This is borne in the main by the individual student or his family directly, and in part by the community through taxes and private endowments. Moreover, earnings from work are foregone wholly or in part during the period of study, a major consideration for lower-income groups. The ability of individuals or families to finance education has increased markedly. The real average per capita income after taxes, for example, increased 42 percent between 1929 and 1951.[1] At the same time, education has acquired a higher priority in the pattern of expenditures of more people. In recent decades, a large percentage of college graduates have been educated in state-supported institutions. The extension of free municipal colleges and the development of community junior colleges, which enable students to live at home, and expanded scholarship aid have also made it possible for more persons to afford college.

About $25 million in scholarship grants and an estimated $50 million in the form of loans or payment for work are available each year.[2] Scholarships vary widely in the amount of assistance they provide and are unevenly distributed over the various fields of study. Ancestry, the accident of birth in a particular community, or other irrelevant factors often determine who are eligible to receive scholarships. Needy students may be deflected from the field in which they are most competent to fields in which scholarships are available.

Living expenses account for the largest part of the cost of education. The fact that college enrollment did not fall during the depression of the 1930's, in spite of the decline in national income, is accounted for in part by a decline in the cost of living. The increasing competition for jobs, the lack of job openings, and increased government and university aid programs also helped to keep enrollments up. The striking increase in enrollments when the G.I. Bill went into effect after World War II was due in part to the fact that college attendance had been postponed for most males who would normally enroll. It also illustrates the important influence of educational costs on the number of persons who attend college. About 20 percent of the veterans entering college in 1946 would not have enrolled if the G.I. benefits had not been available.

In addition to raising the living costs which students must bear, inflation has compelled colleges and universities to raise their tuition charges. These higher costs make it more difficult for some qualified students, who would otherwise go to college, to attend. Increases in tuition have not freed the colleges from financial difficulties. The Commission on Financing Higher Education estimated in 1952 that the colleges and universities of the nation needed an additional $250 million, or 15 percent a year more to meet current operating costs.

The third major factor bearing on the supply of students is the availability of educational and training facilities, including the buildings, libraries, laboratories, and especially the faculties. These facilities do not grow in direct response to the demand for education. Since receipts from student fees never meet even the current operating expenses of colleges, the expansion of facilities depends upon the availability of public or private funds. Originally facilities were provided by private grants, supplemented by some direct and many indirect state aids, such as tax exemptions. More recently, Federal, state, and municipal funds have been used directly and in large amounts to support institutions of higher education. In 1950, the income provided by state and local governments to public colleges and universities came to $493 million, according to the Report of the Commission on Financing Higher Education, with the state governments accounting for about nine tenths of this sum.[3]

Substantial Federal contributions began as early as 1862 with the passage of the Morrill Act, which made possible the creation or expansion of state universities, primarily to train specialists in agriculture and "the mechanic arts." The Report of the Commission shows that by 1950 the Federal government was contributing $468 million annually to institutions of higher education in the form of payments to students to help them attend a college or university; of payments to institutions for services; of grants and gifts for improving their physical facilities; and of grants supporting specific teaching and research activities. Federal, state, and local governments provided almost three fifths of the total annual income of institutions of higher education.[4]

Although the facilities available ordinarily set an upper limit on the number of students enrolled in colleges and universities, the existing facilities do have some flexibility. After World War II, the colleges handled unprecedentedly large numbers by utilizing faculties and physical facilities more intensively and by adding staff members. The problem of facilities, however, has a qualitative as well as a quantitative aspect, and it cannot be taken for granted that the ability of institutions to absorb a heavier student load does not affect the quality of the education they provide.

CHOICE OF FIELD OF STUDY

The choices which students make among fields of study determine the number of new entrants into each field of professional and scientific employment. Some young men and women who attend college as preparation for a professional career have decided upon their field of study and their subsequent career before they enter college. The majority, however, probably make their final choice only after they are enrolled in college. Home influences and individual interests and capabilities incline them to pick one field rather than another. With greater maturity and better knowledge about the content of alternative fields of study and employment opportunities, earlier uncertainties are reduced and final commitments to a field of study and a career are made. In the case of some professions, particularly engineering, the commitment must be made early, because the student frequently enters professional training immediately on graduation from high school. This situation may force a premature choice of career, since the young man may not have had adequate opportunity to learn about himself and the world of work. When a student goes from high school to a liberal arts college, the field of major study may not be decided upon until the second or third year. This later choice will be made with greater awareness of the opportunities for a meaningful career in the physical or social sciences that are not within the horizon of the average high school student.

One factor which enters into the individual's choice among broad fields of study is his ability. The same individual may have widely different capacities for such activities as solving mathematical problems, perceiving spatial relationships, verbalizing, and getting along with people. Some people think more readily about human problems, others about physical problems. These differences contribute to many of the choices that people make between such major areas as the humanities and the physical sciences. The origin of these differences is obscure, but it is certain that they are deeply imbedded. Particular abilities cannot be readily modified by efforts made late in high school or in college.

Since many individuals are as well equipped for study in one broad field as in another, a large part of the decision-making process turns on factors other than ability. In reaching a final choice, the individual weighs not only his abilities, but also the availability and costs of particular kinds of education and the anticipated money rewards of a particular career. He also takes into account noneconomic considerations, which are frequently of major importance. The weight assigned to each of these considerations depends primarily upon the values and goals of the individual. Some students develop a consummate intellectual interest in a given field which dominates all other considerations. Frequently, this is the result of stimulation by an especially able teacher. The way of life which is part of a given professional career may be the key influence in another individual's choice. Thus, a student may become a biologist rather than a doctor because the scientist need not contend with suffering, the responsibility for life-or-death decisions, or the constant demands upon his time which confront the doctor. The decision to work in most scientific fields, particularly in research, is likely to be associated with intellectual values which are not generally shared by a society which assigns great weight to monetary rewards.

The same economic considerations which influence college attendance also play a role in the choice of field of study. One of these is the probable financial reward of a career in a given field. The desire to maximize earnings is not the dominant motive of most students contemplating a professional or scientific career. While the average earnings of professionals and scientists are well above the earnings of the population as a whole, few fortunes are made in these fields. Like other Americans, however, those who prepare for the professions prefer a large income to a small one and a field with abundant job openings to one in which job opportunities are scarce. Some closely related fields offer widely different economic rewards. A large number of industrial jobs with good beginning salaries and good chances for advancement are open to industrial chemists, while the research-minded biochemist may find only a few posts open to him in colleges or universities, most of them at relatively low salaries. The student who prefers to enter a relatively low-paying field obviously places less value upon money rewards than upon noneconomic considerations.

The role of economic incentives in determining most choices made by individuals among professional fields is not clear-cut. The capable student can expect to earn a substantial income in all the fields which offer good opportunities for industrial employment or private practice, such as engineering, chemistry, law, medicine, or dentistry. Although average earnings differ among these fields, the earnings of the individual depend at least as much on his ability and energy as on the field itself. This is likely to be truer in the case of the independent practitioner, such as the doctor or dentist, than it is for the salaried employee. In most scientific and professional fields the range of income from the lowest to the highest is enormous. For teachers and government employees, however, the range tends to be much smaller.

The second economic factor which strongly influences the choice of field of study is the cost of acquiring advanced training in different fields. Medical training, for example, requires at least five years after college. The demands of medical training are so heavy that the student can seldom work part-time. The law also forbids him to practice before his training is completed. If he elects to specialize, he must forego the major portion of his potential earnings for several more years. By contrast, the graduate student in the sciences can frequently earn part of his expenses by teaching, serving as an assistant, or doing other work. Moreover, he can usually interrupt his graduate work at any point to start working and earning in his field, but at less desirable jobs than he could secure had he completed his advanced training.

Medicine is probably the only field in which the number of capable applicants far exceeds the number who can be trained in existing facilities. For every field, however, the concentration of facilities in certain areas and local variations in the quality of facilities have a strong influence on the choices made by individuals. For example, first-rate advanced training in physics is available at a relatively small number of universities. The cost of an advanced degree in physics is raised for most students because they must seek a large university and cannot live at home. On the other hand, the student who finds himself at Cornell or Iowa State may specialize in agricultural science because their facilities and faculties in this field are outstanding. In every college, moreover, some departments are better than others, and this accounts in part for the choices made by many students among different fields of study.

To improve the educational facilities for any field of study it is necessary to strengthen at least the faculty and the library. In the case of the laboratory sciences, new buildings and equipment are also essential. First-rate medical schools cannot be developed except in conjunction with good hospitals. Only a few universities can afford outstanding facilities and faculties in a wide variety of fields, and the high cost of teaching some subjects, such as medicine, dictates their concentration in a few centers of study. An attempt to expand the number of fields in which a college has good facilities may result in uneconomical duplication of the facilities and faculties of other nearby institutions. Yet, where funds are available, the attempt may be justified on the ground that it produces a more balanced and educationally richer institution.

EMPLOYMENT MARKETS FOR SCIENTISTS AND PROFESSIONALS

There are three basic employment markets in which the nation's scientists and professionals are employed. Two are commercial markets: independent professional practice and employment by private industry. The third is noncommercial: employment in nonprofit institutions such as schools and colleges, government, libraries, foundations, and most hospitals.

The distribution of professionals among these markets is affected by income differences. Generally speaking, the independent practitioner earns more than the industrial employee, and the latter more than the employee of a nonprofit institution. Salaries are not the only consideration influencing distribution. The young person who has just completed his professional training is freer to search for a job in a high-paying market than the person who is already established in a job. For the latter, a change of employment may mean a sacrifice of security, pension rights, relations with colleagues, and community ties. Many will be unwilling to sacrifice these for a moderate salary increase. A spirit of public service or the attractions of an academic life hold many professionals in government or education, where they earn less than they could in industry.

In most professions, employment immediately after the completion of formal education is usually a period of continued training. The new graduate may take a relatively low-paying job, either because he wants additional training or because he is unable, without further experience, to enter better-paying employment. The medical school graduate serves an internship and frequently a residency in a hospital before he enters private practice. Most law graduates work at relatively low salaries for law firms, and many young scientists teach in order to continue their education. Industrial employers are becoming increasingly aware of their role as trainers as well as users of manpower. The opportunity for additional training, therefore, may also be an important consideration in the choice of an industrial job.[5]

Most doctors and dentists, many lawyers and accountants, and smaller numbers in several other fields work as independent practitioners. The demand for their services and, consequently, their earnings, fluctuate with the consumers' expenditures. Normally, and particularly in recent prosperous years, the average income of independent practitioners has been higher than that of professionals in other types of employment. The pension rights and greater security of some salaried personnel may counterbalance the higher earnings of independent practice. Nevertheless, higher incomes from independent practice may induce appropriately trained and licensed professionals to shift from the other markets to independent practice.

The services of practitioners are distributed among consumers by means of prices, but not in precisely the same way as commodities are. Physicians, dentists, and other professionals sometimes adjust their charges to the consumers' ability to pay. In recent years, as the demand for professional services has risen, charges have risen, with the result that groups at the bottom of the income scale may either restrict use of professional services to periods of emergency or depend upon free services, such as medical clinics and legal aid societies. In the case of medical service, various community plans, such as Blue Cross, have helped many consumers to meet the financial burden involved.

In the second type of market, scientists and professionals are employed by industry in engineering, research, or managerial positions. Scientists and professionals employed by industry have increased more rapidly than the industrial labor force as a whole because of such long-term trends as increasing complexity of organization and processes, greater investment in product research and development, and the emergence of personnel management, marketing research, industrial training, and other specialized functions within business management.

The distribution of scientists and professionals among commercial employers is determined largely by the availability of jobs in depressed economic periods, and by income differentials in periods of full employment. Income differentials have more effect on the distribution of recent graduates than they do on the movement of older persons who have established positions with a particular company.

Since industry employs a large proportion of the engineers, chemists, and other scientific specialists, the number undertaking training in these fields is likely to respond to changes in technology and economic conditions, which influence trends in job opportunities and earning levels.

Schools, hospitals, universities, and government are the primary employers in the third market for professionals and scientists. Most employers in this market usually make services available to consumers below cost. These institutions seldom provide salaries matching those in the commercial markets. The salaries of noncommercial employers, moreover, are much more inflexible than those of commercial employers. Noncommercial institutions tend, in consequence, to lose employees to industry and private practice in periods of full employment and inflation. There are instances where industry secures scientists, not because of salary differentials, but because they cannot make the grade in the academic world. During periods of deflation and depression, on the other hand, the relative position of those employed by noncommercial institutions improves, since their salaries do not fall as rapidly or as much as the cost of living.

There are important economic differences among employers in the noncommercial market. Hospitals and universities have much in common. They both derive their income from the sale of their services, from gifts, and usually from government appropriations which reach them directly or indirectly. Few private hospitals or universities are able to meet operating expenses solely from income from the sale of services. Since the real value of endowments has fallen, they have encountered serious difficulties in increasing income proportionately to rising costs.

Public schools derive their income entirely from taxes or appropriations. Although other tax sources have become increasingly important, most school systems still rely heavily on income from local real estate taxes. Since real estate taxes are relatively inflexible, school income and teachers' salaries have also fallen behind the general rise of salaries in other fields.

The Federal government employs large numbers of scientists, engineers, economists, and other professionals. In recent decades it has paid them better starting salaries than most other noncommercial employers, and has therefore been able to recruit younger professionals during inflationary periods. A Civil Service position is frequently a good way for a young graduate to gain experience without sacrificing income. On the other hand, government salaries are also relatively inflexible. The government is at a disadvantage in competing with industry and private practice for more experienced personnel, for the top salary levels in the Civil Service scale do not compare with the earnings of competent professionals in industry or private practice. Consequently, government tends to lose its better employees when they are able to step into higher-paying positions in the commercial world.

ARTIFICIAL BARRIERS

The preceding discussion of the factors which influence college attendance and choice of field of study and of employment has ignored the role of artificial barriers resulting from deeply imbedded social attitudes. Although discriminatory barriers against racial and ethnic groups and against women have been greatly reduced in recent decades, they still severely limit the number of Negroes and women in scientific and professional work.

Relatively few Negroes attend and graduate from college,[6] chiefly because the primary and secondary education which many of them receive does not qualify them for or interest them in college education. Most of them leave school before receiving a secondary diploma. These factors, in turn, reflect the fact that a large part of the Negro population is concentrated in areas where income is low and where many communities neglect Negro education.

The scarcity of scientific and professional employment openings for Negroes also discourages them from undertaking advanced education and influences their choice of field of study. Apart from teaching and nursing positions, and these mainly in Negro schools and hospitals, there are very restricted career opportunities in the professions for all but the most unusually gifted. The barriers against Negroes in professional life are an extreme form of the discrimination still felt in lesser degrees by other ethnic groups, especially by Spanish-speaking Americans.

The barriers against women are of somewhat different form. Women receive the same early schooling as men, and nearly as many attend college. Yet relatively few are employed in scientific or professional fields other than teaching and nursing. In part, this underrepresentation reflects the fact that few women expect to pursue professional or scientific careers in other fields. On the other hand, the unwillingness of many employers to hire women discourages them from preparing for certain fields such as engineering and the physical sciences. The problem is complicated because the prejudice of some employers is reinforced by the general knowledge that a young woman hired for a responsible position may well leave within a short time to marry and raise children.

XIII. POST-HIGH SCHOOL EDUCATION AND TRAINING OF WOMEN

The Council Staff

CHANGES IN THE PATTERNS of women's employment outside the home, shortages of personnel in occupational fields in which women are strongly represented, as well as those in which relatively few women are found, and concern with the waste of high ability have combined to give a new significance to the long-debated question of the purpose and content of women's education.

In *Womanpower*, the National Manpower Council urged the broadening of educational and training opportunities for younger and older women alike. It specifically recommended the expansion and improvement of "educational and vocational guidance, in order to help young women make sound decisions with respect to their self-development, the growing and changing opportunities open to them, and the probability that paid employment will occupy a significant place in their adult lives." The Council also called for greater "support of scholarship and fellowship programs, in order to enable more young women of high ability to continue their formal education in college or in professional or graduate schools."

The purpose of this chapter is to present the salient characteristics of post-secondary school formal education and training for women.

> *"Post-High School Education and Training of Women" is reprinted with editorial changes from* Womanpower, *in which it first appeared as "Post-High School Education and Training," Chapter VII, pp. 191–219.*

EVERY attempt to define the purposes of American higher education and to state the most effective means for realizing them is an invitation to disagreement. This is understandable, for its functions and forms, shaped by changing historical circumstances, reflect the needs of a large and heterogeneous student population and the influence of conflicting educational philosophies. Every attempt to specify the purposes of higher education for women in particular encounters additional difficulties.

To inquire how women should be educated, or whether they should be educated in the same way as men, or differently, does not merely raise queries concerning the structure of educational institutions and methods of instruction—it also asks how young men and women are to be prepared to assume those adult responsibilities which society views as distinctive of each sex. Consequently, almost every utterance on the education of women is likely to express a judgment—at least by implication—on the degree to which women resemble or differ from men in general intelligence, abilities, and aptitudes, in "nature" or "psychology," or in functions.

It should not be surprising, therefore, that there has been a continuing debate over whether higher education should serve primarily the needs and interests of women as homemakers, as workers, or as citizens. Enormous changes have occurred in the course of the past century in the status of women in American society, in the ways they conduct their lives, and in the extent and content of their education. These changes have profoundly altered the terms and manner of that debate. They have not, however, resolved the underlying question: Should the primary emphasis in the college education of women be given to preparing them for adult responsibilities and functions which essentially differ from or resemble those of men?

This question is obviously related to the concern which has frequently been expressed that only a small proportion of the girls who graduate from high school go on to college. Even more prominent than those which appear earlier are the differences in the educational behavior and experience of young men and women after high school. As has been seen, fewer young women than young men enter and graduate from college. Women are heavily outnumbered by men in graduate study. In many respects, of course, their college or university education is identical, but, both as undergraduate and graduate students, young men and women differ significantly with respect to the fields in which they specialize. Furthermore, men and women do not make the same use of noncollegiate educational and training facilities.

Yet, there has been less dissimilarity in college attendance and graduation between the sexes in the United States than in most other western societies. Even where, as in France, Italy, and England, the ratio of women to men students is roughly similar to that in the United States, a much smaller proportion of the total population is enrolled in colleges and universities. From a comparative point of view, the extent to which American women are educated beyond the secondary school level is quite remarkable. Since 1949, more than 100,000 bachelor's and first professional degrees have been awarded annually to women—a number which is substantially larger than the total college and university enrollments of Great Britain. From 1946 to 1955, a total of almost one million women earned bachelor's and first professional degrees in the United States. In recent years, about one third of all such degrees have gone to women.[1] In 1950, 2.25 million—or about 43 percent—of the 5.25 million college graduates aged 25 years and over were women.[2]

GROWTH OF COLLEGIATE EDUCATION FOR WOMEN

College education for women, comparable in quality to that available for men, began in the United States in 1837, when Oberlin College opened its doors to four young women. The first women's college, Vassar, was founded twenty-eight years later. By the close of the nineteenth century, women comprised one third of the nation's college and university students. At first, higher education for women, whether provided by establishing separate women's colleges or by admitting women to men's institutions, was staunchly resisted. The early arguments in opposition took for granted the innate inferiority of the female sex and represented college education for women as a device for undermining the superior status of the male. It was maintained that women possessed neither the physical strength nor the mental ability to do college work; that a college education was incompatible with their functions and status; that it would decrease their chances for marriage—for men where repelled by "learned" or "intellectual" women—and destroy their distinctive feminine qualities; and that it would have no utility after marriage.

These and other objections were more than counterbalanced by forces which produced an increasingly vigorous and gradually successful movement for women's rights. This had its educational as well as its legal, social, economic, and political aspects. Much later, however, when the right of women to a college education had clearly been established, the lower marriage and birth rates of women college graduates provided fresh ammunition for those who resisted the break with tradition. They ascribed these developments to college attendance alone and cited them as proof of the undesirable consequences of higher education for women. The proposal that men's institutions be opened up to women was countered on additional grounds. It was contended that this step would "feminize" the institutions, for new courses designed to meet women's needs would be introduced, or men would be discouraged from attending existing courses likely to attract many women, particularly in the liberal arts. Some opponents of educational equality believed that the coeducational system would encourage immorality, or promote early marriages, or weaken the family by leading women to question the superior status of the husband. Such convictions and the weight of tradition contributed to the establishment of the "coordinate college" for women, associated with, but still separate from, the men's institution.

How much had been won in the struggle to provide opportunities for higher education for women, even before the close of the nineteenth century, appears in the fact that women then accounted for more than one third of the still small number of college and university students. Since that time, women have represented from 30 to 50 percent of the enrollments in institutions of higher education.

The growth in college attendance during the present century, which rests upon the foundation provided by the tremendous expansion in high school attendance and graduation, is one aspect of a continuing trend toward more years of schooling for young people. It is a measure of the value which Americans attach not so much to intellectual attainment as to formal education. A growing national income, a substantial rise in family income, and expenditures of public funds for higher education have been crucial in the increase in college attendance. So have the needs of a complex, technological society for highly trained and specialized personnel. These needs are reflected in the extent to which college training is held to be desirable for employment, and in the professionalization of a number of occupations by establishing a college or professional school degree as a minimum requirement.

Young women and men go to college for much the same basic reasons: because they have compelling intellectual interests; because they regard college as essential preparation for a fruitful adult life; because they want to enter one of the professions or prepare for a career in business; because they view college attendance as a means for attaining higher social status; and even because going to college is an acceptable substitute for going to work for those young people who are under no pressure to earn an income. Each of these reasons, as well as others that might be specified, rarely operate alone. The decision to go to college is shaped by social and economic circumstances, a variety of personal considerations, and the influences exerted by parents, relatives, teachers, and others.

It has been seen that the expectation of marriage and of an

adult life defined primarily in terms of functions centered in the home goes far to explain why a smaller proportion of girl than of boy high school graduates go on to college.[3] The available evidence indicates that vocational interests and aspirations are important reasons for college attendance among the young women who do go. These reasons, however, are on the whole still more significant with men. For example, a recent study, "Occupational Planning by Undergraduates of the State College of Washington," found that "women as well as men appeared to be impressed by the vocational importance of college training, although a higher proportion of the men (92 percent) than of the women (77 percent) stated that occupational preparation was the most important reason for coming to college."

TRENDS IN COLLEGE GRADUATION

From 1900 to 1955, there was an elevenfold increase in the number of bachelor's and first professional degrees conferred. Since the number of women graduating from college was twenty times greater in 1955 than in 1900, the proportion of these degrees awarded to women did not quite double between these two points in time. Early in this century, women constituted a much larger proportion of college students than they did of graduates. They accounted for about one third of the students—almost as high a proportion as today—but, as Table 8 shows,[4] for only about one fifth of all recipients of bachelor's and first professional degrees. A partial explanation of this situation is that many young women who intended to teach attended college or normal school for only one or two years, which were then sufficient to meet the requirements for certification. The significant increases in the numbers of women college graduates occurred after 1920, and since that date the ratio of women to men has been about the same for degree recipients as for college students.

Since 1920, moreover, there has been no consistent growth in the ratio of women to men among college graduates. In 1920,

women constituted one third of all the bachelor's and first professional degree recipients. In 1930 and 1940, they received two
fifths of all of the degrees awarded. During World War II, which
temporarily checked the long-run growth in college enrollments
and graduations, women constituted a substantial majority of all
college graduates for the first time. Even though the actual numbers of women graduating from college rose after the war, they
accounted for much smaller proportions of the total recipients of
degrees because of the influx of male veterans into the colleges
and universities. In 1950, only one out of every four degrees was
awarded to a woman. Since then, as Table 8 indicates, there was a
steady growth in the proportion of women among college graduates up to 1955, and a slight decline since then.

The rapid increase in college graduations may also be shown
by comparison with the growth in the numbers of young men and
women in the population. Around the turn of the century, the
number of women graduating from college annually was equivalent to less than 1 percent of the total number of women 22 years
of age. The ratio of men graduating annually to the male population aged 22, however, was 3 percent. By 1958, as Table 8 shows,
the ratio for women came to 11.3 percent, and for men to 22
percent.

Many persons graduate from college when they are in their
later twenties or early thirties. For example, 19 percent of the
women who received bachelor's degrees in June, 1955, are reported to have been 23 to 29 years old, and another 8 percent
were 30 or over. It is, therefore, somewhat misleading to compare
the number of college graduates in any one year with the number
of high school graduates four years earlier. Nevertheless, such a
comparison does help illuminate differences between the sexes
with respect to high school completion and college graduation.
The number of girls graduating from high schools was equivalent
to three fifths of all the seventeen-year-old girls in the population
in 1950. Male high school graduates came to more than half of

Table 8. Bachelor's and First Professional Degrees Awarded to Men and Women, 1900–58

| Year | First Degrees Awarded | | | | Men Receiving First Degrees as Percent of All Men Aged 22 Years | Women Receiving First Degrees as Percent of All Women Aged 22 Years |
	Total	Men	Women	Percent Women of Total		
1900	27,410	22,173	5,237	19.1	3.0	0.7
1910	37,199	28,762	8,437	22.7	3.1	0.9
1920	48,622	31,980	16,642	34.2	3.5	1.7
1930	122,484	73,615	48,869	39.9	6.8	4.3
1940	186,500	109,546	76,954	41.3	9.7	6.6
1942	185,346	103,889	81,457	43.9	8.8	6.5
1944	125,863	55,865	69,998	55.6	4.5	5.4
1946	136,174	58,664	77,510	56.9	4.9	6.2
1947	272,144	175,987	96,157	35.3	14.5	7.7
1948	271,019	175,456	95,563	35.3	14.9	8.0
1949	366,634	264,168	102,466	27.9	22.5	8.6
1950	433,734	329,819	103,915	24.0	29.6	8.9
1951	384,352	279,343	105,009	27.3	25.0	9.1
1952	331,924	227,029	104,895	31.6	21.6	9.2
1953	304,857	200,820	104,037	34.1	19.1	9.4
1954	292,880	187,500	105,380	36.0	17.3	9.6
1955	287,401	183,602	103,799	36.1	17.4	10.0
1956	311,298	199,571	111,727	35.9	19.2	10.8
1957	340,347	222,738	117,609	34.6	20.5	10.9
1958	365,748	242,948	122,800	33.6	22.1	11.3

Source: U. S. Office of Education and U. S. Bureau of the Census.

the seventeen-year-old male population. The number of women graduating from college or professional school in 1954 was equal to 17 percent of the number of girl high school graduates four years earlier. The number of boys completing college in 1954 was 33 percent of the number graduating from high school in 1950.[5] Over the last two decades, the proportions of boys and girls graduating both from high school and college have increased substantially. There have been only moderate gains, however, in the proportions of high school graduates who have gone on to complete college. In each case, the increases for boys have been somewhat greater than those for girls.

All estimates point to a striking growth in the future size of the college-educated population. Such forecasts are based on rapid increases in the college-age population and on the assumption that the underlying social and economic causes for the past growth of higher education will continue to operate in the future. The proportion of young people who complete college may grow at an even faster rate than in the past, particularly if the high level of demand for college-trained men and women continues, as it gives every promise of doing. Projections prepared by the U. S. Office of Education, indicating that women will make up about a third of all college graduates, show 145,000 women recipients of bachelor's and first professional degrees in 1959-60, and 246,000 ten years later.[6] These projections also assume, of course, that teaching personnel and physical facilities required for the expansion in enrollments will be available.

UNDERGRADUATE EDUCATIONAL PATTERNS

Variations in educational patterns appear not only in college enrollment and completion, but also in the types of institutions men and women attend. Three ytpes of institutions award the overwhelming majority of bachelor's and first professional degrees—universities, liberal arts colleges, and teachers' colleges. As Table 9 shows, a much higher proportion of the women grad-

Table 9. *Bachelor's and First Professional Degrees Awarded to Men and Women, by Type of Institution, 1953–54*

Type of Institution	Total		Men		Women		Women as Percent of Total Receiving Degrees
	Number	Percent	Number	Percent	Number	Percent	
Total	292,880	100	187,500	100	105,380	100	36
Universities	141,819	48	102,472	55	39,347	37	28
Coeducational	138,989	47	99,642	53	39,347	37	28
Noncoeducational	2,830	1	2,830	2	..	..	..
Liberal arts colleges	88,384	30	47,136	25	41,248	39	47
Coeducational	67,245	23	39,015	21	28,230	27	42
Noncoeducational	21,139	7	8,121	4	13,018	12	62
Teachers' colleges	34,938	12	13,311	7	21,627	21	62
Technological schools	14,316	5	12,942	7	1,374	1	10
Other	13,423	5	11,639	6	1,784	2	13

Source: U. S. Office of Education, and Richard H. Ostheimer, *A Statistical Analysis of the Organization of Higher Education in the U. S., 1948–1949,* New York, 1951.

uates come from teachers' colleges than is the case among men. A significantly smaller proportion of women than of men graduates earned their degrees in universities in 1953–54, while the reverse was the case in the liberal arts colleges. Women are most poorly represented among the graduates of technological schools.

Coeducation is not nearly as prevalent in American higher education as it is at the secondary level, but it is still characteristic of the college and university scene. In 1953–54, only three institutions classified as "men's universities" did not grant bachelor's degrees to women.[7] Coeducational colleges conferred about three fourths of all of the degrees granted by liberal arts institutions. There are more than twice as many separate women's colleges as men's, and about one third of the degrees earned by women in liberal arts institutions were granted by women's colleges. Only one sixth of the degrees granted to men by liberal arts colleges were awarded by separate men's schools.

Women in the labor force are concentrated in relatively few fields of employment, even though they are found in virtually all occupations. This is also true for the fields of undergraduate study pursued by young women. Thus, almost two out of every five women who graduated in 1954–55 majored in the field of education,[8] and an additional one out of seven prepared for teaching, even though she specialized in some other field. Almost as striking is the contrast between men and women college graduates with respect to specialization in the basic and applied natural sciences. One third of the men graduating in 1954–55 majored in these fields, as Table 10 shows, in contrast to one eighth of the women. Engineering, for men the most important single field of concentration among the natural and physical sciences, claimed less than 1 percent of the women, but in several scientific fields, such as botany, bacteriology, physiology, and mathematics, there were roughly similar proportions of men and women graduates.

The several social sciences accounted for a substantially larger proportion of the men (about one third) than of the women graduates (about one fifth). Within the social sciences, men and women tend to specialize in different disciplines. For example, economics attracted very few women compared to the number of men among graduates in 1954–55, while a much larger propor-

Table 10. *Bachelor's and First Professional Degrees Awarded to Men and Women, by Field of Study, 1954–55*

Field of Study	Percent Distribution		Women as Percent of Total Receiving Degrees
	Men	Women	
Total	100	100	36
Natural sciences, basic and applied	32	13	18
Biological	3	2	28
Physical	5	1	13
Healing arts and medical sciences	9	7	31
Engineering	12	1	..
Mathematics	1	1	33
Science without major	2	1	16
Social sciences	35	19	25
Basic [a]	11	8	29
Applied [b]	20	7	17
Psychology	2	2	46
Other	2	2	41
Liberal art subjects	15	22	45
English	3	8	61
Fine arts	4	8	53
Foreign languages	1	2	60
Religion and philosophy	4	2	17
Arts without major	3	2	27
Agriculture	4	..	2
Education [c]	8	37	72
Home economics	..	7	99
Journalism	1	1	36
Law	4	..	4
Library science	..	1	75
Military science	1	..	..

.. = less than 0.5 percent.

[a] Includes anthropology, economics, geography, history, international relations, political science, and sociology.

[b] Includes business and commerce, social work, and public administration. Master's degrees in social work, where they are the first professional degree granted by a school, are also included.

[c] Most students who prepared for high school teaching are included in other fields of specialization and not in the education category.

Source: U. S. Office of Education.

tion of women than of men had majored in sociology. In liberal arts fields of study, in which about one out of every five women and one out of every seven men college graduates specialized,[9] there were large differences in the proportions of men and women majoring in English, the fine arts, foreign languages, and religion and philosophy.

Four areas of specialization in which the great majority of graduates were women—education, nursing, library science, and home economics—accounted for exactly half of the bachelor's and first professional degrees earned by women in 1954–55. Two thirds of the degrees granted to women were in these four fields and in English and fine arts, where women also outnumbered men. Women were also granted a majority of the degrees in foreign languages, sociology, and social work.[10]

The fields of study which attract women most strongly are those which prepare them for employment in professional occupations long viewed as peculiarly suited to women and in which they are already heavily represented. Teaching, nursing, library work, and the occupations based on home economics study currently account for almost 70 percent of all women employed in professional occupations. The opening up of employment opportunities in science and technology since 1950 has not yet significantly influenced the choices which young women make with respect to fields of college study.

Employment opportunities alone could not determine choices among fields of study, for many young women do not view college in purely vocational terms. There are those who hope that their college years will help them, not so much in paid employment, as in their activities as wives, mothers, and citizens. For some young women, as for some young men, interest in a field of study overrides considerations of employment opportunities. Others might have majored in one of the natural sciences, for example, rather than in one of the "women's" fields, if their high school studies had prepared them for such specialization. Some are greatly influenced in their choices by the strength of a department or even of a single teacher. With others, specialization in college may be affected by the knowledge that their chances of continuing with graduate study are slight. Even if it were possible, it would not be very useful to assign precise weights to these diverse reasons for the relatively heavy concentration of women college students in a few fields of study. For the important points are that a combination of factors results in distinctive and persisting patterns of choice among fields of study and that traditional modes of behavior are not readily altered.

GRADUATE STUDY

At the level of graduate study, women and men behave similarly in one major respect. Just about the same proportions of women as of men college graduates obtain master's degrees. This is not a recent development, for in 1900, when women earned about one fifth of all of the bachelor's and first professional degrees, they also received about the same proportion of master's degrees. In the mid-1950's, about one third of all first degree and of all master's degree recipients were women. In recent decades, the number of master's degrees awarded has increased considerably, in good part because so large a proportion of those entering the teaching profession have gone on to advanced study.

In graduate, as in undergraduate, study women enter almost all fields, but most are found in a handful of specialities. Of the almost 19,500 master's degrees awarded women in 1954–55, about 12,500, or just under two thirds, were earned in the field of education. Two fifths of all the men receiving master's degrees that year earned them in education.[11] Five fields of study—education, English, home economics, nursing, and fine arts—accounted for about four fifths of all of the master's degrees conferred on women.

In only three fields—nursing, home economics, and library science—were the overwhelming majority of the master's degrees granted to women in 1954–55. Even in education, more men than women were granted master's degrees. In social work and some foreign languages (French, Spanish, and Russian) [12] there were more women recipients than men, and in English the master's degrees were equally divided between the sexes. Women who go on to earn a master's degree generally represent a smaller proportion of the total than do those who majored in the same field as undergraduates. Thus, in English and in foreign languages, fields in which women earned about three fifths of the bachelor's degrees, they accounted for about half of the master's degrees granted. In fine arts and psychology, women received about half of the bachelor's degrees, but a third of the master's.

Relatively few women continue with graduate study to the Ph.D. level. The proportion of all doctoral degrees earned by women has fluctuated greatly since the close of the nineteenth century. Women constituted about 6 percent of all doctoral degree recipients in 1890 and 1900, but 12 to 16 percent in the three decades after 1910. At the close of World War II, they earned about one fifth of all the doctoral degrees conferred. Since then, the number of doctorates granted to women has more than doubled, but the increase in the number granted to men has been even greater. Consequently, the proportion of all doctoral degrees earned by women has declined, and since 1949, about one tenth of those granted have gone to women.

As at the bachelor's and master's level, the majority of doctoral degrees earned by women are in education, and this one field accounted for 30 percent of the 826 doctoral degrees conferred on women in 1954–55. Another one third of all of the Ph.D.'s awarded to women were in six other fields—psychology, English, home economics, fine arts, chemistry, and history. At the Ph.D. level, women accounted for most of the few degrees in home economics, Russian language studies, social work, and nursing. On the other hand, they represented a small fraction of the

Ph.D.'s granted in mathematics and the physical sciences, and about 10 percent in the social and biological sciences and psychology.[13]

The vast majority of college men and women do not contemplate further study. In the case of the women, pursuit of an advanced degree is more or less foreclosed by marriage either before or shortly after graduation from college. How significant a role marriage plays can be seen in the findings of a study undertaken jointly by the Women's Bureau and the National Vocational Guidance Association of the women college graduates of the class of June, 1955. Six months later, 12 percent of the single women from this class were enrolled in school full time, most of them in graduate courses. Of the married women, only 4 percent were attending school, and of those with children, 2 percent were in school full time. Of all women graduates of the class of June, 1955 enrolled as full-time students six months later, however, 15 percent were married.

The married woman graduate student was exceptional years ago. It has been estimated that today almost one third of the women working toward an advanced degree are married. Marriage is only one factor affecting graduate study by women. Some young women who do not engage in graduate study would do so if they had the economic means. It has been asserted that some able women do not make the investment of time, effort, and money in a master's or doctor's degree because men are preferred for top positions, even in occupations in which women predominate, such as library service and teaching. There is also reason to believe that most women who look forward to combining paid employment with homemaking do not aspire to top level jobs for which graduate study would be a prerequisite. Most women who enter employment after graduation and who continue to work after marriage see no need to acquire a graduate degree for a successful career, particularly if they find themselves in business or industry. Moreover, there are few professional fields in which substantial numbers of women are found where the opportunities for either employment or advancement depend heavily upon advanced study.

The growing demand for college and university trained personnel in recent years has focused attention upon the nation's resources of individuals with the ability to pursue formal education beyond the high school level. All the available studies demonstrate that there is a substantial reservoir of young men and women intellectually capable of doing successful college and graduate work whose education stops with high school graduation, if not before.

There is certainly little reason to maintain categorically that everyone with the intellectual ability to graduate from college should go to college. Able individuals are needed for a wide range of occupations and functions for which college education and training are neither required nor essential. There is ground for contending that much of the value assigned to college study is a recognition of its worth for attaining social status rather than for developing potential ability. College study, moreover, is only one of several ways in which talents and abilities may be realized. Nevertheless, formal education is the major instrument through which potential ability is developed, and from this point of view the undereducation of those capable of advanced schooling is a measure of wasted ability and talent.

Various investigations have estimated the extent to which potential ability fails to be developed by formal schooling at the high school as well as at the college level. In *Who Should Go to College?* (published in 1952) Byron S. Hollinshead estimates that of the boys and girls who score in the top 25 percent in intelligence, almost one fifth do not graduate from high school; two fifths graduate from high school but do not go to college; and only two fifths enter college. Of the young people who attain an Army General Classification Test score of 120, which is equivalent to the intelligence score of the average college graduate, more than 60 percent do not complete college. Almost all the young people who score in the top 5 percent in intelligence—and are, therefore, considered capable of earning a Ph.D. degree—complete high school, but only about half of them, according to Dael Wolfle, graduate from college. Less than 2 percent of them secure a doctoral degree.

Most investigators agree that about the same proportions of individuals of high ability are found among the members of each sex. Variations between the sexes in intelligence or aptitude test scores are ascribed, as has been seen, not to innate differences but to cultural and motivational factors. A slightly larger proportion of girls than boys capable of doing college work—those with an AGCT score of 120 or over—graduate from high school; of this group, half of the boys, but only one fourth of the girls, enter and graduate from college. Among those with the intellectual ability to earn a doctoral degree, 37 percent of the girls, in contrast to 55 percent of the boys, graduate from college. In this high ability group, one out of 30 men and one out of 300 women actually earn a Ph.D. degree. Among college graduates who are capable of earning a doctoral degree, about 6 percent of the men but only 1 percent of the women do so. Young women probably account for about three out of five of those who have the ability to graduate from college but do not, and for slightly over half of those who could obtain a doctoral degree but do not.[14]

Much attention has understandably been directed to economic reasons in explaining why so many individuals with high ability fail to continue their education beyond the high school level. The evidence is clear that in the absence of economic barriers many more able young people would continue with their formal education. An increase in scholarships providing substantial financial assistance would no doubt enable a significant number of capable young men and women to attend college who today cannot afford to do so. The *Fifth Annual Report of the National Science Foundation* (1955) observes that "a total of from 60,000 to 100,000 seniors have the ability and the desire to go to college, but will not do so. Presumably, if financial support were available, many of this group could be salvaged for higher education."

The Educational Testing Service study cited earlier [15] indicated that scholarship aid can be effective not only in encouraging able students to go to college, but also in inducing them to study in a particular field. It is interesting to note, however, that scholarship aid contingent on a willingness to study in one of the physical or natural sciences seems to be less of an inducement to girls than boys. Financial assistance appears to be more influential with girls when the fields in which they would have to major, in order to secure scholarship aid, are those in which college women normally concentrate—that is, the liberal arts, the fine arts, and education.

There is reason to believe that even if generous scholarship aid were offered to all able young people who do not go to college, a substantial proportion of them would not be induced to do so. For a variety of individual and social reasons, the motivation to do well in high school or to go on to college is lacking in many potentially able young people. Girls are better motivated to achieve good grades in high school than boys, as has been seen, and boys and girls in families at the top of the educational and occupational scale behave very much alike with respect to college attendance. In families at the lower end of the educational and occupational scale, however, able girls are even less interested than boys in going to college.

OTHER FORMS OF POST-HIGH SCHOOL EDUCATION

Full-time regular college and university enrollments represent only part of the entire post-high school student population of the United States. There are, to begin with, summer session students, many, but far from all, of whom are full-time students during the academic year. In addition, there are the part-time, extension, and correspondence students enrolled in college and university programs. Their number has come to about one million in recent years. Another large and rapidly growing group of post-high school students attend junior and community colleges. The American Association of Junior Colleges reported full-time enrollments of 276,000 in 1955. Junior and community colleges also have "adult," "special," correspondence, and other groups of part-time students, many of whom are not high school graduates, and their total student population was estimated at nearly 700,000 in 1955. Technical institutes of various kinds frequently resemble junior and community colleges. In 1955–56, there were over 31,000 full-time and an additional 36,000 part-time students enrolled in the technical institutes covered in the annual survey conducted by Dean Leo Smith of the Rochester Institute of Technology.[16] There are also a number of schools maintained by trade groups, such as the American Banking Association, which provide specialized occupational training. However, no over-all data are available on them. Correspondence schools may be regarded as still another form of post-high school education, even though it is not known how many of their students are high school graduates and to what extent the students take courses above the secondary school level. The number of correspondence school students may be estimated at over one million, with almost one fifth being enrolled in courses conducted by universities.

Information about the many opportunities and facilities for post-high school education and training which are not strictly "collegiate" in character is either fragmentary, outdated, or unreliable. Consequently, it is almost impossible to specify their significance for the education of women or to delineate precisely the ways in which men and women make use of them. There are, however, many indications of differences between the sexes in this large and as yet unmapped area of post-high school education.

The junior and community colleges offer young men and

women an opportunity to continue their education beyond high school at a much lower total cost than is involved in attending an out-of-town, traditional four-year college. They also represent an attempt to build a new kind of two-year terminal education, and an expansion of the facilities of publicly-supported education. Most of these institutions, particularly the newer community colleges, are decisively oriented toward the occupational interests and needs of both their student bodies and local industries. The public junior college has flourished particularly in California, but many other states, Texas and New York among them, have allocated a significant share of their educational expenditures to them. New, ambitious programs for public, junior, and community colleges are under way in Florida, Mississippi, Iowa, Ohio, North Carolina, and other states.

Young women account for approximately the same proportion of total enrollments in junior and community colleges as in four-year colleges. There are about seventy separate women's junior colleges, mainly in the northeastern and southern states, but almost all of the publicly-controlled and the majority of the private institutions are coeducational.

While there are no data on the distribution of students among fields of study by sex, it appears that the curricula of many schools are specially geared to the vocational needs of young women. Training for semiprofessional and office, clerical, and technicians' occupations, in which women are heavily represented, is provided by many junior and community colleges. In California, for example, where special programs are offered in secretarial work and practical nursing, a majority of students in some junior colleges are women. The extent to which these institutions serve adults is indicated by their many part-time students. It is also suggested by the fact that the average age of the student body of one junior college in California is almost 30. In that state in 1952, according to a National Education Association survey, there were about a quarter of a million students participating in junior college adult education programs, half of whom were women. Among the women, 15 percent were housewives.

The student body of technical institutes is overwhelmingly male. In 1953–54, women made up only 13 percent of all full-time students in the 60 institutes included in the annual survey. Eighty percent of the women were enrolled in the state and municipal institutes in New York, while the Rochester Institute of Technology accounted for another 10 percent. Most women pursue courses in fashion design, beauty culture, dental hygiene, and office occupations, and relatively few women follow programs of study in industrial or technological fields.

A variety of schools which do not grant degrees also train both younger and older students for "women's" occupations in the health and other fields. Most student nurses, for example, are trained in hospital and other non-degree granting schools. Practical nurse training has in recent years been offered in almost 300 programs approved by state agencies or the National Association of Practical Nurse Education and conducted by public schools and other institutions. Several programs also specialize in training medical technicians. Note should be taken of the many private secretarial and business schools—about 1500—which offer post-high school instruction, and of the other kinds of proprietary vocational schools in which an unknown number of women are enrolled.

The fragmentary data available on correspondence schooling indicate that women constitute an important segment of the total student body. Housewives preparing to return to work are apparently well represented among women students. In one school with an enrollment of 120,000 in 1956, more than half the students were women, of whom nearly 75 percent were under 25, 35 percent were employed, and 65 percent were housewives. In this school, the "high school" program was most popular with women students, and those enrolled in it showed a particular interest in homemaking, commercial, and retail merchandising courses. Other courses for which women showed a preference provide training for office and clerical jobs.

The return to employment of married women with professional training, for teaching and nursing in particular, has been facilitated by special training and refresher courses. In the case of nonprofessional occupations, this is a responsibility carried by a vast array of vocational training facilities. Adult vocational training, conducted under both public and private auspices in classrooms and on the job, is of special moment to the many women who want to return to work in later life but who lack specialized skills. How many women are participating in such training, to what exent it serves their needs, what role it plays in lifting the skill level of the society, and what bearing it has upon the existing structure of women's employment are all questions which invite study.

THE CONTINUING DEBATE

The women's colleges were founded as part of the larger movement for equal rights for women and out of a need for education and training which was not centered on homemaking functions. There were, however, early critics who took them to task for modeling themselves after the men's colleges in purpose and curriculum and, therefore, for educating women as if they were men. Since then, the purpose and the content of women's college education have been subjects of controversy. The search for an "ideal" college education for women will, of course, continue, but it will not be made easier by the likelihood that more women, as the Commission on the Education of Women has observed, will lead more "complex lives" in the future, "encompassing homemaking, gainful employment, and community service."

In recent years, the proponents of a broad liberal arts education have maintained that it provides the best foundation for individual self-development and, therefore, for meeting the challenges of homemaking, paid employment, and citizenship. Neither the training designed to serve vocational goals alone, nor that shaped to prepare women for their unique functions as wives and mothers, it has been argued, adequately recognizes the extent to which adult women participate in different, if not competing, spheres of activity. A special claim is made for the women's liberal arts colleges on the ground that their students do not compete with men for leadership positions in the college community, and therefore have richer opportunities to prepare for responsible leadership in adult life.

The liberal arts program of education, however, has been charged with several weaknesses. Some of its critics have asserted that, in seeking to prepare young women for all patterns of adult life by stressing their individual self-development, it establishes a goal which cannot be realized. There is, of course, considerable evidence that some liberal arts graduates have found their education severely inadequate in the light of subsequent experiences both in marriage and in paid employment. Whether or not such evidence should be taken as compelling proof that a liberal arts education cannot possibly serve the needs of most women who continue their education beyond secondary school is, of course, another matter.

Other critics have found a liberal arts program lacking because it does not develop in young women a positive motivation toward paid employment, even though it may provide them with some of the knowledge and skills essential for an occupation. The extent to which women are found in college programs which are primarily, if not exclusively, vocationally oriented demonstrates that the liberal arts colleges do not provide the occupational training—whether for short-run employment or a continuing career—which increasing numbers of young women have come to desire.

In spite of modifications in their content, which represent an adjustment to demands for more directly "practical" courses, liberal arts programs still express a belief in the value of an educational experience built upon the needs, capacities, and values which are common to men and women alike. From this point of view, the severest critics of the liberal arts philosophy have been those whom Mirra Komarovsky has identified as "neo-anti-feminists." While rejecting any imputation of inferiority to women, this group insists upon the importance of the differences between them and men, and, therefore, would construct a college education for women based upon distinctively feminine abilities, interests, and functions. One forceful exponent of these views, Lynn White, has called for a curriculum which emphasizes courses of study "dealing with the institution of the family and all that contributes to its well-being through food, beauty and warmth, shelter and security." Some of those who have urged the value of a distinctively "feminine higher education" have maintained that to educate women through a program of study designed for the needs of men is to lay the basis for frustrations in adult life.

The advocates of an educational philosophy which emphasizes homemaking functions are in turn criticized by those who would encourage more professional training among women. The need for this development, they contend, is demonstrated, on the one hand, by the new place of work in women's lives, and on the other, by the society's needs for more highly trained workers. In addition, the economic role of women both within and outside the home has stimulated proposals for changes in the collegiate education of women which call for still a different emphasis. It has been argued by Louis William Norris, for example, that their education should have the effect of encouraging women who want to enter paid employment "to choose work as a means of self-expression and personal enrichment" for themselves and their families, rather than for material gains alone, and to consider what their unique contributions as workers might be. He would also have their education encourage women to make decisions as consumers and investors more effectively and with greater recognition of the consequences, both for their families and the economy, which flow from these responsibilities.

These and still other approaches taken toward the higher education of women in recent years testify to the variety of needs which formal education is called upon to fulfill. They suggest, moreover, that the search for a single educational format which will serve equally well to prepare women for three spheres of activity—the home, paid employment, and the community—may well be self-defeating. A single or dominant mode of education was to be expected when college study was, for practical purposes, the privilege of only a small and more or less homogeneous group of young women. Today, the group which continues formal education beyond high school, while still a minority, is much larger and more diverse in composition. The patterns of women's lives have changed, as have the reasons why young women attend college. These and other developments have been reflected in the growing variety of institutions, programs of study, and purposes which mark the higher education of women. This diversity underscores the plenitude of the facilities and the opportunities for higher education, but obviously makes it difficult to characterize women's college education in simple and precise terms, and it means that the college diploma symbolizes a variety of accomplishments.

CURRENT PROBLEM AREAS

The continuing problem of where the emphasis in women's post-high school education should fall has been both transformed and complicated by the emergence of new issues. How much of the responsibility for the vocational training of women now carried by four-year colleges may be assumed in the future by junior and community colleges is one which has been raised but not yet thoroughly investigated. The rapid growth of these institutions may be viewed as a response to the need for some form of intermediate education between high school and college, which could serve as a bridge to the latter for some, but could also provide highly practical, terminal education for others. For many occupations in which women are well represented, one or two years of post-high school study is adequate preparation, and such training is emphasized in the curricula of junior and community colleges. These institutions have also developed new curricula which have helped to give semiprofessional status to certain occupations. There is good reason to expect a more rapid expansion of junior and community colleges in the future, but it is hard to predict what consequence this will have for four-year college attendance and graduation among young women.

Another new problem area has emerged in connection with the possibilities for undertaking college education later in life. For some time, college attendance has not been narrowly confined to the 18 to 22 year age span. The educational benefits extended to veterans meant a departure from convention at the upper end of this age range, and there is now a conscious effort being made to regularize the admission of able young people to college at 16. The growth of college and university programs of study specially geared to the interests and time schedules of adults has made college attendance and graduation in the later twenties and thirties a commonplace occurrence. How much more can be done to facilitate college attendance by more mature men and women remains to be seen. Meanwhile, some institutions, among them Columbia University's School of General Studies, have already begun to explore what might be done by taking into account the experiences which adult students have had outside the classroom as a basis for experimenting with greater flexibility in programs of study and years of attendance required.

Manpower objectives and changing employment opportunities have given fresh emphasis to two areas of concern. One involves the encouragement of a larger proportion of able young women to undertake undergraduate and graduate study. The second turns on the possibility of reducing, at least to some degree, the tendency of women to concentrate in a few traditional fields of study. The high demand for scientific and professional workers in particular has prompted suggestions for encouraging more young women to specialize in physical science fields in which they are now poorly represented. The point has already been made that altering traditional patterns of choice among fields of study depends upon far more than the existence of new job opportunities. It involves changes in dominant ideas about suitable work for women, in employment practices, and in the way in which young women are guided while in high school and college in planning for the future, and in making decisions about courses of study.

The expansion in the employment of married women whose children are of school age, and the consequent combining of work with homemaking functions, have obviously raised new guidance and counseling problems. Many women would benefit if they could plan their education with an eye not only to marriage and employment early in life, but also to possible re-entry into the labor market later on. Conceivably, such planning might also make it easier to tap the reservoir of ability among married women whose family circumstances permit them to return to work.

It is difficult to do much more at the high school and college level than to establish an awareness and an understanding of the varied kinds of adult lives which women now lead and will be likely to lead in the future. Whether much more than this can be done through early guidance and counseling to help those women who, after a dozen or more years of preoccupation with home and family, may desire to go to work, is an open question. It may not be feasible to attempt to provide ways of helping such women with their educational and occupational problems until they reach the point in their lives when they are interested in and able to work outside the home.

In any case, it may be assumed that greater anticipation of a return to employment will to some degree influence decisions about courses of study and college attendance and completion. Because more and more married women are returning to work in their thirties, and the range of jobs open to them is constantly being broadened, young women in high school and college will be less likely to think about paid employment solely as a short interlude between the completion of schooling and the arrival of the first child. Teachers and guidance counselors can, of course, help create greater awareness of recent trends in women's employment and of their implications for educational decisions. An understanding of the educational experience in relation to an adult life which encompasses both the home and paid employment could have various consequences. It might lead some young women to decide to enter college; to complete their studies rather than drop out along the way; to be more deliberate about the subjects in which they major; to take their studies more seriously; or, finally, to make the added investment of going on to graduate school.

XIV. HIGHER EDUCATION AND THE AMERICAN ECONOMY

Henry David

THE BROAD RELATIONSHIP among manpower resources, education, and economic development and growth is an underlying theme of many of the chapters in this volume. Some of the interrelationships between economic affairs and higher education is the specific concern of the one which follows.

It was initially delivered as an address at the Tenth Annual National Conference of the Association for Higher Education, held in Chicago, February 28–March 2, 1955. Addresses by Dorothy Fosdick and Senator J. W. Fulbright on the same occasion, it may be noted, dealt with "Higher Education and World Leadership" and "Higher Education and the Maintenance of American Freedom," respectively.

"Higher Education and the Economy" is reprinted from Current Issues in Higher Education, 1955 (*Washington: National Education Association, 1955*), pp. 11–18, in which it first appeared.

BY 1890, the United States, already the leading producer of agricultural commodities, had established the base of a predominantly industrial economy. Shortly after that date, it assumed first rank among the nations of the world in the volume of goods manufactured. Today, the United States is responsible for almost half of the goods produced in the world.[1] In 1890, out of every hundred of our young people about three or four graduated from high school, and only one from college. Today, one in every six of our young people graduate from college, and more than six in every ten collect—even if they do not earn—a high school diploma.

America's economic life has left its imprint upon higher education—that convenient abstraction which permits one to deal coherently with not far from 2,000 institutions of learning, diverse in character and involving millions of people engaged in a bewildering variety of activities. The extent and the strength of this imprint will be suggested if you are willing to imagine for a moment that all of the physical evidences and the records of industry, business, farming, transportation, and trade have vanished, and then to ask yourself how much of a picture of the nation's economic activities could be constructed from an examination of the evidence for these activities located in our colleges and universities. The ingenious investigator could fashion a quite revealing, though distorted, picture from sources of funds; scholarship and fellowship opportunities; schools, departments, and divisions of instruction; titles of academic chairs; course offerings and specialized vocational programs; distribution of students by fields of study; degrees awarded; the annual reports of presidents; honorary degrees conferred; the work of placement bureaus; and the composition of boards of trustees.

One could derive no less suggestive an insight into the present character of and functions performed by higher education by reversing the exercise, invoking solely the evidence provided by the economy. The number and kinds of college and university trained personnel employed in different segments of the economy; the alterations in technology; the recruitment policies pursued by industrial and other firms; the use of the college degree as a screening device in selecting managerial personnel; the character of the contributions made by business enterprises to institutions of higher education; their research grants and contracts—these and still other evidences point up the impact which colleges and universities have had upon our economic life.

The exhaustive and definitive study of the part that the growth of higher education has played in the development of the American economy still remains to be written. But it is not necessary to wait on the fulfillment of that undertaking to observe that since the close of the nineteenth century a constantly growing proportion of the highly skilled personnel required for the effective functioning of our technologically advanced and complex economy is college and university educated and trained. It is also clear, as one looks ahead, that the rate and direction of America's future economic development will depend to a critical degree upon the quality and the number of men and women whose preparation for economic functions will be overwhelmingly a responsibility of the colleges and universities.

In seeking to understand the nature of economic development —that is, the nature of the process measured by continuing increases in the per capita production of goods and services—economists and historians have tended to concentrate attention chiefly upon such factors as savings and capital formation, income distribution, scientific and technological knowledge, physical resources, market organizations, entrepreneurial behavior, and political and legal institutions. Until recently, the human resource factor in economic development has been relatively neglected. Moreover, when it was given due weight, it was generally considered in terms of gross labor supply problems from a quantitative and demographic point of view.

True, it was always taken for granted that the abilities and skills of the labor force and, therefore, at least by implication, its educational level and the investment which a society makes in the facilities and opportunities for education, matter significantly to its economic development. It has, however, been much easier to read a rise in educational standards as the result, or as the concomitant, of economic progress than to seek to determine with any precision the interrelationship between a society's investment in education and its economic growth.

There were some strong hints embedded in the late nineteenth and early twentieth century economic history of Japan and Germany, to say nothing of that of the United States, as to what could be accomplished by forcing certain kinds of educational developments. But it is only in recent years that the idea has gained currency—and to this Soviet Russia has, curiously enough, contributed significantly—that a society may be able to manipulate its investment in the facilities and opportunities for education and training, in a fashion similar to its allocation of capital for investment in new plants and machines, so as to influence its future economic growth along certain lines.

Today, we are becoming increasingly sensitive to the role that highly trained manpower and, consequently, higher education play in economic development. Whether this new awareness, which is extremely important, also has certain dangers attached to it, is a question to which I will return.

Our current sensitivity to the critical importance of highly trained manpower must in large part be ascribed to the shortage situations experienced since World War II and to the concern with manpower policies which these engendered on the part of governmental bodies and private organizations. The pinch of shortages of different kinds of professionally and scientifically trained personnel—notably of doctors, nurses, teachers, engineers, and a variety of physical scientists—compelled us to face up to the disastrous effects upon our national security and economic well-being which they would produce if they were to continue unrelieved for a significant time. This experience has produced a new and important, though as yet imperfect, body of knowledge bearing on the problems of manpower supply and demand and utilization; the relationship of education and training to subsequent function and performance; and the viable instrumentalities for policy action in a democratic society.

The experiences of "underdeveloped" societies which attempt to modernize their economies have also helped to make us more sensitive to the role of highly skilled manpower and education. The effective use of capital and the exploitation of the potentialities of scientific knowledge and technology in these areas are always dependent upon the availability of skilled workers, technicians, and scientific and professional personnel, either native or imported. What transpires when "underdeveloped" societies attempt to develop economic techniques and structures modeled on those of the United States or Western Europe helps to illuminate the meaning of pieces of experience buried within our own history.

What occurred in the expansion of research and development expenditures in the United States, from not quite one and one-third billion dollars at the close of World World II to approximately three and one-half billion dollars currently, is significant in this context.[2] The explosive growth of the research and development effort has been a primary factor in the high demand for scientists and engineers on the part of government, industry, and the universities. More important is the fact that manpower availability appears to have been a far more decisive limiting factor on the scale of research and development activities than dollar considerations.

We know far less than we should about the future demand for highly trained manpower. But the indicators upon which we rely point to the judgment that it is unlikely that the United States will produce more college and university trained men and women in the proximate future than the economy will be able to employ at the maximum level of their skills. The big danger, it seems clear, lies not in that direction, but in the possibility that the supply of highly trained men and women will be inadequate to the nation's future requirements. And this danger is enhanced if we fail with respect to three objectives: to increase the supply of young people of ability reaching the colleges; to strengthen the institutions of higher education; and, finally, to reduce the present degree of wastage of potential ability in the population.

It certainly does not lie within the power of higher education alone to realize these objectives. Unless there is early identification of ability, a drastic improvement in the quality of secondary education, a more effective program of educational and vocational guidance, and easier access to more equal educational opportunities for the members of groups presently disadvantaged in this respect, the stream of young people of ability reaching college will remain too small and large-scale waste of potential ability will continue. Without much greater financial support from both private and public sources than they now receive, the colleges and universities cannot be fashioned into stronger centers of intellectual activity than they now are. Note that I am not saying "into more effective training institutions for professional and scientific occupations," for there is a substantial difference between the two.

It is naive to believe, however, that money alone will serve to strengthen the colleges and universities as centers of intellectual activity. For, what also is involved are attitudes, deep-seated in our society, in which a general approval of education—that is, of formal schooling—is accompanied by an amiable contempt for the intellectual and the academic. We are a price-minded people, and it is, consequently, significant that the prices we are prepared to pay for intellectual and educational services are, with few exceptions, relatively low. We place a high value, by contrast, on education for certain professional pursuits, and it is no accident that our medical, law, and engineering schools enjoy the enviable reputations they do. We respond positively when the gospel of higher education is cast in terms of economic worth in future income. Yet, our dominant attitudes assign a low value to intellectual endeavor and to the worth of education for its own sake. Certainly our actions indicate that we even place a low value on education as an essential instrument for liberating the individual by facilitating the full development of his potentialities.

It is a mistake to represent higher education solely as the innocent victim of this deplorable condition, for it has also contributed to it. With a few notable exceptions, higher education has been defensive about its intellectual functions and responsibilities. It has been all too willing to escape from these to grapple with less difficult problems of internal organization, administrative structure, and extracurricular activities. To the extent that it has done this, it has contributed to the poor utilization of much of its energies and brains.

Many institutions of higher education discourage—though not necessarily by conscious intent—disinterested, critical thought and reflection in both their students and their faculties. Too many of them respond so readily to the demands made upon them by the society that they tend to operate as educational service stations rather than as educational institutions. Higher education has fashioned its own professional language—some might prefer the more invidious term "jargon"—and, while this may help its personnel to talk with one another, it has certainly been far more potent in discouraging effective communication with the larger community.

These complaints are familiar, but, as long as they carry substance, there is every reason to reiterate them. Moreover, they do have bearing on the relationship between higher education and the American economy.

I have stated that the quantitative and qualitative characteristics of the future supply of professionally and scientifically trained manpower will be critical determinants of the country's economic well-being, as well as of its security. The education and training of this segment of the labor force is overwhelmingly the responsibility of our colleges and universities. The manner in which this responsibility is appraised and fulfilled will have the gravest consequences.

An urgent and quite valid cry has been raised for some time for extraordinary efforts to be made to increase the supply of our engineers and scientists. It would be unfortunate if the cry went unheeded. But I wish there were equally strong voices to be heard emphasizing the importance of an adequate supply of highly trained and competent men and women in a host of other fields—in the social sciences, in the humanities, in education, in the arts, in religion. I would not think it necessary to assert the nation's parallel need for nontechnological and nonscientific manpower if I were not troubled by certain overtones which, though not dominant, can be heard in the present stress on engineers and scientists. One such overtone conveys the feeling that the nation is more deeply indebted to them than to all other kinds of college and university trained personnel, and that this debt should be paid in terms of significantly differential prestige and income and special treatment for military service. Another suggests that if we wish to observe how a society which truly appreciates its engineers and scientists behaves, we should look at the USSR. True, we are in a race with the USSR in terms of the resources of highly trained manpower, but the means of winning that race must be of our own fashioning and congruent with our own values.

Surely it must be possible to secure the supply of scientists and engineers we need within the context of a broader effort to expand and strengthen our *total* educational resources. It is not necessary, nor would it be wise, to achieve this objective by imposing penalties upon other fields of endeavor and thus seriously distort the larger mission of higher education.

We have already had warnings that some measure of imbalance may now be occurring as a result of the large-scale research and development contracts which the Federal government and industry have been placing with colleges and universities. Through these contracts, higher education, of course, makes a major contribution to the nation's security and to the advance of science and technology. These contracts, moreover, have eased the financial difficulties of some institutions and have made possible improvements in their research facilities and staffs. Research and development contracts, however, are chiefly directed to applied research purposes in the natural sciences. Consequently, there has been concern that they may, over the long run, have the effect of reducing the importance of basic research within the colleges and universities, of their teaching function, and of the humanities and the social sciences.

The college or university moved by a sense of its own integrity and its obligation to serve the larger community will be on guard against such possible distortions in its spirit and structure. It will want to assess—as a number are now doing—the long-term impact upon it of contract research and other opportunities to provide specialized services, however enticing they may be in the short run. It will want its faculty to make important contributions to basic knowledge in the sciences and to the translation of this knowledge into processes, machines, goods, and services. But it will also want to maximize the capacity of its faculty to investigate freely and critically—and with full recognition that error has a positive function in the pursuit of truth—the full range of man's activities and behavior and the meaning of human experience. There was a time when this task was largely the province of nonacademics, when the major historians, political scientists, economists, and literary critics, for example, were not likely to be professors. This undertaking is now almost exclusively located in the institutions of higher education, where it constitutes a responsibility that neither we nor the rest of the world can afford to have indifferently performed.

The injunction to higher education implicit in my argument is quite simple. It must not confuse the economy with society. Consequently, it must not conceive its relationship to the economy as a trainer of highly specialized manpower and as a center for research in such terms that its capacity to fulfill other needs of the society will be severely limited. If the institutions of higher education were geared to respond automatically and with maximum efficiency *only* to the current needs of the economy, they would take on the appearance of high level and expensive service

stations. A system of higher education engaged, in effect, in sup-
plying parts and in repair operations would not only debase its
name, but it would also do the economy a disservice.

What is required for economic development is not the replacement of worn-out parts by their equivalents, but preparation for
the central fact of continuing change: of continuing change in
bodies of knowledge, in ways of doing things and utilizing skills,
in materials and products, in occupational functions, in forms of
organization and structure. From the point of view of manpower
characteristics, flexibility and resourcefulness are key desiderata.
This means that highly specialized manpower must not only be
equipped to perform existing tasks, but, by virtue of the breadth
of education, also prepared to assume new functions without
great strain or sizable new training costs.

Preparation for continuing change has more than a technological dimension. It also means an education which equips men
and women to recognize, if not to cope with, the alterations that
a dynamic technology and economy impose upon other aspects of
their lives. It requires an exposure to experiences that will encourage self-development long after the diploma is won. If I had
any simple prescriptions for bringing about these consequences,
I would readily share them. I do not. But I am persuaded that
the college or university education which does not give these
targets high priority does not provide the economy with the
highly trained men and women required, and makes its own
small contribution to a schizoid society.

Since higher education plays so vital a role with respect to the
effective functioning of the economy and its continued development, what is there to be said about the reciprocal behavior of
business enterprise, particularly of large-scale enterprise, which
has become an increasingly important source of financial support
for the colleges and universities? Happily, a number of distinguished leaders of the business community have expressed more
persuasively than I could the obligation of that community to

maintain and strengthen the institutions of higher education through funds for operating expenses, plant expansion, research and library facilities, and scholarship and fellowship programs. They have recognized that the scale and purposes of their contributions can affect not only the character of the colleges and universities, but also the substance of our culture. Their guidelines for the behavior of business enterprises are sensible. That they are not yet acted on widely enough is self-evident.

It will be sufficient, therefore, to stress the fact that adequate support of our colleges and universities by business enterprises through direct contribution, or indirectly through increased public expenditures requiring higher taxes, is not a philanthropic gesture. It is an act of self-interest, perhaps even of self-preservation. It may even be regarded, in one sense, as an act of justice, for only a small part of the cost of educating the highly trained manpower which our business enterprises require has been directly borne by them.

In the course of this century, both American higher education and the American economy have experienced expansions and structural modifications of revolutionary magnitude. We can now perceive more clearly than we did in the past a system of interdependence in the transformations which have marked these two areas of American life. Their future developments will be linked even more intimately. In both areas, I suspect, Henry Adams' characterization of the crisis of the present century, as a race between education and catastrophe, carries more weight than it ever did.

NOTES

I: MANPOWER PROBLEMS AND EDUCATION

1 See pp. 60–61; 103–57; 267; note 2, chap. II.

2 More recent estimates by the U. S. Department of Labor anticipate a labor force of 87 million by 1970, and the following percentage increases in major occupational groups between 1960 and 1970: professional, technical, and related workers, about 40 percent; clerical and sales, over 25 percent; service workers, about 25 percent; skilled workers, between 20 and 25 percent; and semiskilled workers, less than 20 percent. No change is estimated for unskilled workers, and for farmers and farm workers a decline of over 15 percent.

3 As of 1956. By 1959, these categories probably accounted for about 16 million workers in a civilian labor force of about 69.4 million.

4 This and following figures in this paragraph hold for 1955–56. For more recent data on teachers, see below, note 2, chap. II.

5 During the early 1950s.

6 As of 1955–56.

7 See pp. 227–43; 115, table 3; note 1, chap. XI.

II: EDUCATION AND NATIONAL EFFICIENCY

1 In February, 1954.

2 By 1958, the number of elementary and secondary school teachers had increased to more than 1.6 million. College and university teachers then numbered almost 250,000. There were 6.9 million persons between the ages of 16 and 24—or 36 percent of the age group—enrolled in schools, colleges, and universities. Total expenditures for education in the United States were on the order of $20 million in 1958.

3 In 1959, the average number of school years completed was about 12 years for persons 25 to 44; 10.5 years for those 45 to 54; 8.8 years for those 55 to 64; and 8.3 years for those 65 and over.

4 See pp. 102–5.

5 By 1958, about 60 percent of all young men were graduating from high school, and over one third were enrolling in college.

6 New York: Columbia University Press, 1951.

7 See p. 59; note 1, chap. IV.

8 In 1959, there was one scientific or technical worker for every 32 persons in the labor force. Twenty years earlier, the ratio was 1 to 100.

9 See Eli Ginzberg and Douglas W. Bray, The Uneducated (New York: Columbia University Press, 1953), Chapter 1.

IV: SECONDARY EDUCATION AND PREPARATION FOR WORK

1 In 1953–54. In 1955, exemption from the age requirement was permitted in 24 states for students completing elementary school, in one state for those completing the tenth grade, and in 15 for those graduating from high school.

[2] How rapidly the school population has been growing and other aspects of public education have been changing may be seen by comparing the following statistics with those given in the text. Expenditures for grades nine through twelve in the public high schools probably came to over $2.2 billion in the 1955–56 school year. By 1956, there were 11,771,042 daytime students enrolled in grades seven and above in 26,046 secondary public schools. By 1958–59, there were about 7.8 million students enrolled in grades nine and above in public high schools. A total of almost 8.9 million students were then enrolled in public and nonpublic high schools, compared with almost 360,000 in 1890. In the latter year, only 6.7 percent of all the children in the United States aged 14 through 17 were enrolled in high schools, both public and private, compared to 83.8 percent in 1958. In 1958, 74 percent of this age group were enrolled in public high schools, and the number of high school graduates came to 63 percent of all seventeen-year-old children.

[3] The prediction for 1960 turned out to be accurate. More recent estimates place the high school enrollment above 12 million by 1965.

[4] By 1958, about 90 percent of all young people were acquiring some high school education.

[5] 1953–54.

[6] In 1958, nearly 1.7 million students were enrolled in Federally supported daytime courses in trade and industry, home economics, vocational agriculture, practical nursing, and technician training.

V: SECONDARY EDUCATION AND THE DEVELOPMENT OF SKILL

[1] The most recent data put the number of high school graduates during 1957–58 at 1,507,600. The earlier estimate of 1.7 million for 1960 is likely to turn out to be quite accurate. It is estimated that in 1970 there will be 2.7 million graduates.

[2] In *A Policy for Skilled Manpower*, the National Manpower Council, as one way of strengthening "the contributions of secondary education to the development of our resources of skilled workers and technicians," recommended that: "Boards of education and school officials insure that students are permitted to specialize intensively in vocational subjects only after they have completed two years of high school, and that able and interested students also are provided with the opportunity to qualify for college entrance."

[3] In 1960, Helen Wood of the U. S. Department of Labor estimated that the need for new elementary teachers "will average about 100,000 each year during the 1960 decade unless replacement rates are reduced considerably. This figure does not allow for the employment of additional teachers needed to bring about improvements such as lower pupil-teacher ratios in overcrowded classrooms, replacement of persons not meeting regular requirements, and extension of kindergarten facilities to all areas." She also estimated that "the number of secondary school teachers that must be recruited each year is likely to average more than 50,000 during the 1960's." ("Human Resources for Services to Children and Youth," *Children and Youth in the 1960s: Survey Papers Prepared for the 1960 White House Conference on Children and Youth*, pp. 320–321.)

VI: THE SECONDARY EDUCATION OF GIRLS

[1] By 1958, the number had risen to 1,342,300.

[2] Two years later, the percentage for boys had risen to 60 and that for girls to 66.

[3] See below, pp. 130–32; 138–40.

VII: ISSUES IN VOCATIONAL EDUCATION

1 For a detailed treatment of the ways in which skilled workers acquire their occupational skills, see National Manpower Council, *A Policy for Skilled Manpower* (New York: Columbia University Press, 1954), pp. 208–233.

2 For the fiscal year 1960, nearly $48 million were appropriated for a significantly expanded Federal-state vocational education program. In 1956, two new programs, one for practical nurse training and the other for the fisheries trade and industry education, were provided for, as was an area vocational education program for technicians in 1958.

3 In 1958, over 270,000 students were enrolled in daytime Federal-state trades and industry classes. No comparable figure for industrial arts enrollments has been obtained since 1950.

4 See note 2.

5 In 1958, Federal expenditures for vocational education totaled $38.7 million, or slightly more than one sixth of the $209.7 million expended under the terms of Federal legislation.

6 Of the $38.7 million of Federal funds expended in 1958, $13.6 million was for agriculture, $11.4 million for trades and industry, $8.9 million for home economics, $2.5 million for distributive occupations, and $2.3 million for practical nursing.

7 In 1958, nearly 230,000 boys and 45,000 girls were registered in daytime trades and industrial classes under the Federal-state program.

8 In addition to these, the fisheries trade and industry, and several technicians' occupations are also studied.

9 There were almost 20,000 cooperative trades and industry students in 1958, and there have been as many as 25,000 in recent years.

10 There were 9 percent in 1958.

11 See note 3.

VIII: TYPES OF VOCATIONAL SCHOOLING

1 The questionnaire was circulated and the interviews and correspondence with school authorities and other educators carried on in 1953–54.

2 See Part Three for a fuller treatment of guidance problems.

3 See note 5 in chapter IX, "Vocational Guidance and Counseling," for the expansion of Federal aid for guidance purposes under the provisions of the National Defense Education Act of 1958.

4 See the reports of recent studies of school leavers conducted by the U. S. Department of Labor in "From School to Work: Highlights from a Study on the Early Employment Experience of Youth in Seven Communities," 1952–57."

5 As of 1954. The population is now (1960) over one million.

6 A principal aim of the increased grants for vocational education in recent years has been to introduce many new programs, particularly for technicians and in area vocational education programs.

7 Published in 1954.

8 By 1958, enrollments in daytime vocational agricultural programs had increased to 462,000. Since 1953, enrollments have increased more in trades and industry programs than in agricultural programs, both absolutely and relatively, but enrollments in the former still fall short of the 1942 peak.

9 In 1958, it was not quite twice as many.

10 Since 1953, appropriations and enrollments in distributive occupations programs have increased markedly, although enrollments have not reached the levels

which prevailed from 1948 to 1951. The rise from 209,000 to 283,000 persons enrolled between 1953 and 1958 was wholly among evening students, who now account for over 70 percent of all distributive occupations enrollments. Cooperative students numbered 35,000, or nearly 13 percent.

[11] As of 1954.

[12] In 1958, nearly 57,000 students were enrolled in Federally-aided vocational technical programs: 15,000 of them in aircraft, 11,500 in electronics, and 5,000 in engineering fields.

[13] As of 1951–52. Junior college enrollments had grown to a total of 893,000 by 1957–58. Publicly supported institutions then enrolled 89 percent of the junior college student body.

[14] The U. S. Office of Education now issues an annual report covering organized occupational curricula of at least 1, but less than 4, years in length in junior colleges, technical institutes, and other institutions of higher education. Compare Table 1 with the following table, which shows the enrollments of full-time and part-time students, by type of institution and program, in 1957:

| | Enrollments | | |
	Full-time	Part-time	Total
All organized occupational curricula	124,758	80,037	204,795
In publicly controlled institutions	77,571	49,256	126,827
In privately controlled institutions	47,187	30,781	77,968
In 4-year institutions	41,847	38,880	80,727
In 2-year institutions	82,911	41,157	124,068
Engineering related	40,068	36,239	76,307
Nonengineering related	84,690	43,798	128,488

Source: Henry H. Armsby, Walter Crosby Eels, and S. V. Martorana, *Organized Occupational Curriculums, Enrollments and Graduates, 1957,* U. S. Office of Education, Circular No. 568.

[15] As of 1953–54.

[16] In 1957, organized occupational curricula were offered by 790 institutions of higher education, 380 of them public and 410 of them private, including 233 public and 152 private 2-year institutions. The leading states were California with 68 and New York with 60 such institutions. Total enrollments in these curricula increased 42 percent between 1956 and 1957, and even more rapidly in nonengineering related curricula, for part-time students, in publicly controlled institutions, and in 2-year institutions.

[17] Graduates from organized occupational curricula in institutions of higher education in 1956–57 were distributed as follows:

| | Graduates | | |
	Men	Women	Total
All organized occupational curricula	24,312	20,474	44,786
In publicly controlled institutions	12,975	11,731	24,706
In privately controlled institutions	11,337	8,743	20,080
In 4-year institutions	8,830	9,723	18,553
In 2-year institutions	15,482	10,751	26,233
Engineering related	13,145	170	13,315
Nonengineering related	11,167	20,304	31,471

Business and commerce accounted for 35 percent of the graduates, education for 15 percent, and electrical technology for 12 percent.

[18] Compare with the following data for 1957:

	Enrollment	Graduation
Occupational therapists	4,532	490
Physical therapists	798	750
Medical record librarians	161	139
Medical record technicians	58	37
X-ray technicians	4,113	2,019
Practical, attendant, and vocational nurses	16,843[b]	10,666
Dental hygienists	n.a.	945
Medical technologists	3,099	2,285

n.a. = not available.

[b] = admissions during school year, 1956–57.

Source: American Medical Association, American Dental Association, and American Nurses Association.

[19] As of 1953–54.

[20] These data are for 1954.

IX: VOCATIONAL GUIDANCE AND COUNSELING

[1] Compared with the 433 occupations listed in the 1951 *Occupational Outlook Handbook*, the 1959 edition of the *Handbook* describes employment opportunities in 600 occupations in 30 major industries. In 1955, Supplement 1 to the *Dictionary of Occupational Titles* contained 2,260 new and revised job definitions.

[2] Based on the 1951 edition of the *Dictionary*.

[3] The situation has changed since 1952–53. According to the U. S. Office of Education, in 1959 there was one full-time counselor for every 750 high school students. The ratio recommended by Dr. James B. Conant is one full-time counselor for every 250 to 300 students.

[4] As of 1954. Here, too, there has been a change. In September, 1959, state supervisors of guidance were employed by 47 states, the District of Columbia, and the two territories. The data in this paragraph which follow were for 1952–53.

[5] In the fiscal year 1958, about $440,000 in Federal funds for guidance programs were expended under the George-Barden Act. The states and local school systems reported that they spent nearly $1.3 million in qualifying for Federal aid. In addition, Congress, under the National Defense Education Act, appropriated $5.4 million for grants-in-aid to the states for guidance, counseling, and testing for the fiscal year 1959. An additional $2 million was appropriated for grants to establish training institutes to improve the qualifications of those who are, or will be, engaged in guidance in the secondary schools. These appropriations are expected to increase toward the authorized maxima of $15 million for grants to the states and for $7.25 million for grants to training institutes. Matching of these Federal funds was not required during the first year. In subsequent years, the grants to the states for guidance, counseling, and testing must be matched on a fifty-fifty basis by either state or local funds, or both. Where Federal funds are allocated by the states to pay for testing in nonpublic schools, the matching must be from nonpublic funds. Matching is not required for grants for training programs. Total appropriations for the fiscal year 1960 for guidance activities under the NDEA came to $20 million.

[6] This directory is now compiled by the American Board on Professional Standards in Vocational Counseling, Inc., which was created by the APGA. In 1958, there were 153 such services. Only 13 states lacked approved services.

[7] Up to July 1958, about 55,000 disabled veterans had received training and counseling under the Korean Vocational Rehabilitation Program (Public Law 894). Under certain conditions, nondisabled veterans and war orphans may also receive counseling from the Veterans Administration. During the fiscal year 1958, counseling was provided to 63,800 disabled and nondisabled veterans and war orphans.

[8] Between 1953 and 1960, the total appropriations for vocational rehabilitation programs increased from $24 to $66.3 million.

[9] The 1959 edition devotes as many as 4 pages to many occupations. In consequence of this and the inclusion of more occupations and industries, the *Handbook* has grown from 577 to 785 pages since 1951.

[10] Up to 1954. A subsequent survey showed that by June, 1957, mandatory certification had been adopted by 30 states and the District of Columbia; that 7 states had optional certification; and that 12 states certified school or counseling psychologists.

[11] About 37 percent by 1958.

X: VOCATIONAL GUIDANCE AND THE SKILLS OF THE WORK FORCE

[1] In 1959, according to the U. S. Office of Education, "More than half of the counselors in the U. S. are in only 7 states, which serve only one-third of the Nation's school children . . . an estimated two-thirds of today's school counselors do not meet minimum certification requirements. . . . Only 19 states have testing programs; 14 states have none at all."

[2] See note 3.

[3] The stimulating effect of the National Defense Education Act of 1958 appears in the report of the U. S. Office of Education that, since its adoption, 17 states and the District of Columbia have added at least one special consultant to help develop their guidance programs, and that some states have added as many as five. Demands for stronger counseling and guidance services were also made at the 1960 White House Conference on Children and Youth.

[4] The National Manpower Council has, of course, continued to stress the importance of improved guidance in its work subsequent to the publication of *A Policy for Skilled Manpower*. Through its staff it has also contributed to the work of other organizations concerned with guidance, as in the case of the National Association of Women Deans and Counselors.

[5] Robert A. Wendorf, "State Wide Guidance Survey" (Unpublished doctoral dissertation, Western Reserve University, Cleveland, Ohio, 1954).

[6] For practical purposes, the National Defense Education Act of 1958 broke the link with vocational education at the Federal level. The statute, according to the U. S. Office of Education, has encouraged the reorganization of state guidance services and changes in state and local guidance practices along the lines recommended by Mr. Odell.

[7] "Biennial Survey of Education" (Unpublished data on *Offerings and Enrollments in High School Subjects*, U. S. Office of Education).

[8] Edward R. Cuony, Unpublished doctoral dissertation (New York University School of Education, New York City, 1953).

[9] Robert Shosteck, "How Well Are We Putting Across Occupational Information?" *Personnel and Guidance Journal*, XXXIII (January, 1955), 265.

[10] Joseph S. Kopas and Wiley Garrett, *Achieving Your Career, A Vocational Guidance Manual for Use in Schools*, Industrial Information Institute, Youngstown, Ohio, 1953.

[11] *Your Career Opportunities in Evansville Industry*, Evansville Manufac-

turers and Employers Association, Public Relations Division, Evansville, Indiana, 1953.

12 See p. 185.

13 Jones and Miller, *The National Picture of Pupil Personnel and Guidance Services,* Washington, D. C., U. S. Office of Education, 1954. There appear to be no more recent data available than that which are presented on p. 215 for enrollments in "guidance oriented" classes.

14 This estimate for 1954, according to subsequently available data, appears to have been too high. In 1959, the number of high school graduates benefiting from the services mentioned was between 350,000 and 400,000.

15 Howard M. Bell, *Matching Youth and Jobs,* Washington, D. C., American Youth Commission, 1940, p. 257.

16 It should be added that disabled school-age youths are eligible for guidance, as well as training and medical services, under the Federal-state vocational rehabilitation program.

XI: THE POTENTIAL FOR HIGHER EDUCATION

1 Compare the following percentages for 1958 with those for 1951–52 shown in Figure 2: less than 1 percent of all high school graduates became Ph.D.'s or M.D.'s; 28 percent became college graduates; and 47 percent college entrants. Of the college age population, less than 1 percent became Ph.D.'s in 1958; 16 percent became graduates from college; 29 percent enter college; and 63 percent graduated from high school.

2 This was as of 1951–52. The rapid growth of the college population is shown in the change which had taken place by 1958, when three out of ten in the college-age group entered and one out of six graduated from college.

3 The current proportion is 17 percent, but this does not affect the contention that there is a significant reserve in view of the fact most college students and half of the college graduates still score below 120 on the AGCT.

4 See note 3.

5 For more recent data, see Richard L. Plaut, editor, *Interim-Report—Southern Project, 1953–54* (New York: NSSFNS, 1955).

6 In 1958, 35 percent of all college graduates were women. See pp. 260–88, for the factors affecting college attendance by women.

7 Almost 16,000 men and women received doctoral degrees and M.D.'s in the school year 1957–58.

XII: FACTORS INFLUENCING EDUCATION FOR SCIENTIFIC AND PROFESSIONAL OCCUPATIONS

1 By 1958, real per capita income after taxes had increased 12 percent over the 1951 level and 58 percent over the 1929 level.

2 In 1955–56, according to the U. S. Office of Education, universities and colleges had scholarships available in the amount of $65.7 million for undergraduate students; fellowships amounting to $18.2 million for graduate students; loans amounting to $14.3 million for graduate and undergraduate students; assistantships amounting to $35.0 million mainly for graduate students; and $65.9 million for employment for undergraduates. State scholarship programs are not included in these figures. Funds for scholarship, fellowship and related purposes have increased since then. Under the National Defense Education Act, the Federal government distributed $30.5 million to colleges and universities for student loan funds in the fiscal year 1959.

3 This figure understated the income for 1950 by over $25 million. Six years

later, state and local governments provided $969 million to public colleges and universities for current purposes.

4 Federal contributions amounted to $494 million in 1956, and the share of current income of all colleges and universities contributed by all levels of government had declined to two-fifths.

5 For expenditures for education and training by private employers, see Harold F. Clark and Harold S. Sloan, *Classrooms in the Factories* (Rutherford, N. J.: Institute of Research, Fairleigh Dickinson University, 1958).

6 This is still true in spite of the significant rise in recent years in the level of educational attainment for the Negro population as a whole. Today, about one fifth of all nonwhite adults have completed high school, in contrast to less than one tenth in 1940. In 1940, only 1.8 per cent of the nonwhite population aged 25 years and over had completed four or more years of college, compared with 4.6 percent of the total population 25 and over. In 1959, 3.2 percent of the nonwhite population in this age group had completed four or more years of college, compared with 7.9 percent for the total population 25 and older. Among younger adults aged 25 to 29 the rise in the proportion with four or more years of college between 1940 and 1959 was even more striking: for the population as a whole it increased from 5.8 percent to 11 percent, and for the nonwhites from 1.3 to 4.6 percent.

XIII: POST-HIGH SCHOOL EDUCATION AND
TRAINING OF WOMEN

1 The number of bachelor's and first professional degrees earned by women increased to 122,800 in 1957–58. During the decade 1950–1959, such degrees were awarded to 1.1 million women, who accounted for one third of the total.

2 By the close of the decade, about 3 million—or about 40 percent—of the 7.5 million of all college graduates aged 25 and over were women.

3 See pp. 117–18; 120–26.

4 This table originally covered the period 1900–55. Data added for the three succeeding years has required only one modification in the original text.

5 Nearly seven out of ten young girls were graduating from high school in 1959, compared to about six out of ten boys. 1958 college graduates amounted to about 19 percent of the number of girls and 40 percent of the number of boys who graduated from high school four years earlier.

6 These estimates have since been revised on the basis of actual experience through to 1958. The numbers of women receiving bachelor's and first professional degrees in 1959–60 and 1969–70 have been estimated at 134,000 and 238,000, respectively.

7 A subsequent check showed thirteen institutions called "universities" which did not grant bachelor's degrees to women in 1957–58.

8 In 1957–58, nearly half the women graduates majored in education.

9 In 1957–58, over one out of every six women and one out of every nine men graduates were in the liberal arts fields.

10 In 1957–58, women were also a majority of the graduates in secretarial studies and in several paramedical fields.

11 Of the 21,362 master's degrees awarded women in 1957–58, some 14,633, or over two thirds, were in the field of education. Three out of eight master's degrees awarded to men were in education.

12 By 1958, more men than women received master's degrees in the Russian language.

[13] In 1957–58, education accounted for 35 percent of the 964 doctoral degrees. Women now account for 15 percent of the doctorates in psychology.

[14] These estimates, prepared by Dr. Dael Wolfle, are based on data collected around 1950.

[15] See above, pp. 110 ff.

[16] See notes 14 and 17, p. 304.

XIV: HIGHER EDUCATION AND THE AMERICAN ECONOMY

[1] By the close of the 1950's the United States was probably responsible for closer to two fifths of all the goods and services produced.

[2] This was for 1954–55. Total public and private research and development expenditures have been estimated at over $10 billion for 1958 and $12 billion for 1959.

INDEX